CROSS-BORDER WARRIORS

CROSS-BORDER WARRIORS

Canadians in American Forces, Americans in Canadian Forces

From the Civil War to the Gulf

FRED GAFFEN

Dundurn Press
Toronto • Oxford

Editor: Judith Turnbull
Printed and bound in Canada by Best Book Manufacturers

The publisher wishes to acknowledge the generous assistance and ongoing support of the Canada Council, the Book Publishing Industry Development Program of the Department of Canadian Heritage, the Ontario Arts Council, the Ontario Publishing Centre of the Ministry of Culture, Tourism and Recreation, and the Ontario Heritage Foundation.
    Care has been taken to trace the ownership of copyright material used in the text (including the illustrations). The author and publisher welcome any information enabling them to rectify any reference or credit in subsequent editions.

J. Kirk Howard, Publisher

Canadian Cataloguing in Publication Data

Gaffen, Fred
    Cross-border warriors : Canadians in American forces, Americans in Canadian forces

Includes bibliographical references and index.
ISBN 1-55002-225-3

1. Canada – Armed Forces. 2. United States – Armed Forces. 3. Canada – History, Military. 4. United States – History, Military. 5. World War, 1939–1945 – Canada. 6. World War, 1939–1945 – United States. 7. Americans – Canada. 8. Canadians – United States. I. Title.

FC226.G35 1995   355'.00971   C94-932664-X
F1028.G35 1995

Dundurn Press Limited	Dundurn Distribution	Dundurn Press Limited
2181 Queen Street East	73 Lime Walk	1823 Maryland Avenue
Suite 301	Headington, Oxford	P.O. Box 1000
Toronto, Canada	England	Niagara Falls, N.Y.
M4E 1E5	0X3 7AD	U.S.A. 14302-1000

CONTENTS

PREFACE

Canadians and Americans have served in one another's forces, have fought side by side in the First World War, the Second World War and the Korean War. They have also been in prisoner of war camps together. Others have jointly served in NORAD, NATO and peacekeeping operations. There is ever-growing contact and cooperation between both countries' military forces and veterans' organizations. It is time to recognize these growing ties.

Most people want some recognition for what they have accomplished. For those who risked their lives fighting in a war, some kind of acknowledgment is all the more important. This book is intended to give recognition to those who have been ignored or forgotten because they were not citizens of the country in whose armed forces they served in wartime. This does not mean they did not serve as well or with as much dedication as others; in fact, the opposite is more often the case. They did their full share and it is appropriate that they, too, should receive their due.

I wrote this book because none existed on the subject. Those men and women often gave up their citizenship as well as put their lives on the line. A considerable number were killed or wounded. Following hostilities, most returned home.

Although generals plan battles, it is the individual soldier who must carry through the plan. Success or failure often depends on his will to fight. Historians can write about strategy, tactics and leadership, but the most important factor in the entire equation is the individual soldier. This book helps honour those individuals and their contribution by giving them an opportunity to tell their stories in their own words.

Throughout Canada's history there have been influxes of Americans, from the Loyalists of the American Revolution to the draft evaders and deserters of the Vietnam War. During the American Revolution, Americans loyal to the Crown joined British regiments and irregular forces, notably the provincial corps. From the American Civil War to the turn of the century, the trend was for Canadians to go south to enlist in the American forces. During the First and Second World Wars, Americans came north to enlist, while a good number of Canadians enlisted in the U.S. forces after Pearl Harbor. During the Korean conflict some Canadians and Americans ended up in the armed forces of each other's country. The Vietnam War witnessed a large movement of Canadians into the American forces. In the war against Iraq, some Canadians who had enlisted in the American forces found themselves at war in the Persian Gulf. However, their numbers were a tiny fraction of the number of Canadians who fought in Vietnam. There has been a program to allow Canadian service personnel to serve on loan for certain periods in the American armed forces as well as in those of other Allies. However, in the face of reductions in the armed forces of both countries, and as citizenship requirements become more and more restrictive, the chances of citizens of one country serving as enlistees in the armed forces of another become less and less.

Looking at the personal stories of Americans who enlisted in the Canadian forces in the Second World War, I am filled with admiration for their courage. They could have avoided military service until the United States entered the war but instead followed their principles with action. As the number of such veterans is declining, I think it important now to obtain their stories firsthand. Their accounts have been arranged by date of enlistment.

The stories span the last century and a half, from the Civil War to the Gulf War. During that time the nature of warfare has changed significantly. Weapons of the Civil War were augmented by more efficient killing weapons such as the machine gun. The aeroplane, tank and submarine increased the ability of the military to employ greater destructive power on air, land and sea. By the time of the Gulf War, weapons had become more efficient through computerization.

In all these conflicts, those who fought had a sense of duty, a belief their cause was right. Whether in the American Civil War or in the world wars, the purpose was to conquer the enemy. As war became more horrific so did the conduct of those taking part. The treatment of prisoners and civilians did not improve with the technical development of weaponry. Fighting did not become less brutal even though the treatment of battlefield wounded improved remarkably, thanks to strides in medical technology. One new characteristic of modern warfare was the appearance of women as support troops on the battlefield.

It is appropriate that this book should appear as we commemorate the fiftieth anniversary of the end of the Second World War. We have passed the fortieth anniversary of the end of the Korean War and are also marking the twentieth anniversary of the end of the Vietnam War.

The British North Americans who fought for the North and some for the South in the Civil War were akin in motivation to Canadians who fought in the U.S. forces in Vietnam – they sought adventure, the chance to fight against communism (slavery), monetary gain, or a sense of belonging. Americans who fought in the CEF (Canadian Expeditionary Force) in the First World War and the Canadian forces in the Second World War did so for different reasons. Many Americans in the CEF were of British stock and thus were motivated by a sense of loyalty. The same is true, though to a lesser extent, of Americans who joined the Canadian Army in the Second World War. Those who enlisted in the RCAF (Royal Canadian Air Force) were additionally motivated by a strong desire to fly. There were even some who managed to join the Royal Canadian Navy. The plight of Britain, a democracy, standing alone against Nazi Germany was the most significant motivating factor. Many of these individuals believed that doing "what was right" was more important than their citizenship.

Although there have been many conflicts and wars since the Second World War, none has been on a world-wide scale. The fear of mutual annihilation by nuclear war has prevented a major conflict between the superpowers. On this anniversary of the end of the Second World War, another global war seems unlikely.

ACKNOWLEDGMENTS

I am grateful to the following individuals and institutions: Jean Langdon-Ford and Carol Ann Kennedy of the Canadian War Museum library; Myron Momryk at the National Archives; Claire Leblanc, senior research clerk, National Personnel Records Centre; Edward F. Murphy, Medal of Honor Historical Society; Dominic Rotondo of Canadian Vietnam Veterans, Quebec; and Gary Befus of Canadian Vietnam Veterans, Hamilton. I owe a very special debt to the Ontario Arts Council for its support. My publisher, Kirk Howard, encouraged me to do this book. To all those who responded to my advertisements in various publications, my sincere thanks. My appreciation goes to Frank McGuire for editorial assistance. My wife, Susan, allowed me the use of weekends to work on this book. Thanks also to Judith Turnbull, my editor once again, for her superb work. Above all, I would like to express my gratitude to those who contributed their stories.

PART ONE

From the American Civil War until the Second World War

Canadian Cross of Sacrifice in Arlington National Cemetery.
U.S. Army

INTRODUCTION

In the American Revolution (1775–83) many Loyalists fought on the British side against independence. Some formed Loyalist provincial corps. The King's Royal Regiment of New York under Sir John Johnson, Butler's Rangers under John Butler, and Mohawk Loyalists led by Joseph Brant are a few notable examples.

While there have been and remain many differences between those living on either side of the 49th parallel, there has been a steady flow of people back and forth across the border. This has continued even in time of war. The last serious military conflict between the two countries was the War of 1812; ever since, men from both countries have honourably served in the others' armed forces.

Nevertheless, on Armistice Day 1927, while officials of the Canadian and American governments were honouring Americans who had fought with the Canadian forces in the First World War before the U.S. entered the conflict, the military staffs of both countries continued to plan for possible war against each other. Canadian-American relations have always had two faces. By 1927 there had developed numerous friendly ties through intermarriage and commerce, but there was still a streak of anti-Americanism in Canada. It was only very gradually that American-Canadian military cooperation on a governmental basis emerged. Friendships with Americans were one part of the wartime military experience.

The stories in this book are not of generals, air marshals or admirals; they are the stories of ordinary Canadians and Americans. But these individuals are different in that they left their own country to fight in the armed forces of the neighbouring country in time of war.

THE AMERICAN CIVIL WAR

CANADIANS IN THE AMERICAN CIVIL WAR, 1861–1865

In the mid-nineteenth century, Canadians with a taste for adventure usually volunteered to fight on foreign battlefields under the British flag. No exact statistics as to their numbers are available. In May 1861 Britain proclaimed that it would not intervene in the American Civil War, but many Canadians, in disregard of British neutrality, enlisted in the armies of both the North and the South.

In 1863 Congress passed a conscription or draft law for the North. To avoid service, any man could come up with a commutation fee or find a substitute willing to serve in his place. Some British North Americans were enticed to replace a draftee for money. Other Canadians were crimped, that is, forced by military procurers into the Northern armies. British soldiers deserted their own forces to enjoy the better pay in the armies of the North or South. While draft evaders crossed the border into the British colonies, Canadians moved to the United States to seek employment. While it is known that the American Civil War had a profound impact on that country, it also affected the British North American colonies politically, economically and socially.

Some 2,500,000 men served in the Union and Confederate armies, and about 600,000 died.[1] According to the American census of 1860, 250,000 people living in the United States gave a place of birth in British North America. Of the many recruits listed as British North Americans several reached the rank of general, including Jacob D. Cox, John F. Farnsworth and John McNeil. The number of Canadians who fought in the American Civil War is unknown. Estimates have ranged as high as 40,000,[2] but it was likely much lower.

SARAH EDMONDS

Sarah Emma Evelyn Edmonds served in the Civil War mainly as a "male" nurse with the Union forces. She was born in December 1841 in Maguadavic, New Brunswick. There were already several girls and one boy in the family. Her father, a farmer, wanted only male progeny and considered the birth of yet another girl a cruel act of God. He arranged for Emma, at age fifteen, to marry an older man she detested. She ran away from home and eventually disguised herself as a man, ending up in Flint, Michigan. There, as "Franklin Thompson," she became a book agent for a Connecticut publishing company.

Sarah Emma Edmonds in male disguise as Franklin Thompson.
Lucy Sterling Seelye

When the Civil War broke out Emma, then twenty, enlisted as Franklin Thompson on 25 May 1861. She served for three years as a member of Company F, 2nd Regiment, Michigan Infantry, accompanying that unit to Virginia. She was a field nurse. Emma also served as a spy. On a good number of occasions, she used various male and female disguises to learn the number of Confederate troops and assess the strength of their fortifications prior to battle. She contracted malaria while on a spying mission in the Chickahominy swamps in May 1862, and in the following year it flared up again. At the end of her physical and mental resources (what we would now call battle exhaustion) and fearing certain exposure in hospital, Emma at Lebanon, Kentucky, deserted on 22 April 1863.

Emma moved to Oberlin, Ohio, and stayed in a boarding house. There, with medical attention, she recovered, but it took longer than she expected. A healthier "Franklin Thompson" left for Pittsburgh as a man, but returned as a slim attractive woman, Sarah Emma Edmonds, still in need of rest. During this second convalescence, Emma wrote *Nurse and Spy*. In it, she drew not only from her own experiences but from those of others as well, using fictional names. The book was published by her former employer in Hartford and sold over 170,000 copies. Emma gave the royalties to the Sanitary and Christian Commissions for the benefit of sick and wounded Union soldiers.

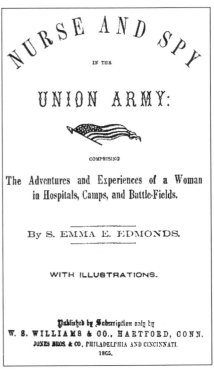

NURSE AND SPY

IN THE

UNION ARMY:

COMPRISING

The Adventures and Experiences of a Woman in Hospitals, Camps, and Battle-Fields.

By S. EMMA E. EDMONDS.

WITH ILLUSTRATIONS.

Published by Subscription only by
W. S. WILLIAMS & CO., HARTFORD, CONN.
JONES BROS. & CO., PHILADELPHIA AND CINCINNATI.
1865.

In 1864 Emma returned to hospital duty as a female civilian at St. Louis, Missouri, during January and February of 1864, and at Harpers Ferry, Virginia, in the fall. There she met Linus H. Seely, a widower from West Saint John, New Brunswick. His family were originally United Empire Loyalists from Virginia. Seely was a carpenter by trade. On 27 April 1867 Emma married him in Cleveland. She soon added an "e" to the surname. None of their offspring survived past early childhood and they adopted two young boys. The Seelyes settled in Fort Scott, Kansas, and remained there for a dozen years.

About twenty years after the war, poor health persuaded Emma to apply for a pension. She obtained affidavits of her war service from 1861 to 1862 from former comrades. On 5 July 1884 Congress approved her claims and granted her a pension of twelve dollars a month. Two days later President Chester H. Arthur approved the bill. In October Emma attended a reunion of her regiment in Flint. On 3 July 1886, after further lobbying, a charge of desertion against Franklin Thompson, alias S.E.E. Seelye, was removed by act of Congress and signed four days later by President Grover Cleveland.

The Seelyses' last move was to La Porte, Texas. On 5 September 1898 Emma died. On her tombstone appear the words EMMA E SEELYE, ARMY NURSE. That was how she wished to be remembered.[3]

EDWARD E. DODDS

Some 1,500 Medals of Honor were awarded during the American Civil War. Among the approximately thirty Canadian winners was Sergeant Edward Edwin Dodds (1845–1901). Born near Port Hope, Canada West, in 1845, he was a volunteer with Company C, 21st New York Cavalry. He received the Medal of Honor for bravery at Ashby's Gap, Virginia, on 19 July 1864, for rescuing his wounded captain from death in the face of the enemy and carrying him from the field to a place of safety. A commemorative plaque in his honour was erected near his grave at Canton Cemetery in Hope Township.

Edward E. Dodds while clerk of Hope Township, Ontario.
Richard Gardiner, East Durham Historical Society

Of the Canadians who were awarded the Medal of Honor, about one-third were navy. Four of the naval Medals of Honor were earned at the Battle of Mobile Bay on 5 August 1864 and two of these were awarded to Canadians, Landsman William Pelham and Coxswain Thomas Fitzpatrick, both serving on Admiral David G. Farragut's flagship.

THE WOLVERTONS

Enos Wolverton came from Ohio in 1826 at age sixteen, settling with his family in Oxford County, Canada West. By 1834 he had begun farming on his own nearby and raising a family. Newton, his son, was born there in 1846. In 1849 Enos moved to a piece of land on the River Nith in the Eighth Concession. This was the origin of the village of Wolverton. At age thirteen Newton was sent to Cleveland, Ohio, to attend school with his two elder brothers, Alfred and Jasper, who had left home to receive an education.

When civil war broke out in the United States in 1861, the three brothers enlisted in the 50th New York Infantry. When it was learned they were experienced horsemen, they were transferred to the quartermaster's department. Alfred was given charge of over a hundred six-horse teams. Newton was made wagon-master of twenty-five of the six-horse teams. A fourth brother, Alonzo, came to Cleveland and enlisted in the 20th Ohio Artillery. Jasper died early in the war from typhoid fever. Newton himself was hospitalized for three months as a result of exposure during the winter of 1861–62. He was assigned clerical work for a time in Washington.

In consequence of the *Trent* Affair (the seizure by the North of two Confederate emissaries from a British ship) in late 1861, pressure was mounting on Lincoln to declare war on Britain. Newton Wolverton, just sixteen, now in Washington, served as a spokesman for the Canadians serving in the Northern army. He led the delegation of British North Americans in the Union forces to point out to the president that they had not enlisted to fight against Britain. With the settling of the affair, the threat of war subsided.

Newton Wolverton, 1864, a member of the 22nd Oxford Rifles.
Oxford Historical Society

Early in 1863, Alfred died of smallpox while in the service. In June, Newton's term of service expired and he returned home. Alonzo remained in the army until war's end.

Newton resumed his education, became a Baptist minister, then a teacher and principal of the Canadian Literary Institute, later renamed Woodstock College. He died in Vancouver on 31 January 1932 after a long and distinguished career.

OTHER BRITISH NORTH AMERICANS

Canadian blacks living in British North America, especially in towns in what is now southern Ontario, crossed the border to fight for the Union cause. Many were former slaves.[4] A considerable number of recent immigrants from Ireland crossed the border and enlisted in the Union forces to join fellow countrymen. Many went only with the intention of serving in a support role as engineers, labourers, doctors, even musicians. Among the now better-known Canadians who joined the Union forces were Calixa Lavallée, the composer of Canada's national anthem, and Frederick Howe, son of a prominent Nova Scotian, Joseph Howe.

One individual who joined the Union Army was Alfred F. Armstrong, born 10 August 1840 in Kent County, Canada West. For him, taking part in the Civil War was a way to escape the humdrum existence of daily life and to make more money than he could in Canada. He enlisted at Grand Rapids, Michigan, on 19 September 1861 for three years, and was assigned to Company D, 1st Michigan Regiment. By 1 February 1864 he had risen to the rank of quarter-master sergeant. He was honourably discharged at the expiration of his service in October. Like a good number of other Canadian soldiers, his army life often had more to do with coping with daily existence than with exciting action.[5]

William W. Cooke was born in Mount Pleasant, Canada West, on 29 May 1846. His father was the local doctor. William resided in Canada until the age of fourteen when he continued his studies in Buffalo. During the Civil War he enlisted in the 24th New York Cavalry. He became a second lieutenant on 26 January 1864 and a first lieutenant on 14 December. He fought at Petersburg, Virginia (17 June 1864), near Charleston, Virginia (29 March 1865), and Sailors Creek, Virginia (6 April 1865). He was honourably discharged 25 June 1865. After the Civil War, Cooke re-enlisted on 28 June 1866 in the 7th Cavalry. On 25 June 1876 he was killed in action, along with General Custer, by Sioux Indians at Little Bighorn, Montana.[6]

John A. Huff was born on 14 November 1816 in East Gwillimbury Township (north-east of Toronto), Ontario. He was a carpenter. John moved to

Lieutenant William Cooke of Brantford, Ontario, c. 1875.
Little Bighorn Battlefield National Monument

Royalton, Niagara County, New York, where he married on 3 July 1841. He eventually settled in Armada, Macomb County, Michigan. Like many other British North Americans then living in the northern United States, he joined the Union forces. It is generally accepted that as Private John Huff of Company E, 5th Michigan Cavalry, he killed Confederate Lieutenant-General J.E.B. Stuart on 11 May 1864, near Richmond, Virginia. Huff himself was wounded at the end of May and died about a month later.[7] Raymond Huff of Toronto, the great, great, great nephew of John, is a director of the American Civil War Historical Re-enactment Society.

Some Canadians served in the Confederate forces. Their numbers, although considerably fewer than in the Union Army, are unknown. A majority of British North Americans in the Confederate ranks were already living in the South before the war. If a few individuals from one village or township from Canada enlisted in a particular unit, other locals would frequently follow their example. Some French Canadians from Quebec found their way into Louisiana regiments as well. French Canadian names also appear on the nominal rolls of many New England regiments.

Enlistments from British North America were enhanced by crimping. The crimps initially concentrated on British soldiers and militia, later turning to younger members of the civilian population. Male crimpers often used liquor while female crimps utilized drugged tea. Various forms of deceit and enticements were used to lure able young British North Americans across the border to fill enlistment quotas.

The American Civil War created a sudden need for large numbers of medical practitioners. Many came from British North America. Francis M. Wafer, a Queen's medical student, was an assistant surgeon to the 108th New York Regiment. He recorded his experiences in letters home. Dr. Solomon Secord from Kincardine, Canada West, was captured serving as a surgeon to a Georgia regiment. There is a memorial to him in Kincardine. William Cannitt, a physician from Canada West, returned home to write a history of Ontario. A plaque in his honour is located at Cannifton-Corbyville School, Hastings County.

Captain Jonathan George Ryan, a printer from Toronto serving in the Confederate army, had the notoriety of being incarcerated for nearly four months without trial as a suspect in Lincoln's death. A wave of hysteria swept the United States following the assassination and all possible suspects were sought. Ryan had written a letter to a Jackson, Mississippi, newspaper on 26 April 1865 praising the assassination twelve days before. Following his release from prison, Ryan became a lawyer in Chicago.

As a neutral country, Canada became a haven for secret agents, mainly from the South. Confederates used the area as a base. William Collins of Montreal and three other Confederate supporters tried unsuccessfully to rob a bank in Maine and were charged. Perhaps the best-known Confederate raid was a successful bank robbery in St. Albans, Vermont, by a small Canadian-based guerrilla force.

Brigadier General Edwin Gray Lee, a second cousin of Robert E. Lee, was forced by tuberculosis to leave the Confederate army in late 1864, and moved to Montreal where the cold, dry winter climate was supposedly to help his condition. He served there as the representative of the Confederate government. He gave moral support to the St. Albans raiders during their trial and offered financial assistance to prominent Confederate refugees living in Montreal, such as General George E. Pickett of Gettysburg fame, who had fled after the fall of Richmond. Lee helped John H. Surratt Jr., a suspect in Lincoln's assassination, to escape to Italy. Lee returned to the South after the war and finally succumbed to his illness on 25 August 1870 at age thirty-four. The famous Confederate spy Belle Boyd (1883–1900), after spending August to December 1863 in Washington's Carroll Prison, was paroled to Canada. She soon left for England, where she took to the stage to support herself. After the war she returned to the United States and offered dramatic one-woman re-enactments of her career as "The Cleopatra of the Secession."

After the Civil War, a good number of veterans moved to Canada. For example, Private William Barnett, the last survivor of Pickett's charge on 3 July 1863, is buried at Bottrel, near Calgary, Alberta. He died there in 1933 at age eighty-nine while visiting his sons who had moved from Virginia.

American draft-evaders or -dodgers were also referred to as skedaddlers. So many draft-dodgers settled around Mapleton, New Brunswick, that the area was named Skedaddle Ridge. There was also a Skeddaddler's Reach on Campobello Island, and settlements of draft-dodgers appeared along the Maine–New Brunswick border.

Problems arising from the American Civil War did not end in 1865. In 1866 and 1870 there were incursions by Fenians, Irish nationalists whose aim was to seize parts of British North America as ransom in exchange for independence for Ireland. Many of them were Union veterans.

TURN OF THE CENTURY

Throughout the latter part of the nineteenth century there continued to be small numbers of men born in Canada serving in the United States Army. Some others served in the U.S. Navy. Willard and Harry Miller were two brothers from Nova Scotia who served in the navy in the Spanish-American War and who both won the Medal of Honor, the highest American award for valour.

Of the 112 Americans who served with the Canadians during the South African War, 1899–1902, most were young, single, Protestant, from rural areas, and without previous military experience. Most came from west of the Mississippi River. Perhaps the best known was American-born Major A.L. "Gat" Howard, named after the Gatling gun he operated during the North-West Rebellion of 1885.[8] After the war, most returned to the United States.

THE FIRST WORLD WAR, 1914–1918

While Canada was at war with Germany in August 1914, it was two and a half years before the United States entered the conflict. In the meantime, significant numbers of Americans crossed the border to enlist. At the time of the First World War there was a good deal of anti-Americanism in Canada. The presence of American citizens in Canadian units did not always help assuage some stereotypical beliefs about "the Yankees," even among those with whom they served. Initially Prime Minister Robert Borden discouraged the enlistment of Americans in Canadian Expeditionary Force (CEF) units, but his attitude changed when he was informed that Lord Kitchener, British secretary of state for war, wished to encourage it. Thus, thousands of Americans entered the CEF.

The zealousness of Canadian recruiters at border points eventually caused a rift between Borden and the governor general, the Duke of Connaught. The American Foreign Enlistment Act of 1818 had made the recruitment of American citizens on their own soil for service against a country with which the United States was not at war a criminal offence. This law had been extended to include the offering of inducements to entice Americans to go abroad to enlist. The governor general felt that Canadian actions were breaching imperial policy, endangering relations with the United States, and permitting German agents to infiltrate Canadian forces. Borden insisted on the right of Canada to enlist American volunteers and succeeded in asserting Canadian independence in this area. However, abuses in Canadian recruiting practices were subsequently curbed.[9]

AMERICANS IN THE CANADIAN EXPEDITIONARY FORCE

During the First World War, 35,612 persons of American origin who were resident in Canada in August 1914, or who later crossed the frontier into Canada, independently and voluntarily enlisted in the Canadian Expeditionary Force. Over 600,000 persons served in the CEF. In the First Contingent, which sailed from Canada 33,000 strong in October 1914, were 791 men born in the United States. Before the U.S. came into the war, some Americans would join Canadian battalions recruiting near the border in the autumn. They would spend the winter training with these battalions but desert in the spring. Some who re-enlisted, however, soon found themselves headed overseas. Americans made up 20 percent of recruits of some border battalions in southern Ontario prior to 6 April 1917.

Sam Hughes, Canada's minister of militia and defence, offered to create a battalion of American citizens resident in Canada. The 97th Battalion, based in Toronto, was recognized in December 1915 as the unit for Americans to join. It was to be the nucleus of a brigade consisting of Americans recruited in the United States. Several Canadian officers of the 97th crossed the border to recruit men. Militia funds were also used to pay transportation costs of potential soldiers who were accompanied into Canada by enlisted men in civilian clothes from the 97th. The 97th Battalion developed a reputation for disciplinary problems because the men became frustrated when they weren't sent overseas promptly. The battalion finally went overseas in August 1916, but it was broken up and its men were absorbed by other units.

In February 1916 four more battalions for Americans – the 211th, 212th, 213th and 237th – were formed in Vancouver, Winnipeg, Toronto and Sussex, New Brunswick. These were unofficially designated "The American Legion." Over 2,700 enlisted in this so-called legion; 1,619 of these sailed from Canada; and 1,049 served in France. The American Legion's formation and existence exposed the Canadian government to a charge of disregarding the neutrality of the United States. The American government protested. As a result, by November 1916, four of the five battalions had ceased to exist, and when the 211th was disbanded in March 1917, the legion finally disappeared. Hughes had been replaced as minister of militia in November 1916, and without him the scheme to create a brigade of American volunteers came to an end.[10]

BRITISH AND CANADIAN RECRUITING MISSION

At the outbreak of the war in 1914, many British and Canadian subjects were living and working in the United States. Being neutral, the United States did not openly allow recruiting on its territory. When it entered the war, recruiting of British subjects for the British and Canadian forces was permitted.

On 8 May 1917, President Woodrow Wilson signed a bill permitting recruiting for the Canadian and British forces. The British and Canadian Recruiting Commission thus began to function, establishing depots east and west in all the leading American centres so that British and Canadian residents of the U.S. could join the British Army or the Canadian Expeditionary Force. Lieutenant-Colonel J.S. Dennis of Montreal was the senior Canadian member of the commission. Some 45,000 recruits were enlisted.

To bolster enlistments, there were parades, mass meetings, displays of captured German equipment, official British war pictures, and aeroplane demonstrations. A British tank was even brought over. The Jewish Legion attracted young Canadian and American men of the Jewish faith to enlist. This legion served as part of the British forces in Palestine.

A CEF battalion, the 97th "American Legion," parades down Toronto's University Avenue.
City of Toronto Archives, James Collection

With the implementation of the draft in the United States and conscription in Canada, the need for the British and Canadian recruiting mission ceased. It was agreed between Britain, Canada and the United States that American citizens in Canada or Great Britain of draft age would be conscripted into the Canadian or British Army and that British or Canadian subjects of draft age residing in the United States would be drafted into the American Army.[11]

While the Vietnam War is well known for bringing a large influx of American draft evaders to Canada, the two world wars also affected the movement of young men, and at times families, across the border. When Canadian males of military age living in the United States became subject to American draft laws upon the U.S. entry into the Great War, Canadians ceased moving to the United States as a way of avoiding military service.[12] Britain, Canada and the United States permitted voluntary reciprocal military service of their subjects and citizens on 30 July 1918.[13]

THE BRITISH AIR SERVICES

The British air services proved popular among American citizens who wished to see action as pilots. Reasons for joining, besides a wish to fly, included a desire to help Britain and, in some cases, rejection by the American aerial service.

Initially, unless an American could prove that he was of pure European descent, which usually meant being the son of a natural born or a naturalized British subject, he was automatically disqualified from enlistment in the British air services. The Royal Flying Corps (RFC) displayed some latitude in allowing a few Americans who were serving in the Canadian Expeditionary Force to train as observers or as pilots. However, the Royal Naval Air Service (RNAS) policy was more restrictive. In the closing months of 1917, the RNAS also specified that the applicant must be "no more than 25 years of age nor less than 18 years of age on date of application," a greater restriction than the maximum thirty years of age they had originally found acceptable. They also had higher academic requirements, accepting only those with high school diplomas or, preferably, university degrees.

These barriers to the enlistment of Americans remained steadfastly in place until Lieutenant-Colonel Cuthbert G. Hoare, RFC, was sent by the British War Office to organize and command the

RFC Training Brigade in Canada in January 1917. This venture arose from increasing demands from the War Office for more aviators. Many of the Americans who came to Canada to enlist in the RFC (later the Royal Air Force) did so in 1917–18, especially after the United States declared war on Germany on 6 April 1917. Frustrated at not being accepted into the American air service, they crossed into Canada and joined the Royal Flying Corps. By the end of the war there were 1,717 Americans who had served in the RFC/RNAS and RAF.

Britain made an important contribution to the training of American pilots in Canada and the United States during the First World War. After the American entry in April 1917, close cooperation grew between the Royal Flying Corps, Canada, and the U.S. Signal Corps. The Royal Flying Corps trained individuals for the Signal Corps with Canadian equipment at existing aerodromes in Canada. In exchange, the aviation section of the Signal Corps erected and equipped two aerodromes in Texas capable of accom-

Launching the Seaplane. A. Lismer shows a U.S. Navy plane being launched at Eastern Passage, N.S.
Canadian War Museum

modating ten squadrons. In July 1917 about 1,400 men arrived from the United States and trained in Canada during the summer. In October and November the American squadrons in Canada and the 42nd and 43rd Wings of the RFC proceeded to the aerodromes that had been constructed at Fort Worth in Texas, and remained there during the winter. The 42nd and 43rd Wings as well as a school of aerial gunnery maintained active training from November 1917 until April 1918 and in time turned out over 1,900 pilots in addition to thousands of mechanics and technicians. The association that developed inspired a great number of Americans from Fort Worth to enlist in the RCAF early in the Second World War.

As Canada did not have an air force of its own in the First World War, a detachment of the U.S. Naval Air Service (USNAS) arrived at Halifax on 6 August 1918 with two flying boats for anti-submarine duty. By the end of the war, fourteen HS-2L flying boats were being operated by the USNAS from the stations at Dartmouth and Sydney. These machines carried out patrols and convoy flights.

Among those Americans who served in the British air services were Oliver LeBoutillier, Raymond Chandler, and George V. Bell.

OLIVER LEBOUTILLIER

Oliver LeBoutillier was born in Montclair, New Jersey, on 24 May 1895. His father was originally from the Isle of Jersey, United Kingdom, and his mother from Quebec. He trained at Wright School, Mineola, Long Island, New York, and on 21 August 1916 joined the Royal Naval Air Service in Ottawa. LeBoutillier was assigned to No. 9 Squadron in 1917. With the amalgamation of the RNAS and the Royal Flying Corps into the Royal Air Force on 1 April 1918, his squadron was renumbered No. 209, RAF. LeBoutillier was one of four

Lieutenant Oliver LeBoutillier.
Department of National Defence

American-born airmen in the RAF who took part in the last two battles of Manfred von Richthofen (the Red Baron), in April 1918. The others were William John Mackenzie of Memphis, Lloyd Andrews Hamilton of Troy, New York, and Mark Curtis Kinney of Mount Vernon, Ohio. Returning to the United States after the war, LeBoutillier became a barnstormer. He was also a stunt pilot in Hollywood. From 1948 LeBoutillier was a resident of Las Vegas, where he was president of a pharmaceutical firm. He died on 12 May 1983.[14]

RAYMOND CHANDLER

Raymond Thornton Chandler was born in Chicago on 23 July 1888. He is the author who created the well-known fictional character Philip Marlowe, a private detective. Chandler was a resident of Los Angeles when the First World War began. On 14 August 1917 he enlisted in the Canadian Expeditionary Force in Victoria, British Columbia. On 26 November he embarked from Halifax aboard the *Megantic.* In England he was put in a reserve battalion in December. As a private, Chandler served in France for a few months with the 7th Battalion until wounded. As an acting sergeant, Chandler joined No. 2 Cadet Wing, RAF, in the summer of 1918 in England. His training was cut short by the Armistice. He returned to Canada in February 1919 and was honourably discharged in Vancouver.

    After the war Chandler went back to California, where he was a successful oil company

Private Raymond Chandler in the kilt of the 50th Regiment of Victoria, B.C. He went on to become a famous author of detective fiction and a Hollywood screenwriter.
R. Chandler Estate

executive until the economic crash of the 1930s. He went on to become a successful writer of novels, such as *The Big Sleep* (1939), and screen plays, notably *Double Indemnity* (1944) and *Strangers on a Train* (1951). He died 26 March 1959 at La Jolla, California.[15]

GEORGE V. BELL

George V. Bell was born in Liverpool, England, on 26 May 1884. As a young man he moved to Detroit, where he worked as a printer for several years. When war broke out, he enlisted in Windsor on 8 August 1914. He served overseas with the 1st Battalion, then transferred on 25 January 1916 to the 3rd Battalion, and finally to the 10th Battalion on 2 September 1918. He never rose above the rank of private. He married while on leave in England on 23 January 1918.

Bell was gassed twice, in April 1915 and September 1918. As a result of the latter, he was hospitalized in England and Canada and honourably discharged on 26 March 1919. Bell continued to suffer from bronchitis for many years. He died in St. Petersburg, Florida, on 29 January 1963.[16] His account is typical of what he and other American volunteers as well as Canadians experienced.

Going In

When newsboys of downtown Detroit shouted "war extra" one fine morning in August 1914, curiosity led me to Windsor, directly across the river. I had no intention of enlisting. To be sure, I was born in England but had lived several years in the United States, had taken out my first naturalization papers, and in a few months I would receive my citizenship.

In Windsor curiosity was replaced by a desire for excitement and, besides, the homeland was threatened. I felt that the war would last only three to six months. That would give me transportation to England, a few days' leave to visit relatives and boyhood friends, and perhaps a chance to participate in the final battle of the war, with transportation furnished back to Canada. I found myself in a line at the Windsor armoury where I underwent a preliminary medical examination and was told that I would be notified when wanted.

After several days orders came for me to report at once. With others, I became a small cog in the gigantic war machine that was being built. A few days later we were rolling eastward to Valcartier, the great camp near Quebec, where thousands of young men were pouring in from all parts of the Dominion. We were the raw material out of which was forged the 1st Canadian Division. With daily drilling the feeling of awkwardness wore off, and the individualism which each man possessed disappeared as we began to find our places. The individual soldier thought less of himself and began to think in terms of sections, platoons, companies and the battalion, of cooperation and coordination.

In late September we were considered sufficiently trained to go to England which we did in October. We entrained at Mount Plymouth for the great camp at Salisbury Plain to complete our training and settled down for an English winter with mud which thousands of marching feet churned into a thick soup. But it was good experience, for in France we found more mud.

Time came when I was entitled to a pass and I went to Liverpool, my birthplace, and the home of my brother John, whom I had not seen in ten years. There I met John's wife's family and I was particularly attracted to a little brunette, her sister.

France

We crossed to France in February. We were a long way from the front line where we wanted to be. Our impressions of St. Nazaire were that it was a tremendously busy place, as shipload after shipload of troops and supplies were unloaded. We were quickly bundled into the famous "40 hommes ou 8 chevaux" type of box-car which French military authorities said could transport forty men or eight horses. Our officers explained the lack of comfort by reminding us "there's a war on," which I later learned covered everything that could not be accounted for otherwise, from rainy weather to failure of rations to come up.

Though we disembarked in the French mud of mid-winter, marching was a relief and it was with light hearts that we hiked a few miles to Merris, about twelve miles from the front line, arriving there on 13 February 1915. Our progress could be traced by the goatskin vests beside the road. These, designed to be worn under the overcoat, were copied from the Russians, but we found them so uncomfortable that we dumped most of them beside the road.

After six days of Merris we moved up to Armentières. Late in the afternoon orders came that we were to go into the line that night. At dark we were ordered to fall in. Pipes and cigarettes were extinguished and into the darkness we marched. We were now on our way to the front line trenches after travelling all the way from

Canada. Guides from a Leicester battalion holding the trenches were detailed to lead us up.

We found many things unlike what we expected. Trenches were scarcely trenches at all, merely parapets made by piling sandbags of earth on top of each other, about six bags thick at the bottom and three at the top. But as we filled fresh bags we kept lowering the level of the trench floor and thus bettered our protection. Some built dugouts by putting bags of earth on corrugated iron, giving fairly good security against shrapnel.

Taddy Callan, a young bugler, couldn't resist the temptation to take just one peep at what lay beyond. He raised his head above the top and almost instantly slumped and spread grotesquely on the ground, a bullet hole in his forehead. We were all solemn as we carried him back to the rear for burial – our first casualty.

One night Private Cope and myself are detailed to a listening post. Out there in the cold and darkness, ankle deep in freezing water, I reflect on the passing of martial glory. Gone are the immaculate uniforms, blaring bands and cheering crowds on the sidewalk; instead are mud, eerie silence broken by occasional rifle fire, and ahead darkness, punctuated now and then by a star shell which sheds a ghastly light on broken stumps, barbed wire posts and weeds nodding in the breeze. Things take on strange forms, the star shell fades and darkness settles down. It is a terrible lonely place.

We found that both sides had a common enemy. They came by the millions in massed formation up and down the seams of our underwear, and then deployed in extended order. Each of us conducted his own campaign, going over clothing and routing the enemy as much as possible. But it was a hopeless task. We gave up in despair and settled down to make the best of it, looking forward to the day when we could get to a hot shower and clean clothes. The cootie was victorious. He lived on us and we lived in mud. War had resolved itself down to the point where the lousiest and the dirtiest, the one who could best stand the filth and muck of the trenches, was the best soldier.

Gas

So peaceful were our surroundings in this village of Vlamertinghe that officers arranged a sports day for the battalion on a field just outside the village. That date was 22 April 1915. As we cheer our favourite athletes we hear the thunder of artillery increasing in intensity, and we stop for a few minutes to watch shells bursting in the distance, flecking the sky with fleecy smoke. About five in the evening a pitiable procession comes streaming past our billets. They're all coughing and gasping ...

Leave to England
Seven days' leave!

What a thrill comes to a man in the trenches when he gets word that he is actually going to get away from it all for a whole week.

"Liverpool?" asks a government guide. "Go to Paddington station." As I shuffle through the streets I see clean faces, well-pressed suits. What beautiful girls. Fresh, rosy complexions, well fed and not wan and war torn as they are in France. Was I once like these people or am I from another planet? No one notices me and I am unspeakably lonely, a solitary figure in that city of millions. The crowds do not know my bewilderment. I feel that I don't belong in their sphere. I've been living in the jungle of savagery for a year, shut off from the civilized world.

Liverpool! I get off the train and there is my older sister with her family of youngsters waiting for me on the platform. I unhitch my equipment and lay it down as they rush toward me.

"George," is the only word she says as we embrace each other. I can't say a word. I'm weak in the knees, a mist comes over my eyes and my throat begins to fill.

So I'm tough, am I? I who have gone through a year of hell am about to blubber like a baby. Great guy, I am.

The youngsters are scrapping to see who will carry my rifle and who my kit bag. This is different. No longer am I among strangers. I am among my own kind, my own kin.

"Why do they call you Canadians white Ghurkas?" asks my sister. In as bold a tone as I can muster I reply, "Because we're so damn tough," and make a motion for all to enter the parlour of a little inn across the street.

"How many Germans have you killed?" "What does a battle sound like?" "Are we going to win?" "What do you have to eat?" – and so on almost without end.

My sister and the kids do not monopolize all my time. There is that little brunette whom I met for the first time the year before when on leave from Salisbury Plain, the sister of brother John's wife. Events move quickly in time of war and before I am ready to return to France she has pledged herself to be my wife.

The end of my leave is near. Will I ever see my sister, the kids and my sweetheart again? It is a solemn day for me.

Shot at Dawn

We receive a hurried order to "roll out and fall in." What has happened? It is pitch dark. Has the enemy broken through and are we to be rushed in to stop his advance? Only on occasions when the enemy is near are verbal orders given, rather than by a bugle. We turn out quickly in full battle array and the roll is called. Then comes the mystifying order to take off our equipment and fall in again. Why should we be routed out in the middle of the night and ordered to fall in again without arms?

We are quickly lined up and in the darkness the battalion begins a march across the open country for about three miles. I, like everyone else, am trying to figure out what it means. Toward the end of the third mile, I hear an automobile coming down the road from our rear, and as it passes I see it is a motor ambulance. What is an ambulance doing this time in the morning with no battle going on? Five minutes later we are halted, the colonel gallops up and orders: "Battalion will stand at attention and not a sound made until further notice."

The eastern sky is faintly flushed with the first rays of dawn. It seems like an eternity as we stand there in the ghostly light. Figures are unreal in the dawn that creeps over us as the sun rises higher and higher. It is not light enough to see plainly, but I note to myself that it is going to be a nice day.

From an old barn in front of us comes the sound of chanting, growing louder as the processional in a church swells with the approach of the choir. The door opens and a figure in uniform shuffles out, an armed escort on each side, the chaplain walking behind and chanting the prayers for the dead.

I now realize that we are about to see a man die. We had grown accustomed to killing and to seeing men die, but only in battle. This is different. That shuffling figure is one of us. He has fought with us, slept with us, eaten with us. We, who have seen thousands die, are called out at this unearthly hour to see one man die. What an ironic thing it seems to be.

The little procession of four reaches the sides of the barn, the escort and chaplain stand to one side, the latter continuing his chant. I close my eyes. The solemn notes are torn apart by the crash of rifle fire. As I open my eyes I see a huddled heap on the ground and the ambulance being driven toward the spot.

The adjutant faces the battalion and reads: "Pay attention to proceedings of general court martial of Private – – –, third battalion, charged with desertion. Accused was found guilty and sentenced to suffer death by being shot. Sentence was duly carried out at dawn."

Orders were given and, deep in thought, the battalion marched back. Not a word was spoken during the return.

The condemned man was only nineteen years old. He had received a bad shaking up a few days before when a big shell exploded near him. I knew how he felt. After that the sound of every shell seemed magnified a thousand times. One particularly dark night as the battalion was moving up to the front line, an explosion of shrapnel sent him diving into the ditch beside the road. Unlike the others, he failed to rejoin the battalion after the shelling had ceased. He waited until the battalion had gone forward and then made his way back to the base.

Vimy Ridge

Once more we were taken a few miles back of the lines where we went through a full dress rehearsal for the capture of Vimy Ridge. I am back at the headquarters, a member of a composite company

The battlefield as seen from Vimy Ridge, looking towards the German lines, May 1917.
National Archives of Canada, PA-1809

detailed to carry ammunition and rations in and the wounded out ... We have captured the ridge, taken thousands of prisoners and gained much territory, including some villages, but are disappointed in not having been able to take full advantage of this success ...

Passchendaele
Capture of Passchendaele was the objective and British troops were opening the way. We moved forward in November. The enemy, during this long interval, had been pushed miles further back and the country he left was unrecognizable. Practically everything had disappeared and I realized more than ever the terrible destructive force of war.

It was now near winter and the mud was sticky and ankle deep. We went up to the front lines on duckboards laid by the engineers to keep us out of the mud as much as possible. Most of the wounded had to make their way back as best they could, as it was impossible to send up a sufficient number of stretcher-bearers. It was bad enough for an able-bodied man, but for those weakened by wounds it was sheer torture. A pitiable procession limped back from the front. Many slipped off the duckboards and into the mud which gripped them in its sticky embrace, while they floundered about helplessly. It was hours before many could be reached and then it was too late. Deeper and deeper they sank until death ended their sufferings. For eight days the battle went on, one day like the rest except that our morale was sinking as we floundered in the mud.

Amiens
On 8 August 1918, our artillery opened a terrific bombardment. We had at last assumed the offensive and there was a feeling that the critical time had arrived. The Canadian Corps was on the right of the attack on the Hindenburg Line, with Australians and British on the left and French on the right of the British Fourth Army. Much further to the right there were Americans, I was told, although I did not know it at the time.

After artillery had sufficiently pounded the German lines, we went forward at a signal and from the start it was easy going, easiest we had ever experienced. We cleared the first two lines of trenches in a few minutes, assisted by tanks which were doing better work now. The tanks lumbered along, flattening machine-gun positions. We bumped into some exceptionally strong isolated machine-gun posts, but the tanks disposed of them. The end of the third day found the Germans falling back rapidly, giving our cavalry a chance to get into action.

Hindenburg Line

The whole corps was massed there and on 2 September we kicked off with the famous Hindenburg Line as our objective. This was supposed to be the last word in entrenchment systems and was considered to be impregnable, but we were so bucked up with our previous success that we considered ourselves invincible.

The battle started early in the morning with a terrific bombardment from our artillery. It was still dark and it was an impressive sight to see the thousands of shells bursting in and over the enemy trenches. Nothing, so far, had come from them.

I was now in the machine-gun crew of the fourth platoon of A Company, and within two minutes after the attack I could see that we were in for tough going. We were not having the easy time of it we enjoyed in the south. We had no tanks to aid us and we had to go it alone.

We were on the left flank of the attack and south of the Arras-Cambrai road and there we were being held up. We had but sixteen men left out of the platoon. Eight of us were organized in two sections of four men each, and with a Lewis machine gun in addition to our rifles, were ordered to clean up a machine gun post lately established in front of us.

One man dropped dead with a bullet through his head. Another was hit in the jaw, the bullet ripping out all his lower teeth and gums. Another man, a newcomer, was hit and we dropped into a shell hole in No Man's Land, leading to a small communication trench or sap.

We were now able to move underground without being seen. I talked it over with the rest of the crew and arranged that some move be made further to the right. Both our sections were below the surface and about thirty yards from our objective directly in front. After our other crew had crawled about fifty yards to our right, they started firing into the air from the bottom of the sap. The enemy gun crew thought them the attacking party and swung their gun around, sending a stream of bullets in that direction to prevent them from emerging to make an attack. This gave our section the chance they were looking for, and we dashed across the broken ground, covering the thirty yards before the crew could swivel the gun around in our direction with any effect. We bayonet-ed the crew and I shot one from the hip, being unable to take aim because we were so close. The others threw up their hands and the whole thing ended in about three minutes, but for sheer excite-ment there was as much packed in that brief time as in three days of ordinary battle. We were now in a position to post our gun on this new place of entrenchment.

Blighty at Last
Bump, bump. I seem to be moving. I look around. A few feet from me I see two men stretched out in bunks, one above the other. I collect my scattered wits and it dawns upon me that I am in an ambulance. I ache all over. Every time I move pains shoot through me and it hurts to breathe.

It was several days before I knew what had happened. A shell had hit the dugout in which we were "quite comfortable." I was knocked unconscious and those of us who were still alive were dug out of the dirt. Some of the other boys had been killed, however. Both my ankles had been badly wrenched, my collar bone had been dislocated and I was badly dosed with gas, while buried unconscious beneath the earth, gas from shells which the enemy now used almost entirely.

During the next ten days I suffered severely from this gas which affected my throat, chest, eyes and head. At first they thought I had pleurisy, but decided I had escaped it. I was taken to No. 26 British Field Hospital at Etaples, France. There I was given excellent treat-ment for two weeks and then shipped to that heaven on earth – Blighty. My ticket read "general debility and war worn" which cov-ers a multitude of incapacities.

Eight weeks of splendid care and treatment made me feel human again. I was sent to the Canadian Military Hospital at Shorncliffe near Folkstone in Kent. As I looked at the hills on the French side of the Channel I thought of the millions of lives that had been spent trying to take them and the millions spent to hold them. What an expensive piece of real estate!

Armistice and Home
Bells ringing! Whistles blowing! Crowds in the streets cheering! What is it? The armistice. The war is over. Germany has quit.

While at Folkstone I was finally passed through a medical board in December and marked "medically unfit for further military service."

I was sent to the collecting station at Liverpool where about a thousand Canadians, all invalids, were awaiting their turn to sail on hospital ships to Canada. Luck was still with me. Here I was in the city of my birth, the city where I was married when on leave.

It is Christmas Eve, 1918.

I had two days' leave from the hospital. It was the first Christmas of peace in five years. I go to the home of my wife and with relatives we had planned a real old-fashioned English Christmas, a day of thanksgiving.

We finally embarked on the hospital ship *Araguaya*, but instead of sailing for Canada we landed at Portland, Maine. It was winter and navigation in the St. Lawrence was closed. What a reception! We expected to land with little ceremony and board the Red Cross train immediately. What did the Yankees care about some Canadian soldiers? They had soldiers of their own to welcome. But we had not reckoned on Yankee hospitality. It made no difference if we were Canadians; American soldiers could not have received a warmer welcome. The dock was crowded and what a cheer went up as our ship warped into place.

By train we were sent to different dispersal areas. My battalion area was London, Ontario, and there we went through the usual form of medical examination.

Those who were able to travel were given fourteen days' leave, and I was soon in Detroit, the first glimpse I had of it since that day in August 1914. What a thrill it was to get my feet on those familiar pavements. How good Woodward, Gratiot, Jefferson and Michigan avenues and Grand Circus Park looked to me.

In the CEF in France, one out of 22 were born in the United States. Of 344,596 who served in the CEF in France, there were 15,221 Americans, and 63 of these were nursing sisters. Out of a total of 61,112 fatal casualties in the CEF, 2,138 were of U.S. birth, that is, about one out of every 29. Americans serving with the CEF came mainly from northern states such as Massachusetts. Many, like Bell, had family connections in Great Britain and Canada.[17]

VICTORIA CROSSES WON BY AMERICANS

Five Victoria Crosses were awarded to Americans serving in the Canadian Expeditionary Force. George Harry Mullin of Portland, Oregon, a member of Princess Patricia's Canadian Light Infantry, was awarded the VC for his actions at Passchendaele on 30 October 1917:

Lieutenant G.H. Mullin, VC. This photo was taken after the First World War.
National Archives of Canada, PA-6946

For most conspicuous bravery in attack, when single-handed he captured a commanding "Pill-Box" which had withstood the heavy bombardment and was causing heavy casualties to our forces and holding up the attack. He rushed a sniper's post in front, destroyed the garrison with bombs, and crawling on to the top of the "Pill-Box" he shot the two machine gunners with his revolver. Sgt. Mullin then rushed to another entrance and compelled the garrison of ten to surrender.

His gallantry and fearlessness were witnessed by many, and, although rapid fire was directed upon him, and his clothes riddled by bullets, he never faltered in his purpose and he not only helped to save the situation but also indirectly saved many lives.

"Tackling a pill-box."
Canadian War Museum, 71-5961

The Victoria Cross.
Canadian War Museum

Although Frederick George Coppins gave his place of birth as London, England, he was, in fact, born in San Francisco on 25 October 1889. At the outbreak of the war, he joined the 19th Alberta Dragoons in Edmonton. He went to France with the 1st Division and was awarded the VC for his courage on 9 August 1918 in the Battle of Amiens.

For most conspicuous bravery and devotion to duty during an attack when his platoon came unexpectedly under fire of numerous machine-guns. It was not possible to advance or to retire, and no cover was available. It

Frederick George Coppins.
National Archives of Canada, PA-6766

became apparent that the platoon would be annihilated unless the machine-guns were silenced immediately. Corporal Coppins, without hesitation, and on his own initiative, called on four men to follow him and leapt forward in the face of intense machine-gun fire. With his comrades he rushed straight for the machine-guns. The four men with him were killed and Corporal Coppins wounded. Despite his wounds, he reached the hostile machine-guns alone, killed the operator of the first gun and three of the crew, and made prisoners of four others, who surrendered.

Corporal Coppins, by his act of outstanding valour, was the means of saving many lives of the men of his platoon, and enabled the advance to be continued.

Despite his wound, this gallant N.C.O. continued with his platoon to the final objective, and only left the line when it had been made secure and when ordered to do so.

Sergeant Raphael Louis Zengel of Faribault, Minnesota, with the 5th Battalion, also received the VC for his bravery during the Battle of Amiens, 9 August 1918:

Sergeant Raphael Louis Zengel, VC.
National Archives of Canada, PA-6796

> For most conspicuous bravery and devotion to duty when protecting the battalion left flank. He was leading his platoon gallantly forward to the attack, but had not gone far when he realized that a gap had occurred on his flank, and that an enemy machine-gun was firing at close range into the advancing line. Grasping the situation, he rushed forward some 200 yards ahead of the platoon, tackled the machine-gun emplacement, killed the officer and operator of the gun, and dispersed the crew. By his boldness and prompt action he undoubtedly saved the lives of many of his comrades.
>
> Later, when the battalion was held up by very heavy machine-gun fire, he displayed much tactical skill and directed his fire with destructive results. Shortly afterwards he was rendered unconscious for a few minutes by an enemy shell, but on recovering consciousness he at once continued to direct harassing fire on the enemy.
>
> Zengel's work throughout the attack was excellent, and his utter disregard for personal safety, and the confidence he inspired in all ranks, greatly assisted in bringing the attack to a successful end.

Tending a wounded soldier.
Canadian War Museum, 71-5985

Captain B.S. Hutcheson of Mount Carmel, Illinois, with the Canadian Army Medical Corps, attached to the 75th Battalion, won the VC during the Battle of the Drocourt-Quéant Line, 2 September 1918:

> For most conspicuous bravery and devotion to duty on September 2nd, when under most intense shell, machine-gun and rifle fire, he went through the Drocourt-Quéant Support Line with the battalion. Without hesitation and with utter disregard of personal safety he remained on the field until every wounded man had been attended to. He dressed the wounds of a seriously wounded officer under terrific machine-gun and shell fire, and, with the assistance of prisoners and of his own men, succeeded in evacuating him to safety, despite the fact that the bearer party suffered heavy casualties.
>
> Immediately afterwards he rushed forward in full view of the enemy, under heavy machine-gun and rifle fire, to tend a wounded sergeant, and having placed him in a shell hole, dressed his wounds. Captain Hutcheson performed many similar gallant acts, and, by his coolness and devotion to duty, many lives were saved.

Lance-Corporal William Henry Metcalf of Waite Township, Maine, also earned the VC in the Drocourt-Quéant Line on 2 September 1918 as a member of the 16th Battalion:

> For most conspicuous bravery, initiative and devotion to duty in attack, when, the right flank of the battalion being

Lance-Corporal William Henry Metcalf, VC.
Canadian War Museum

held up, he realized the situation and rushed forward under intense machine-gun fire to a passing tank on the left. With his signal flag he walked in front of the tank directing it along the trench in a perfect hail of bullets and bombs. The machine-gun strong points were overcome, very heavy casualties were inflicted on the enemy, and a very critical situation was relieved.

Later, although wounded, he continued to advance until ordered to get into a shell-hole and have his wounds dressed.

His valour throughout was of the highest standard.[18]

BETWEEN THE WARS

If I should die, think only this of me;
That there's some corner of a foreign land
That is for ever England.
                              – *Rupert Brooke*

In cemeteries, particularly in western Europe, are the graves of
Canadians killed in the First and Second World Wars. Their
final resting places have made that ground a part of the world
that is forever Canada. Similarly Americans killed fighting in
Canadian uniform and Canadians killed fighting in American uniform have left a part of themselves with those countries.

The official figure of men who on enlistment in the Canadian
Expeditionary Force gave their birth place as the United States or
Alaska is 35,612.[19] An act passed at the end of the war by Congress
allowed individuals in this category to reclaim their American citizenship.

In May of 1925 Prime Minister Mackenzie King requested
American permission to erect a memorial in the United States to
pay tribute to the citizens and residents of that country who had
enlisted in the Canadian forces and lost their lives in the First
World War. The Canadian government pointed out that one of the
most significant features of British military cemeteries was the
Cross of Sacrifice. In June 1925 President Calvin Coolidge gave his
approval for the erection of such a memorial in Arlington National
Cemetery. The monument, located northwest of the Memorial
Amphitheatre, was unveiled 11 November 1927 by Canadian
Minister of National Defence J.L. Ralston. Vincent Massey, the
Canadian first minister at Washington, presented it to the people
of the United States, and American Secretary of State Frank
Kellogg accepted it on their behalf.[20] The Canadian government
sent over 200 Canadian troops to participate in the unveiling and
dedication ceremony. The Canadian guard of honour was com-
posed of men from the Royal Canadian Regiment and Royal 22nd

Dedication of the Canadian Cross of Sacrifice at Arlington National
Cemetery, 11 November 1927.
National Archives of Canada, C139756

Regiment in scarlet tunics, blue trousers and white helmets with red puggarees, together with the brass band of the RCR and the pipe band of the 48th Highlanders in full Highland kilt as well as three trumpeters from the Royal Canadian Horse Artillery and three from the Royal Canadian Dragoons. The American guard of honour was represented by men from the 3rd Battalion and 12th Infantry and by buglers from the Third United States Cavalry.

In his address at the dedication of the Cross of Sacrifice, Dwight F. Davis, U.S. secretary of war, said: "This monument will always be a source of pride to the citizens of the United States … In the years to come, this monument shall stand as a symbol of that friendship which has been sealed by the blood of our heroic sons."[21]

Unfortunately the monument was not maintained and the Canadian Department of Veteran Affairs has had to pay for the repair work to this "gift" to the United States.

Additional inscriptions were placed on the monument by the Canadian government to commemorate those killed during the

Second World War and the Korean conflict. As well as its commemorative aspect, the monument was to be "a symbol of the friendship and goodwill between the governments of the two countries." Most Canadians and Americans are unaware of the monument's existence or of what it represents.

President Coolidge and Vincent Massey, Canadian minister to the United States, with guard of honour, Washington, D.C., 1927.
National Archives of Canada

PART TWO
The Second World War, 1939–1945

INTRODUCTION

C anada has long had a love-hate relationship with United
States. While circumstances in the eighteenth and nineteenth centuries generated animosity between the two countries, those of the twentieth century have generally drawn them
together. In 1918 there was some cooperation between Canadian
and American aircraft and naval vessels in the battle against
German boats on the Atlantic coast. There was also limited cooperation during the Allied intervention in North Russia and Siberia.
Even following the First World War, however, both countries made
contingency plans for war against each other. Defence Scheme No.
1 by Colonel J. Sutherland Brown, the director of military operations and intelligence at National Defence Headquarters in Ottawa
from 1920 to 1927, saw the United States as the major threat to this
country. In the U.S. there were also studies and contingency plans
at the Army and Navy War Colleges in the event of war with Great
Britain. "Plan Red" called for the occupation of Canada by four
armies.

Cooperation between Canada and the United States in the
Second World War was close, although the Americans were the
dominant partner in the relationship. For example, the First
Special Service Force, which saw action in the Aleutians, Italy and
France, was 70 percent American and 30 percent Canadian. Home
defence units of Canadian Army troops also took part in the invasion of the Aleutian Islands. RCAF squadrons participated in the
defence of Alaska. The construction of the Alaska Highway
between Dawson, B.C., and Fairbanks, Alaska, was undertaken in
1942 with the United States government the dominant player. The
Americans on the east coast were active in Gander and Argentia,
Newfoundland (then a British colony), and in the North Atlantic
protecting their shipping. As well there was economic cooperation
and the strong influence of American culture.

When Canada entered the Second World War on 10 September
1939, only Canadian citizens and other British subjects could legally

The Hollywood film *Captain of the Clouds,* starring James Cagney
and shot in the summer of 1941 at Ottawa, promoted the idea of
Americans joining the Canadian forces.
Canadian Forces Photo Unit

be enrolled in the Canadian forces. But things changed quickly. By
an order-in-council issued four days later, Canada created the Royal
Canadian Air Force Special Reserve which could accept volunteers
from other countries. A few months later, the Canadian Army made
similar provisions to permit the enlistment of Americans and others. U.S. citizens could enlist in the Canadian forces in the spring of
1940 without loss of citizenship if they did not take the oath of allegiance; rather they took an oath of obedience.

U.S. citizens living in Canada could be recruited there, but the
recruiting of American nationals in their own country to fight in
foreign wars was a violation of the United States' Neutrality Act.
Consequently, Americans crossed the border in order to enlist.
And many did so.

Americans were seen as being good recruit material. They were
viewed as adventurous, brash, brave and with initiative. The movie
Captain of the Clouds starring James Cagney typified the general
stereotype of American flyers. While generally the Americans were
well behaved and served quite honourably, some deserted, leaving
debts, bad feelings and even broken hearts.

During the filming of *Captain of the Clouds* at RCAF Station
Uplands (Ottawa), James Cagney chats with an American flying
instructor, July 1941.
Department of National Defence

Similarly, Canadians were seen as good recruit material by
Americans. Qualities such as industriousness, steadiness under fire,
self-discipline and general reliability were viewed as desirable traits
for their military forces. Thus, there was a reciprocal willingness to
recruit military personnel from each other's population.

As a result of the German offensive in April and May 1940,
Norway, Denmark, The Netherlands, Belgium, Luxembourg and
France fell. When France signed an armistice on Germany's terms
on 22 June, Britain and the Commonwealth stood alone until June
1941, when the Soviet Union also found itself at war with Germany.
It was not until the Japanese attack on Pearl Harbor, 7 December
1941, that the United States was brought into the war. Four days
later Germany declared war on the United States, which then
declared war on Germany.

Between the wars many Canadians had moved to the United
States. When the U.S. entered the war, a good number of them
joined the American forces. Most of this group remained in the
United States after the war and became American citizens.

The historical events in the years leading up to the Second

World War no doubt had some influence on the Americans who enlisted in the Canadian forces. The Depression, above all, left its mark on that generation. For a good many, three square meals a day, a place to sleep, and some money made the Canadian forces seem attractive. For those who had longed to fly, an opportunity to serve in the RCAF or RAF was a dream come true. Travel, adventure and the possibility of earning a commission were other reasons why youngsters enlisted. Not to be overlooked, and perhaps most important, was the resolve to defend democracy against fascism. The latter motive became increasingly important after the fall of France in May 1940.

PATTERNS OF ENLISTMENT

With the United States' entry into the war, about a third of the Americans serving in the RCAF transferred to their own air service. By the end of the war that proportion had risen to a half. The responses from Americans serving in the Canadian Army were similar to those of their air force brethren.

Of those Americans who joined the RCAF most eventually ended up with Bomber Command because that was where the casualties were highest and replacements most needed. Upon U.S. entry into the war, many transferred to the U.S. Army Air Forces.[1] Because of their previous experience flying in combat, the transferees were usually assigned to comparable combat positions in the American air force.

A smaller though still significant number of Canadians joined the U.S. Navy. There were also some Americans who joined the Royal Canadian Navy at the outbreak of war. Better pay and living conditions aboard American ships were two main factors for Canadians enlisting in the U.S. Navy.

The war generally brought out the best and occasionally the worst in the young American volunteers. Most recall it being an important – a good number would say the most important – time of their lives. Some of the friendships made have lasted a lifetime. For those who survived emotionally and physically, the experience gave them confidence in their abilities.

Military cooperation between Canada and the United States during the Second World War is usually thought of in terms of developments after Pearl Harbor. This cooperation, however, had its most tangible expression in the Clayton Knight Committee. The committee derived its name from the first American brought into the scheme, Clayton Knight, a First World War pilot known for his illustrations in many books on wartime flying.

The primary aim of the Clayton Knight Committee was to recruit American pilots into the RCAF. Unable to advertise, recruiters depended on word of mouth and brochures. The leading figure was Air Marshal W.A. (Billy) Bishop, the Canadian air ace. After the Munich Conference of September 1938, approving Germany's acquisition of the Sudetenland, Bishop became convinced that war was less than a year away. Remembering the contribution of the Americans who had flown with British squadrons in the First World War, he wanted Canada to accept American pilots in the RCAF. Under U.S. neutrality laws, however, there was a $10,000 fine or a prison sentence of two years, or both, for recruiting American citizens for service in a foreign war. As a partner for Knight, Bishop chose Homer Smith, a Canadian with extensive experience in business.

With the establishment of the British Commonwealth Air Training Plan (BCATP) by Canada, the United Kingdom, Australia

Air Marshal W.A. (Billy) Bishop presenting a pilot's wings to an American in the RCAF.
Department of National Defence

and New Zealand on 17 December 1939, making Canada the main centre of air training for the Commonwealth, it became evident that Canada would need experienced pilots. The Americans quietly let the Canadians and British know what would and would not be acceptable as far as recruiting. Recruiting could be discreetly carried out in the United States but enlistment would have to be on the Canadian side. In June 1940, when it was clear that events in Europe had become unfavourable for the Allies, the Air Training Plan was put into full operation ahead of schedule.

Recruits from the United States could become either commissioned officers or sergeant pilots. They did not have to take the oath of allegiance because Canada, on 7 June 1940, officially dropped that requirement for foreign nationals enlisting in the armed forces. Those airmen looking for an early overseas posting to a war theatre were soon disappointed, since the most pressing need was for instructors under the BCATP.

AIR FORCE ENLISTMENTS

The Clayton Knight Committee became the agency that helped the British obtain pilots for the Atlantic Ferry Service, the Air Transport Auxiliary, which ferried aircraft within the United Kingdom, and three "Eagle" squadrons of the RAF.

Most of the Americans who went to Canada to become pilots did so because they did not possess the academic qualifications to get into the U.S. army or navy aviation cadet programs – a minimum of two years of college. The Clayton Knight individuals claimed already to have some flying time – enough to get into an abbreviated training program and then a posting to England to an Operational Training Unit.

Many an American youth with no air training had, since the beginning of the war, been making his way to Canada attracted by the opportunity of becoming a pilot in the RCAF. The air training schools, however, were crammed with Canadian recruits and those from other parts of the Commonwealth. At that time, American applicants without any flying experience were usually put on a waiting list unless they were willing to be enrolled in a ground trade.

The decline of Allied fortunes combined with the importance of air power led to an expansion of the BCATP. Quite apart from applying through the Clayton Knight Committee, which began to obtain American aircrew trainees, U.S. citizens were crossing the

A group of American pilot trainees in the RCAF.
Fred Hatch

border to enlist on their own. In 1941 the number of Americans enlisting in the RCAF increased as the number of Canadians began to fall.

The number of American enlistments began to fall off after Pearl Harbor. Starting on 19 December 1941, negotiations were undertaken to release Americans from the armed forces of Canada and enlist them in those of the United States. Americans in active service in a war theatre were to remain with their units until they could be advantageously employed in American fighting formations. On transfer the Americans were to be enlisted in the service of their choice: army, navy or marines. In general they could keep their rank on transfer. For example in the army, a pilot officer would be commissioned as a second lieutenant and a flying officer as a first lieutenant.

At the time of Pearl Harbor over 6,000 American citizens were serving in the RCAF and several thousand in the RAF. To allow those Americans who had lost their citizenship upon enlisting in the Canadian armed forces to regain it, an amendment to the U.S. nationality code came into effect on 2 April 1942. All the individual was required to do to regain U.S. citizenship was take another oath renouncing allegiance to any foreign state or sovereign in front of a diplomatic or consular officer abroad or before a naturalization court in the U.S. This also applied to those Americans who had lost their citizenship in the First World War.

A Canadian-American Military Board was set up to travel across Canada between early May and early June 1942 to transfer to the American armed forces those citizens and ex-citizens of the United States in the Canadian armed forces who wished to transfer. The board affected the transfer of some 2,000 of the approximately 5,000 Americans stationed in Canada of the total of some 16,000 remaining in the Canadian forces.

After Pearl Harbor the Americans urged the RCAF to keep its lists open to applicants from the United States, but Canada declined. Long afterwards applications still came from Americans seeking to join the RCAF. A form letter informed the American applicants that RCAF regulations had been altered and no longer permitted the acceptance of U.S. citizens. These regulations did not apply to Americans already resident in Canada or to those whose homes were in Canada.

Exactly 18,848 American citizens served in the Canadian Army in the Second World War.[2] Some 9,000 joined the RCAF. While a high percentage of English-born Americans had crossed the border into Canada to enlist in the First World War, the vast majority of those who crossed over to join the Canadian army or air force in the Second World War were native-born Americans.

From available service records and those contacted, it appears that most of the Americans who joined the RCAF came from California or New York. Many already had some flying experience. Of those who joined the Canadian Army, most came from states along the U.S.-Canadian border, although some came from states such as Kentucky and Texas where there was very high unemployment.

A number of Americans who had served in the ranks of Canadian units received commissions upon transferring to the American forces. Some of them later returned from overseas to visit their former units to renew acquaintances. One ex-member of the Royal Canadian Regiment, who had a less than clean slate, even returned to dine with his former officers.

Some 30,000 Americans likely joined the Canadian air force, army and navy during the Second World War. Of the Canadian battalions overseas, the Essex Scottish had the highest proportion of

Americans, at least several hundred. One of the major problems in trying to obtain accurate statistics is that many Americans gave Irish or Scottish as their background and the YMCA as an address.

A good number of Canadians from border areas, in turn, joined the United States forces during the Second World War. Members of some ethnic and religious minorities did so because they felt there was less discrimination in the U.S. forces. Pay rates and opportunities for advancement were also better.[3]

RECIPROCAL INDUCTION AGREEMENT

Under part of a Canada-U.S. reciprocal induction agreement, Canadians living in the United States could elect to serve in either the Canadian or the American forces, and Americans living in Canada had the same option. If the individual had already entered the military, he might request a transfer to the forces of his own country. The largest group in this category to be affected upon U.S. entry in the war were some 2,500 airmen who transferred to the United States Army Air Forces (USAAF) from the RCAF.

Canada, like other countries with whom the U.S. had entered into mutual induction agreements, discovered that only a small minority of its citizens in the United States preferred to serve in the Canadian armed forces. This was because American service personnel were better paid.

When the United States declared war on Japan on 8 December 1941, more than 3,000 Americans were under training in Canada or waiting their turn to begin. Some would fly with the RCAF and some with the American air force but all had received a running start. The most significant contribution made by Americans who joined the RCAF was that of the American flying instructors and staff pilots who helped put the BCATP into full operation so quickly.

The Clayton Knight Committee's successor, the Canadian Aviation Bureau, was disbanded in June 1942 after 900 experienced American pilots and 1,450 air-crew trainees has been recruited for the RCAF. Those recruits, however, represent less than half of the 6,000 Americans in the RCAF at the time of Pearl Harbor. The American contribution was an important step in the growth of the BCATP and the RCAF and in the development of Allied air power. Of the 8,864 Americans who had come to Canada to enlist in the RCAF some 800 were killed.[4] Several hundred of the 2,000 who transferred to the USAAF also were killed.

An American sergeant pilot in the RCAF gets his kit bag and steel
helmet in preparation for overseas posting. A New Zealand pilot
and a British observer wait in line.
Department of National Defence

Many Americans decided to stay in the RCAF in spite of its
lower pay rates. A lot had developed friendships with their crews
and did not want to leave. They also felt a sense of loyalty to the
RCAF, as it had accepted and trained them. Some pilots stayed with
Bomber Command because they preferred to be the sole pilot, for
example, of a Halifax or Mosquito, rather than a second or co-pilot
of an American Liberator or Fortress.

Those who had already enlisted in the armed forces of Canada
and the United States were volunteers. However, military service
became compulsory. The Selective Service Act was enacted by
Congress in May 1917 during the First World War and in
September 1940 during the Second World War. In Canada conscription became law in April 1917. During the Second World War
conscription came into effect in the spring of 1940 for home
defence and in November 1944 for overseas service.

While the Canada-U.S. reciprocal system generally worked well,
it seems that Canada did not observe the agreement in its entirety

with regard to citizens of dual nationality. In 1944 Canada conscripted such individuals as though they were only British subjects.
The Americans politely objected but nothing was done to change
the situation.[5]

THE EAGLE SQUADRONS

The "Eagle" squadrons were made up of a small proportion of the
Americans who had volunteered for service in the Royal Air Force
and the Royal Canadian Air Force before Pearl Harbor. In their
final form the Eagles comprised three fighter squadrons totalling
some 240 fighter pilots who had served with them at one time or
another. They flew for the British for almost two years, were credit-
ed with shooting down about seventy-five German aircraft, won one
Distinguished Service Order and thirteen Distinguished Flying
Crosses, and suffered about a hundred casualties.

The Eagle squadrons owe their origin to Colonel Charles
Sweeny, an American soldier of fortune. The German invasion of
France in May 1940 put an end to his scheme to have an American
squadron within the French air force. Instead, three American
pilots already in France escaped to England, where they obtained
permission to form the nucleus of an American squadron in the
RAF. Colonel Sweeny, working in California, recruited other expe-
rienced pilots. This was occurring about the same time as the
Clayton Knight Committee was recruiting American pilots for the
RCAF.

After completing flight training, the first three Americans from
France were assigned on 5 August 1940 to 609 Squadron and flew
Hurricanes during the Battle of Britain. On 19 September 1940,
No. 71 (Eagle) Squadron came into existence at RAF Station
Church Fenton. A second Eagle squadron, No. 121, was formed on
17 May 1941, consisting mainly of Americans who had indepen-
dently volunteered and had been sent to various RAF squadrons.
On 1 August 1941 the third Eagle squadron, No. 133, was created.

In October 1941 the RAF recognized the growing ability of the
three Eagle squadrons by replacing their Hurricanes with the more
modern Spitfires. Positive results were soon forthcoming. No. 71
Squadron engaged in many combats in that period and was named
the highest scoring squadron of the month. The fighting over
Malta offered an opportunity for members of Eagle squadrons to
transfer there for greater action, and seventeen Eagles did so.

Squadron Leader John J. Lynch, a Californian who scored
thirteen times with the RAF. Here he has just scored Malta's
1,000th victory.
Imperial War Museum

On 19 August 1942 the Eagles took part in Operation Jubilee,
the raid on Dieppe. Their group, No. 11, supplied air cover for the
landings. Every squadron in the group made at least three flights.
No. 133 Squadron had its best day, shooting down four enemy
fighters and two bombers.

Soon after Dieppe, the British and American governments
began negotiating for the transfer of the squadrons to the U.S.
Army Air Force. They were formally transferred on 29 September
1942. This transfer included many who were not in one of the
Eagle Squadrons. Now the pilots would earn three times as much
money as they had in the RAF. They became members of the 4th
Fighter Group, U.S. Eighth Air Force, and served on bomber
escort duty. From that day until the end of the war, the former
Eagles were to destroy a thousand German aircraft, a performance
made possible by their previous training and experience.

Several hundred Americans served in RAF operational
squadrons other than the Eagles. Some Americans arrived too late
to see any action; others experienced only a brief tour with an
operational RAF unit before transferring to the American air force.
Some went on to see a lot of combat, some very little.

THE PILOT POET

One of the most well known volunteers from the United States to join the RCAF was John Gillespie Magee. He was born on 9 June 1922 in Shanghai to two missionaries – his father from Pittsburgh, Pennsylvania, his mother from Helmingham, Suffolk. Both parents wanted their four sons to receive their schooling in both England and the United States. John, the eldest, attended Avon School near Hartford, Connecticut, and was planning to attend Yale University in the fall of 1940 but instead joined the RCAF. He received his wings on 22 June 1941 and was posted to Great Britain. At the training station of Llandow in South Wales, a fellow flyer suggested that as John was interested in writing poetry, he ought to put his feelings down in words. John then quickly scribbled out what was to become the world's most famous poem about flying, "High Flight":

> *Oh! I have slipped the surly bonds of earth*
> *And danced the skies on laughter-silvered wings;*
> *Sunward I've climbed, and joined the tumbling mirth*
> *Of sun-split clouds – and done a hundred things*
> *You have not dreamed of – wheeled and soared and swung*
> *High in the sunlit silence. Hov'ring there*
> *I've chased the shouting wind along, and flung*
> *My eager craft through footless halls of air.*
> *Up, up the long delirious, burning blue,*
> *I've topped the windswept heights with easy grace*
> *Where never lark or even eagle flew –*
> *And while with silent lifting mind I've trod*
> *The high untrespassed sanctity of space,*
> *Put out my hand and touched the face of God.*

Soon after joining No. 412 Squadron RCAF near Digby (Wellingore), Lincolnshire, in September 1941, John sent a copy of the poem to his parents. His time henceforth was spent practising manoeuvres, but he did see some action. While undergoing further fighter training on 11 December 1941, he collided in the clouds with another aircraft from the nearby RAF College at Cranwell.

At the time of his death, John's father printed the poem in his church magazine. It was spotted by a reporter who published it in a

J.G. Magee, future author of "High Flight," beams as he receives
his wings from Group Captain W.A. Curtiss.
Canadian Forces Photo Unit

Washington newspaper. From that moment the poem captured the
public imagination. President Reagan referred to it in his speech
following the explosion of the space shuttle *Challenger* on take-off
in January 1986.

SEVERAL NOTABLE AMERICANS

Wherever British airmen fought, Americans were present – the
Battle of Britain, Malta, North Africa, Sicily and Italy, and
Northwest Europe. Some individuals achieved considerable fame.
Squadron Leader Lance C. Wade, the "Arizona Wildcat," became
the highest-scoring American-born ace* with the Royal Air Force,
with twenty-five victories; he met an untimely death in an air accident on 12 January 1944. Squadron Leader David C. Fairbanks, a
native of New York, scored fifteen victories flying with the RAF and
RCAF. Wing Commander James H. Little of New Orleans rose to
command No. 418 Squadron RCAF and just narrowly missed ace-
dom by scoring four victories.

---

* Ace – unofficial status given to a fighter pilot with five or more victories.

Squadron Leader Lance C. Wade, the "Arizona Wildcat," who became the top-scoring American-born ace with the Royal Air Force, with twenty-five victories to his credit.
Imperial War Museum

Squadron Leader David C. Fairbanks, a native New Yorker who scored fifteen victories flying with the Royal Air Force and Royal Canadian Air Force.
RCAF

John Godfrey (left) with Don Gentile while flying P-51s with the
4th Fighter Group, USAAF.
Glover Collection

John Godfrey was born in Montreal on 28 March 1922 and grew up in Woonsocket, Rhode Island. In 1941, after graduating from high school and trying unsuccessfully to enlist in the USAAF, he had no problem enlisting in the RCAF in Montreal. At 57 Operational Training Unit in England, he trained on the Spitfire. After that he transferred to the USAAF, in which he became an ace. Along with Major Don Gentile from Piqua, Iowa, he formed a top-scoring fighter team with the Eighth Air Force's famed 4th Fighter Group.

FERRY COMMAND

Ferry Command was established early in the Second World War to improve aircraft deliveries from U.S. factories to Britain. Surface shipping was too slow and the space was needed for other cargoes. Lord Beaverbrook, the Canadian-born minister of aircraft production in Britain, asked Sir Edward Beatty of the Canadian Pacific Railway to assemble an organization to fly new multi-engined aircraft across the Atlantic. A handful of experienced transatlantic flyers from British Overseas Airways Corporation (formerly Imperial Airways and British Airways) worked together with servicemen and civilians (many of whom were from the United States) from head-quarters in Montreal. At the time transatlantic flight was still in its infancy. Sceptics who believed such a scheme to be impossible were proved wrong. The CP Air Services Department, established in July 1940, and its successors, Royal Air Force Ferry Command and No. 45 Group of RAF Transport Command, eventually delivered more than 900 warplanes – losing only about 100. Ferry Command paved the way for mass postwar transatlantic air travel.

AIR TRANSPORT AUXILIARY

During the Second World War, Air Transport Auxiliary, a British civilian organization, took over the task of ferrying RN and RAF aircraft from the factories to the airfields, thus releasing service pilots for more active duties. Among its members were Americans who had joined in Canada. It was controlled functionally by the Ministry of Aircraft Production, operationally by No. 41 Group, while being administered by the British Overseas Airways Corporation.

NAVY

Among the Americans who joined the Royal Canadian Navy at the outbreak of the Second World War were former members of the Royal Navy who had moved to the United States. Some of them had even become U.S. citizens. One such individual was Commander Edmund Johnson, who was in Personnel. Another American was John Farrow, originally from Australia. He became director of Naval Information. Farrow, who was married to the actress Maureen O'Sullivan, would be familiar to most as the father of Mia Farrow.

NEWFOUNDLAND

Many Newfoundlanders served in the Canadian forces in the First and Second World Wars, before Newfoundland had become part of Canada. A significant number also joined the American forces. The Second World War brought large numbers of outsiders, including Americans, to the island. More than 25,000 of the American servicemen stationed in Newfoundland between 1940 and 1990 married inhabitants.

SECOND WORLD WAR EXPERIENCES

RICHARD DUNHAM
Theatre: Northwest Europe   Service: RCAF/USAAF

I was born in Rochester, New York, on 28 April 1923. I had to go to work on a farm, but through hard work I managed to survive and eventually graduated from high school at Moravia, New York. One day, while I was sitting under a brown Swiss cow, the cow managed to kick me and a milk bucket clear across the barn. I contemplated my future and decided that war might be hell but that it beat milking cows. I struck out for the border of Canada, at Buffalo, still wearing everything that I owned, pledging myself to serve King and Canada, as long as neither owned any cows. I was welcomed with open arms at the recruiting station in Toronto

Sergeant Richard Dunham,
Cambridge, England,
October 1942.
R. Dunham

and then was completely ground into the dirt by the only dude that was uglier than me – my drill instructor. As he stood over 6 feet 3 inches and had large muscles even in his eyelashes, his slightest wish was my command. Under him, I quickly grew up and went on to graduate at Aylmer, Ontario (No. 14 Service Flying Training School), as a sergeant-pilot. I did not lose my American citizenship as I took an oath of obedience, whereas the Canadian lads took an oath of allegiance.

After combat with No. 222 Squadron, and being returned to the American service in 1943, I went back to England with the American air force (78th Fighter Group) and stayed until the war ended.

I look at the wall over my head where I'm sitting now, at my many medals for what a lot of folks think of as heroism but which I call (when no one is around) lucky cowardice or unmitigated good fortune. The war has been over so long and there are so few of those pilots left that I find I can now tell some very fine, lying war stories without too much fear of getting caught.

I retired from the service in 1964, went into civilian law enforcement in Maryland, and was retired in 1980 as a chief of police – I was retired because I was still ugly, despicable, and if it looked anything like a brown Swiss cow, I was very apt to shoot it. (There were a lot of folks around the nation's capital that looked like brown Swiss cows.) Now I sit here without a great deal to do except correspond with curious military historians.[6]

BEN BRINKWORTH
Theatre: Northwest Europe   Service: Army

I was born in Chicago on 10 November 1917. I enlisted in the Essex Scottish on 14 September 1939. My motives for joining were a combination of adventure and a sense that I was on the right side of history. I lost my American citizenship upon enlisting but regained it in October 1945 upon application to the U.S. State Department.

As a corporal, I was captured on the beach at Dieppe 19 August 1942. I spent most of the war at Stalag VIII B. I found life there monotonous, fearful and boring. My main memory, however, was always being hungry, and in winter, being cold. Initially my hands were tied with rope for six to eight weeks and then handcuffs for another ten to eleven months from 7:00 a.m. to 8:00 p.m. each day. I was transferred to Stalag II D from about April 1944 to February 1945. Living conditions there were better. When we were lucky two of us shared a Red Cross parcel – one to two per month. German daily rations were two to three potatoes, one cup of soup and two to three inches of black bread. The last three months of the war had the most marching – fifteen to eighteen miles per day to prevent us being liberated. There was almost no food. What shelter we were given was in barns. We were all literally lousy. On 5 May 1945, the ordeal ended.

I was liberated near Lubeck by the U.S. 6th Armored Division. I was eventually moved to hospital in Aldershot, England, for six weeks convalescence, then I was sent home by hospital ship. I was honourably discharged from the Canadian forces in August 1945.

In March 1946, I joined the U.S. Army which I made my career until 1967. I retired with the rank of lieutenant-colonel and now reside in Petaluma, California with my wife and two dogs.

Would I enlist again? Probably, if I was twenty-one or twenty-two and knew as little as I did then! I was bitter for years at the British and Canadian officials. Dieppe was incredibly stupid. And, I have never read what I consider a valid excuse for the raid. With age has come a forgiving process. To stay angry is really counterproductive. I was also angry and bitter toward the Germans. That too has passed with time.[7]

Corporal Ben Brinkworth, an American from Chicago, in the Essex Scottish, Aldershot, England, 1940.
B. Brinkworth

TERRY GOODWIN
Theatre: U.K. and Northwest Europe   Service: Air Force

I was born at Schenectady, New York, on 2 August 1920 but moved from there when I was three months old and was raised in Philadelphia and suburbs. I had been attending the University of Pennsylvania when I came to Canada in February 1941 to join the RCAF.

Why did I join up? Simply because I was the right age. I was not at all pleased with the American position of non-intervention. Roosevelt was doing all he could. As an individual, I could be more useful by joining the RCAF.

I did guard duty at Camp Borden and buried ten student pilots while I was there. It was a poor introduction to the flying business. No. 1 Initial Training

Sergeant H.T. Goodwin of Philadelphia, December 1941.
H.T. Goodwin

School was followed then by No. 1 Elementary Flying Training at Malton – now Toronto's Pearson International – on Tiger Moths. I got my wings on 5 December 1941 at Dunnville on Harvards. Two days later at home I heard the radio tell about Pearl Harbor. I spent Christmas of 1941 at "Y" Depot in Halifax waiting for a boat to England during a blizzard.

My first mission was on 31 July 1942, to Dusseldorf on the Ruhr, flying Hampdens. I converted to Manchesters and then to Lancasters and flew a tour with 61 Squadron at Syserston near Nottingham. After that they had me instructing on Wellingtons at Silverstone and Turweston. By December of 1943 I was at Marham learning to fly Mosquitos. I was one of the original crews forming 692 Squadron at Gravely, eighteen miles west of Cambridge, in January 1944.

We did not know how long a tour was to be when we first got there. It was thirty for Lancasters with twenty-five for the second tour at the time. I thought it should be about thirty-five on Mosquitos and found out later it was fifty!

The Mosquito aircraft I flew was the Mark IV. It was designed for 1,000 pounds of bombs. We got it with 2,000 pounds. Then shortly they brought in one with a pregnant belly for a 4,000 pounder!

I kept on flying after my fiftieth mission and did seventy-five. My Distinguished Flying Medal was awarded after the Lanc tour and the Distinguished Flying Cross while I was on Mossies although it did not catch up with me until I was back after being overseas.

There was no promotion in the Mossie squadrons. We had an establishment for four flight lieutenants and had fourteen, so my promotion just came through three days before I got out of the service in April 1945. Although I married and stayed in Canada after the war, I only became a Canadian citizen in 1961 when I was asked to serve on Vaughan Township Public School Board. In 1974 I was elected to the Council of the Town of Vaughan. I served until the end of 1978. I am retired from the trucking business.[8]

JOHN DACY
Theatre: North Africa, Sicily,   Service: Army
            Northwest Europe

I was born on 14 April 1907, in Mansfield, Massachusetts. In February 1940 I had broken my ankle and while recovering was sitting around the house, clubs and bars, listening about Hitler. I felt I should be helping out in some way. One day, after a few drinks, I took a bus to Montreal to join up to fight. At Customs, just past Swanton, Vermont, they asked me why I was going to Montreal. I told them, to visit a cousin who lived on Main Street. They told me there was no Main Street in Montreal and sent me back to Swanton. The next morning I went back to Customs and met the same man. He again asked me why I was going to Montreal. I told him the truth – in order to join the army. He said, "Why the hell didn't you say so last night?"

I enlisted in the Canadian Army in Montreal on 21 May 1940. I lost my citizenship as I pledged allegiance to the king but I got it back when I joined the U.S. Army. I was posted to the 14th General

Hospital, Royal Canadian Army Medical Corps. Later I transferred to the 5th Light Anti-Aircraft Battery, C Troop, located at Craig Street Armoury in Montreal. Because my hair was grey, I was known as "Whitey." We lived at Place Viger. We sailed to England early in January 1941. I was stationed at Colchester and later all along the south coast between Dover and Lands End. My rank was gunner.

I transferred to the U.S. Army on 3 July 1943, ending up in Northern Ireland with a Minnesota infantry regiment. I then transferred to Battery B, 103rd Anti-Aircraft Artillery Battalion (Medium). Our anti-aircraft unit was attached to the 16th Infantry Regiment, 1st Division, most of the war. I was a gunner on a 40-mm Bofors. My North African service began at Tafaraoui and La Senia airfields, Oran, Algiers, and then to Tunis. Just prior to

John Dacy of Mansfield, Massachusetts, in England, 1941.
J. Dacy

landing in Sicily, our sergeant came down with malaria, so I took the gun onto the beach. I got a navy full-track vehicle to haul us to the top of the dunes and we had a 360 degree arc of fire. We were the first to open fire on incoming planes and I saw our first hit. Our firing alerted the whole beach and soon everyone got into the act. Our unit got a citation. We went across Sicily and then back to England.

We hit Omaha Beach about three days after D-Day and were at the St. Lo breakthrough. I ended up for a while with a small infantry unit along with two 105-mm guns, two Bofors and two half-tracks, at the southern end of the Falaise Gap behind enemy lines. After we bypassed Paris, I took over a half-track with four 50-calibres and four men. We usually served on the left flank of the 16th Infantry.

After the Battle of the Bulge, I ended up in the hospital in Belgium – not wounded, just worn out – no sleep, arthritis, etc. Everyone guessed I was about fifty-five. After a stay in hospital, I returned to my unit about V-E Day.

They were sending soldiers home by the point system and my Canadian time counted. Thus, I had more points than anyone in the outfit and so was about the first to go home. I was discharged as a corporal at Fort Devens, Massachusetts, on 14 July 1945.

I got married about a month after returning home to my old girl friend. We had a good life together. In 1946 I began work for the U.S. Postal Service. After many years as a supervisor, I retired in 1971 to take care of my wife, who had come down with Alzheimer's disease. She is now in a good nursing home. I visit her every day.[9]

JAMES HUNTER
Theatre: Northwest Europe   Service: Army

I was born in Brooklyn, New York, on 14 December 1917. As a young boy I had cut out a picture of a member of the Black Watch of Scotland and put it on my bedroom wall. After Dunkirk in May 1940, I decided with family encouragement to join up and save England. I enlisted in the 1st Battalion, Black Watch of Canada in September 1940. I took my training in Aldershot, Nova Scotia. At that time I had a strong Brooklyn accent and I quickly found out there was a good deal of anti-Americanism in that community. Prior to my arrival, a considerable number of Americans who had joined the Canadian Army had run up debts and then deserted.

Overseas in England after Pearl Harbor, I was asked whether I wished to transfer to the U.S. Army. I declined. I had decided I was going to remain in Canada after the war.

On 18 August 1942 I was told I would be going on an exercise. The next day I was on a LCT (landing craft tank) headed for Dieppe. I was part of the company support mortar platoon. A machine-gunner on the LCT was severely hit as we landed. I with my friend private Kevin Gallagher went up to help him. Enemy fire was intense and the LCT left the beach before we could disembark.

I fought in Normandy during the summer of 1944, including the battle of Verrières Ridge. When we reached Belgium, I was promoted to sergeant. The ensuing fighting in the Scheldt campaign was intense. I remained non-wounded until 26 October 1944. I was part of a crew trying to flush out some German paratroopers. The last sight I ever saw was the heads of three dead German soldiers. A shell must have landed in the trench they were in. The blast had killed them and collapsed the walls of the trench. The three heads caused me to pause and that's when I was hit with a blast from an anti-tank weapon. I was knocked down but not out. I got up right away. I used to box (being a 2nd Division champion) and at first I thought I was blind only because there was blood in my eyes. I wiped with my hands and discovered that I didn't have eyes.

I was sent back to England. Here I was blind with only Grade 5 formal education. I had been a construction worker. I didn't seem to have much of a future.

I went to the centre for blind training in Toronto (Baker House), and with the help of wonderful volunteer readers earned a master's degree in social work from the University of Toronto. Upon graduation, I was hired by the Saskatchewan government. Much of my working career there was spent in Regina counselling people injured in work-related accidents. I was later offered a supervisory job with the John Howard Society in Winnipeg, which I accepted.

I consider myself lucky. Out of the platoon I started with I believe only three of us survived. I hope the world has reached the point where men will not be asked to make these kinds of sacrifices again.

I married a Canadian girl in 1949 and we had three children. I am now retired. In spite of blindness, I keep busy making furniture as a hobby. I am a member of the Sir Arthur Pearson Association of War Blinded, a section of the Canadian National Institute for the Blind.[10]

HOLLIS HILLS
Theatre: Northwest Europe   Service: RCAF

I was born in Baxter, Iowa, on 25 March 1915, although our home was Iowa Falls. I wanted to be a fighter pilot from the time I was just a tad. The First World War and the exploits of the flyers in that war were part of my boyhood. They were the subject of much prose, both factual and fantasy. I had applied for the U.S. Air Corps but they were not really geared up for accelerated training in 1939 and 1940. I thought the RCAF might be a chance and it turned out to be a good choice.

I joined the RCAF in June 1940 and was called up for training in September. Due to problems in the starting of the Training Plan, I did guard duty at Brantford, Ontario, until pre-flight training started mid-December 1940 at the Hunt Club in Toronto. I reported to No. 7 Elementary Flying Training School mid-January 1941. There I was trained on Fleet Finches, graduating in March. I then went on to No. 10 Service Flying Training School at Dauphin, Manitoba, on Harvards. We were the first class at that station. I received my wings and was designated a sergeant pilot on 22 June 1941, the day Hitler invaded Russia. I received orders as an instructor and a commission as pilot officer while on leave. I was able to swap the orders with an eighteen-year-old for overseas posting.

Pilot Officer Hollis Hills, Croydon, 1941–42.
H. Hills

I sailed from Halifax on 21 July 1941 aboard HMS *Ascania*. It was a Cunard liner that had been converted to an armed escort. We started north the first night, ran into icebergs and lost seven vessels to collisions. About eight or nine days into the voyage we were notified by the captain that we were detaching and charging north to intercept a pocket battleship and try to delay it long enough to save the convoy. He was quite emotional and stated the obvious, that we were going to our destruction. You can well imagine how that hit us after all our training as pilots and aircrew to realize it was all for naught. In any case, the battlewagon never hove over the horizon and we didn't have to "die like men." That happened to a majority of us later in the air. The *Ascania* left us off in Iceland on 2 August 1941. On the 11th we boarded the *Leopoldville* and were dropped off in Scotland on the 14th. That ship went on to a tragic end when it was sunk in the Channel by a U-boat on 24 December 1944 with the loss of over 800 U.S. troops.

I was sent to operational training at Old Sarum in Wiltshire, on Lysanders and Tomahawks. It was then on to No. 414 Squadron RCAF at Croyden (Greater London) on 13 October 1941, along with Ray MacQuoid, Frank Chesters and George Dunaway, another American from Arkansas.

George was accidentally killed in a Tomahawk on 21 October while we were on a navigation hop to Land's End. We both hit thunderstorms in the stratus clouds. I came out of the mine with two black eyes from banging around the cockpit. George's airplane crashed. Ray MacQuoid was killed 1 April 1943 train busting. Frank Chesters survived the war but died quite young from a heart attack.

We trained and did some operations in Tomahawks, hours and hours in practice air fights with Spitfires and Hurricanes from operational squadrons based at Biggin Hill, Kesley, and Red Hill. We got Mustang Is in June of 1942 and flew a number of operations on them. I particularly liked train busting. Another satisfying job we did was to stop bombing raids on the south-coast towns.

Pilots of No. 414 Squadron. Front row, left to right: Frank Chesters and Charles Stover. Back row, left to right: Sandy Sanderson, Chappie Champlin, Freddie Clarke, Bill Blakely, Hollis Hills and Chappie Chapman.
H. Hills

Mustangs at Dieppe

No. 414 Squadron received the North American Mustang fighter in the first week of June 1942. The Dieppe operation started for our squadron on 18 August 1942. We flew our planes from home base Croydon, near Gatwick. In the pitch black of early morning on 14 August, Flight Lieutenant Freddie Clarke and I took off as the first mission of the day for the Mustangs, four squadrons strong. Our task was a road reconnaissance of the route from Abbeville to Dieppe. We were to check on movement of armour. We set course for our penetration point a few miles south of the planned troop landing point. About halfway across the Channel, an inverted cone of anti-aircraft fire and searchlights hove into view. We later learned that Bostons were attacking the heavy guns in the cliffs north of the Dieppe beach. They had a terrible time of it. Our navigation problem was solved by all this action. It was a mixed blessing, for as soon as we crossed the coast, Freddie's plane vanished in the inky black. Nothing was visible. We both returned shortly thereafter with no damage.

My second mission later in the day was the same. Again, we were to look for armour en route to the Dieppe beaches. The weather had turned out fine and sunny, not a cloud in the sky. We set off on the same course. However, this time starting at sea level and going all the way up to the contrail level, the sky was full of fighters in one massive dogfight. I was busy but in hurried glances counted seven parachutes at one time.

A couple of miles short of landfall I spotted four Fw. 190s off to our right at about 1,500 feet. Their course and speed was going to put them directly overhead when we crossed the beach. We reached the road we were to reconnaissance in no time and Freddie turned right towards Abbeville. My plan was to cut off the lead 190 before he could fire on Freddie. My timing all went to pot when a crashing Spitfire forced me into a sharp left turn to avoid a collision. That gave the Fw. pilot time to get into firing position as he hit Freddie's Mustang with his first burst. It wasn't a very hard hit but was obviously terminal. I was able to get a long-range shot at the leader but had to break right as the number two now was having a go at me. He missed and made a big mistake sliding by my left side. It was a very easy shot and I hit him hard. His engine caught fire smoking heavily. The cockpit canopy came off so I hit him hard again. I knew he was a goner as he didn't move up, falling off to the right towards the trees. The last pair of 190s had vanished so I turned back toward Dieppe looking for Freddie's Mustang. There he was heading for the harbour at 1,000 feet with the Fw. trailing behind.

The glycol stream from the Mustang was very thin so I knew the engine had little time left. Before I could get into good gun range of the 190, the pilot started to slide dead astern of Freddie. I gave a short high deflection burst at the 190. I was hoping to get his attention and it worked. He broke hard left into my attack. I now had my hands full. The fight seemed to go on forever. Just as I would be getting into position to fire he would break off and streak inland. It never entered my mind to follow him deeper into France. He would come back at me as soon as I started for the coast. We would start our turning competition all over again. It was apparent to me that my opponent was highly competent and I was ready to call it a draw as soon as I could. As the entire fight had taken place in the treetops, a high speed stall would have been the end of it. The planes of those days lost speed in our ring-around-the-rosies. As our speed decreased, the other pilot would use the superior power of his BMW engine, breaking away inland. He could pull out of range before I could dive. The timing of these breaks was such that I could get my Mustang up to speed and head for the coast. The last break had given me a good start and I headed for the south end of the harbour. All the ships were under attack so they let fly at me. I don't blame them because with all the smoke, there was no way they could recognize my plane. The 190 did not follow me over the harbour and I was not hit by anti-aircraft fire. Halfway across the Channel I flew directly under a gaggle of Ju. 88s and Me. 109s. They were the survivors of an attack on Southampton and had taken heavy losses. We ignored each other and the rest of the trip was without thrills.

There was talk of a third mission. We later learned that the other RAF fighters had been under orders not to cross the coastline. It is no surprise that the heavy losses were sustained by Mustangs as they tried to penetrate inland in pairs. Our squadron returned to Croydon. We spent a very sombre evening in the mess. Freddie was missing, our only loss. The two RAF Mustang squadrons had taken severe losses. The day had been a disaster. There was no cause for celebration.

About five the next morning, my door burst open. I was grabbed in a bear hug by what smelled like a huge clump of seaweed. It was Freddie Clark. His head sported a huge bandage covering the severe cuts he had received in the ditching. He had been rescued.

Post-RCAF
On 8 November 1942 I transferred to the air arm of the U.S. Navy. I flew missions in the South Pacific. I served in the regular navy after the war. I retired in 1964 and spent the next sixteen years retired in England and Spain. In 1980 I returned to the United States. I now live in Melbourne, Florida.[11]

ROBERT GLADNICK
Theatre: Sicily/Italy   Service: Army

I was born on 29 June 1914 in Vyazma, Russia. My parents died within a year. I came to the United States in August 1923 with two older brothers and an elder sister. My sister and I went back to Siberia, now Khazakstan, where she married. From 1923 to 1927 I lived with my grandmother, who put me into a rabbinical school, as they fed me there. Conditions were generally horrible so in March 1928 I returned to the United States. I lived with an older brother for two years and then went on the bum, living as a hobo.

From April 1930 until the end of 1931 I rode freight trains, worked in the harvest fields in North Dakota, lumber camps in Washington State, and the oil fields of Texas. There were millions of unemployed and vagrants. I scrounged food from Salvation Army soup kitchens and slept on park benches. In 1932 I joined the Young Communist League (YCL) in Texas. I began organizing the unemployed. For this activity I think I often spent more time in jail than outside. I then made my way back to New York City where I worked as a union organizer and merchant seaman prior to going to Spain.

I do not consider myself the "average" American volunteer in the Canadian Army in World War II. You see I was a veteran of the Spanish Civil War. I was one of the first American volunteers for that conflict. I sailed from New York on 26 December 1936. I served at the front (Jarama) as company commander and on or about 15 March 1937, for bravery in action, was transferred to the Soviet tank corps.

When I left for Spain, I was a red hot communist. I was the

YCL's secretary on the New York waterfront, having also served as a YCL organizer in Texas, Oklahoma, North and South Dakota, and in California as well as Black and Spanish Harlem in New York. I certainly was not a parlour pink sympathizer.

At the front in Spain I became disillusioned with communism and was one of the founders of an anti-communist underground organization called FONIC (Friends of the Non-Intervention Committee). Wherever the XV International Brigade (American, Canadian, British) went, walls and stones were painted with the FONIC sign. What I am proud of is that the executioners of SIM (Servico de Investigacion Militar), a secret police comparable to the KGB-NKVD, were unable to find even one of our lads, although dozens of innocents were shot in a desperate attempt to catch one of us. How to conduct an underground organization in a totalitarian state is a story in itself.

Upon return to the U.S.A., I and other American veterans of the Spanish Civil War tried to form an anti-totalitarian vet-

Sergeant Robert Gladnick, in summer dress worn in Sicily. Photo taken in Chicago, September 1945.
R. Gladnick

erans organization. But of approximately 4,000 volunteers who went to Spain only about 1,500 returned. Most were killed by the ineptness of our Moscow commissars and their lackey-appointed officers. Of the thousand or more who returned, most just disappeared into American society and were unwilling to join an anti-communist group. The rest remain communist zombies – they just couldn't function outside the atmosphere of the party.

At the time of the Stalin-Hitler pact, 29 September 1939, I became disillusioned with the social democratic movement. Based on my combat experience in tanks in Spain, I submitted an article to the *New Leader* (a social democratic publication) in November 1939, saying that the British and French armies were no match for the Wehrmacht. While the latter was trained to fight at ten to twelve miles per hour, the movement of the French and British armies was around one mile an hour. The article was rejected as being too pessimistic.

Second World War

Taunted by communists who had become Nazi allies, after the fall of France in June 1940 and during the Battle of Britain, I went to Montreal to join the Canadian Army and enlisted on 6 September 1940.

When I joined the Canadian Army, I stated I was an American and there were no questions asked. Americans then took no oath of allegiance to the king. We signed a statement that we would obey our superior officers. In early 1942, following Pearl Harbor, many U.S. citizens in the Canadian forces transferred to the U.S. forces. I was going to, but decided against it on the advice of a friend who transferred before me.

I never made a secret of my service in Spain. Upon arrival at Camp Borden, I informed my regimental commander, Lieutenant-Colonel J.G. "Jake" Vining of the Three Rivers Regiment (Tank), to be also later known as the 12th Army Tank Regiment, of my background. As our commander, he was a Colonel Blimp of the old school. His reaction to me was "once a Red, always a Red." Colonel F.F. Worthington, commander of the 1st Canadian Armoured Brigade, came to see me about my experiences in Spain and his reaction was not much better: "Spain, well I observed a guerrilla war in Nicaragua." When I tried to tell him there was no comparison – in Spain there were battles with 250 tanks just on our side and just as many aircraft – he shrugged it off as a "guerrilla war." Colonel Vining added, "I told you this guy was full of bullshit." From then on, I withdrew into my shell as an ordinary trooper. I must admit that until we went into action almost three years later, service in the Canadian Army was *cafard*, an expression I learned from a French foreign legionnaire in Spain. It roughly translates into army life as a mindless hell, broken up once in a while by drunken bouts. I am not much of a drinker so I escaped into non-interrupted reading until we landed in Sicily. There on 10 July 1943 I was immediately promoted to sergeant.

In Camp Borden there was a six-foot-two corporal who bragged of how much he hated Jews. I am a proud Jew so I took a swing at him and it was the last thing I remembered. The corporal brought me to. "You damn fool, I am a professional boxer," he said. "You're a brave man, so let's shake." After that he constantly begged me to tell him about Jews. He was from a farm in Saskatchewan and had never even met a Jew. We became close friends. He was killed in Italy. I must admit that I truly miss that "anti-Semite."

There were other incidents of anti-Semitism in the forces. My attitude was very simple. Real anti-Semitism is when they tie the hands of a Jew then beat him for not fighting back. As long as I can have the freedom to fight back, I don't consider it anti-Semitism.

The army gave me dog tags marked C. of E. (Church of England). I protested to our chaplain, Padre J.L. Wilhelm (a saint of a man), that as a Jew I wanted my own religion on my dog tags. He told me it was for my own protection in case I was taken prisoner. I told him that if taken prisoner I wanted the Nazi swine to know Jews also were front-line soldiers and my dog tags were changed to read HEB.

After Pearl Harbor many of the Americans in the Canadian Armoured Corps ended up with General Patton's II Corps. He welcomed them and told them that those unwilling to start as new recruits would be formed into a reconnaissance unit consisting of those with Canadian armoured experience. During the American withdrawal from the Kasserine Pass in February 1943, U.S. troops retreated but the ex-Canucks stood their ground and fought almost to the last man. Unfortunately, their reconnaissance tanks were no match for the German tanks.

The two years of 1943–45 were ones of active combat service. Thank God just before sailing from Scotland to Sicily Lieutenant-Colonel Vining was replaced by Lieutenant-Colonel E.L. Booth. He treated me as his eyes and ears as did the most outstanding officer I remember, Lieutenant-Colonel Fernand Caron, who took over in March 1944. I saw a lot of action as the point man of my reconnaissance troop.

I remember the breakthrough of the Gustav Line below Monte Cassino in May 1944. I served as the liaison troop between the tanks on the extreme right flank and the infantry on the left. It was a beautiful manoeuvre carried out with very few casualties under Colonel Caron's leadership. We had advanced, fighting for each inch of ground, from the Liri River. We were relieved by the North Irish Horse, who got a bloody nose as they approached the reinforced German line the following morning. They were relieved, in turn, by the 5th Canadian Armoured Division – at this time parade-ground disciplined but not combat worthy – a unit that had abandoned me in early 1944 at the Ortona salient. The 5th did no better than the North Irish Horse. We were called back and, as mentioned, we succeeded in breaking through the Gustav Line with very few casualties.

Sometime in late February 1945 orders came to leave the front. Rumours had it we were to head for Yugoslavia. Instead we moved to Leghorn on the west coast of Italy and learned we were destined for Holland. We were loaded on U.S. LSTs (landing ship tank) and sailed to Marseilles. It wasn't long before we found where the food was stored on board. We soon were gorging on huge sides of beef, bacon, eggs, and canned peaches. The captain seemed beside himself when he saw the pilferage but he knew in a day or so he would be rid of us.

In the Marseilles freight yard, as we were tying down our tanks onto the railroad flat cars, an American staff sergeant began mouthing off about "kikes back home making money while you guys are getting killed." My men wanted to beat up the guy, but I figured it was my responsibility. I took the marlinspike I was using to tighten the tank cables and knocked him down. An American major appeared wanting to know what happened. Our commander, Major East, came to my defence. The American major was amazed at how the other Canadians also backed me up. The major apologized, saying the man had been warned about having a big mouth. He came over to me shook my hand and with a grin quietly said "Shalom" (greetings).

A night or so later we arrived in Menin, Belgium. We were billeted in private homes. The women of the house laundered all our clothes, polished our badges and shone our shoes until they looked like mirrors. Our sergeant-major, "Fritz" Prevost, had reintroduced regimental parade. His system was to gather a roster for KP or other unpleasant jobs from those not up to his dress standards. On the periphery of the parade ground that morning stood wooden-shoed Flemish housewives with whom we had been boarding. Somehow the women got wind of what Fritzie was doing. Hell hath no fury like a Flemish or Dutch woman accused of improper polishing or washing. Soon a gaggle of women rushed the parade square and taking off their wooden clogs began to clobber the R.S.M. (regimental sergeant major). Poor Fritzie was a brave man but no match for these gals. He rushed off the parade ground and took shelter in the sergeants' mess.

After a few days, sometime in early April, we left for the front. As our advance began in earnest, we ran into 2nd Canadian Corps soldiers who called us zombies and accused us of still having Canadian water in our canteens. They soon learned we were not draftees from Canada but veterans of the Italian campaign.

When we got to Hilversum, on the outskirts of Amsterdam, negotiations for a cease-fire had begun. I persuaded the squadron commander to allow a fast reconnaissance up ahead. When I entered Amsterdam, German soldiers were still armed to the teeth in a few parks, but the rest of the city was in an orgy of celebration. I got drunk as hell. As the day wore on, I lost consciousness and later woke in bed with a half-Dutch, half-Indonesian girl who was married. I then realized that I had better get back to Hilversum and the regiment as soon as possible, which I did.

Post-war

When I returned to New York after the war, I got a job with an English company to sell silver antiques but found myself out of character. I had also met the girl I was to marry. Her parents raised holy hell when I suggested she should go with me to Palestine. If I was to get married, I had to have a job. I finally got a job as an organizer for the International Ladies Garment Workers Union in Virginia, then West Virginia, Cleveland, Puerto Rico and Miami. I had two sons along the way.

In 1967 I thought the union should become part of Martin Luther King's campaign in the South. The higher-ups disagreed and I quit. I got a job for a while in Montevideo, Uruguay, with the American Institute of Free Labour Development. After two years I quit. I next worked in public relations for Histadrut, the Israeli Federation of Labor in San Francisco. As a spokesman, I was very good, but I couldn't bring myself to be subservient to the rich donors. A stint as a union organizer for hotel and restaurant workers was followed by a stint as a real estate vendor in Florida. I am now retired and live in West Palm Beach, Florida.[12]

GWILYM JONES
Theatre: Italy, Northwest Europe   Service: Army

I was born 16 July 1920 in Liverpool, England. My family emigrated to the United States from Wales when I was a few months old. I grew up in Pennsylvania and eastern Ohio. While attending Columbia University, in New York City, I was recruited for the RAF. I was sent to Montreal but my papers did not arrive and I ran out of money. On my fourth day in Montreal I saw a smartly dressed soldier and asked him how to find the Black Watch armoury, but he would not hear of it. He, too, was a Yank in the Canadian Army. He persuaded me to join his regiment. On 13

Sergeant Gwilym Jones,
Holland, 1945.
G. Jones

January 1941, I enlisted in the Canadian Grenadier Guards. I swore allegiance to King George VI, and thus again became a British subject.

Our draft arrived at Camp Borden late at night towards the end of January. After debarking, a massive non-commissioned officer carrying a swagger stick began extolling the virtues of belonging to such a regiment. It took some time for my ear to become attuned to his bark-type commands.

We finally departed Canada and arrived at Aldershot on 8 October 1942. Spit and polish returned. The parade square took a beating and supplies of Silvo and Brasso began to run low.

The regiment was finally issued with tanks. We moved to the Brighton-Hove area, then to Worthing for manoeuvres. I took commando training and a mine demolition course.

In late summer of 1943 I was selected to participate in an exchange project with the Central Mediterranean Force in order to get some battle experience. I (Corporal Jones) would relieve one man of equal rank in Italy for six months for reciprocal training and experience.

By the time we arrived in Naples in early November 1943 the Allied troops were fighting their way up the Italian boot. I chose to go to the Three Rivers Regiment of the 1st Canadian Armoured Brigade, an independent brigade which was part of 13th Corps, Eighth Army. As an independent brigade it was called upon to support whichever division was committed at the time. At the time the Three Rivers Regiment was engaged in heavy fighting at Ortona (December 1943). When I arrived, the infantry was still flushing German troops out of Ortona. I was put to work with a sapper sergeant clearing mines and booby-traps.

We spent the winter months concentrated in the Ortona area, each regiment of the brigade holding static positions. In April 1944 we moved to just south of Cassino in the villages of San Pietro and St. Vittore. The task of the 1st Canadian Armoured Brigade for the major offensive against the Gustav Line of 11 May was to assist the 8th Indian Division. Although it had been decided that the Three Rivers Regiment would be in reserve, the reconnaissance troop was assigned to go with the tanks of the Ontario and Calgary Regiments. My patrol went to the Ontarios for the crossing of the Rapido River, then rejoined the regiment after the third day.

A day or so before the attack some of us decided to have a haircut. Wally Burnett was selected to be the barber. Wally was a big lumbering bear of a man. He was from the Bronx in New York City, and had attended New York University before enlisting in Canada. Most of us went into battle wearing bowl haircuts courtesy of Wally.

At 2300 hours on 11 May the artillery barrage started. As the tanks moved forward towards the river, it was necessary to keep within the white tapes previously laid down by the sappers. The Gustav Line was eventually breached and Cassino fell.

On about the third day, after the higher ground had been secured, my patrol (two Honey tanks and eight men, four in each tank) moved back to the river to try and find Wally, who had been killed crossing the flat ground. His body was moved to a plot near where the Canadian dead were being buried. I went across the river to fetch the padre, a Roman Catholic. The padre checked Wally's dog tags then exclaimed "un juif" and told me he would not bury him. I pulled out my side arm, pointed it at him and said, "Padre, you bury him or we'll bury you." And he did.

The next day I received orders to report to regimental headquarters. When I got there the padre was with the colonel (Lieutenant-Colonel Fernand Caron). Colonel Caron asked me to explain what had happened and I told him. I never saw that padre again.

Following the breakthrough of the Gustav Line and the capture of Cassino, it was on to the next German line of defence, the Hitler Line and the Liri Valley, barring the natural route to Rome. By this time I had been promoted in the field to troop sergeant and Mentioned in Despatches.

Following this breakthrough, the 5th Canadian Armoured Division got its first taste of real action when it successfully crossed the Melfa River. The American forces were given the honour of taking Rome on 5 June 1944, while we forced our way towards Florence.

By mid-June we had reached the German's next line of defence around Lake Trasimene. We then lost more men here than in any other battle. The regiment lost five officers and fifteen other ranks killed, four officers and forty other ranks wounded, and five prisoners of war.

I was awarded the Military Medal on 17 October 1944. The citation reads:

> Seven Stuart tanks of the Reconnaissance Troop, 12th Canadian Armoured Regiment, loaded with ammunition and engineer explosives, were parked north of the village of Castel del Rio. Between them and the road was an ammunition dump. On the road an ammunition party with lorries was at work moving the dump. At about 0915 hours the enemy commenced to shell the immediate area with a heavy concentration. A direct hit was made on a pile of ammunition between two Stuarts. Sergeant Jones, regardless of exploding shells and burning ammunition, remained in the area until all his men were under cover and carefully checked each tank to ensure that no wounded men remained. At about 1000 hours a loaded ammunition lorry was hit and set on fire. Realizing that the Stuarts were in danger of catching fire, Sergeant Jones rushed out of cover and, under a shower of exploding ammunition, extricated one from behind the burning lorry and drove it away. Handing it over to its own driver, he returned and brought out two more.

Encouraged by his fearless example, the drivers of the tanks and ammunition vehicles left cover and commenced to drive their vehicles away. Sergeant Jones remained behind with a Stuart to pull out a loaded ammunition lorry which had gone off the road. As a result all Stuarts and all but one ammunition lorry were safely evacuated to the shelter of the buildings.

The outstanding courage, initiative, and example displayed by Sergeant Jones under great personal risk and under enemy observation was directly responsible for averting serious losses and is in the highest tradition of the service.

V-E Day was 8 May 1945 and we were in the Netherlands. The people decorated our tanks with flowers and hugged and kissed us. My feelings as all this was taking place was that after all the mud and blood we had been through and seen, it was well worth it to see the joy in their faces, especially those of the children.

Following discharge in Montreal I returned to university, obtained a bachelor of commerce degree from Sir George Williams University, married a Canadian girl, and became a Canadian citizen. After thirty years service with DuPont Canada I took early retirement, returned to university and earned a master's degree in social work at McGill. I am retired now and live in Toronto.[13]

LIONEL PROULX
Theatre: Europe   Service: Air Force

I was born in Southbridge, Massachusetts, on 14 July 1918. I enlisted in the Royal Canadian Air Force in Montreal on 3 February 1941 because I became impatient with President Roosevelt's lack of action toward Hitler. My father was born in St. Hyacinthe, Quebec. He was brought to Massachusetts as a pre-schooler and never returned to Canada to live. But he grew up not realizing he was still a Canadian citizen and a British subject.

In 1917 my father joined the U.S. Army, was sent to France and was wounded. While he was convalescing in hospital overseas, his records were reviewed and it was discovered that he was a

Canadian. He was told then he either had to apply for U.S. citizenship or remain a British subject. He decided in favour of U.S. citizenship and became an American citizen after returning to the U.S.A.

To confuse and complicate the matter I was born in the U.S.A. I became automatically a U.S. citizen, but since my father was still a Canadian at the time, I also unknowingly was a British subject as well. This fact was not made known to either my father or me.

When I enlisted, the RCAF authorities examined my birth certificate, which showed that I was born in Southbridge, and accepted me at face value as a U.S. citizen. I went through training, served in RAF Ferry Command out of Dorval, and then went to RAF General Reconnaissance School at Squires Gate near Blackpool before being transferred to RAF Coastal Command at Limavady, Northern Ireland.

Later, in 1942, I was ordered to report to the United States Army Air Forces Headquarters in London, England. There I was told that I had to transfer from the RCAF/RAF or lose my

Captain Lionel Proulx (left), Watton Field, Norfolk, England, August 1944.
L. Proulx

American citizenship. So, on 28 October 1942, I was sworn in as a second lieutenant in the U.S. Eighth Air Force.

I was sent to the Bovingdon Airfield near London to serve as a navigator instructor and eventually headed the navigation school. All this time, no one, including myself, realized that I had lost my American citizenship when I enlisted in the RCAF.

Later, in 1944, I was transferred to the 25th Bombardment Group (Reconnaissance), which was the only USAAF unit which flew the de Havilland Mosquito (as many as two squadrons). During the course of my service with the 25th Group, I was assigned as the group navigation officer and flew thirty-five combat missions, including one on which my pilot and I landed in the Soviet Union.

After World War II, I decided to remain in the air force and was sent to the Army Language School at the Presidio of Monterey, in California, to study the language and culture of the U.S.S.R. During the first several months there my previous personnel records and background were checked.

One day in June 1947 I was ordered to appear before the commanding officer and informed that I was an alien and as such was confined to the post until it could be determined whether I should be court-martialled. The language school was part of the intelligence structure of the U.S.A. and was off limits to aliens. However, I was permitted to continue with my classes. Finally, it was decided that I was innocent and told to apply for U.S. citizenship. In 1947 I was sworn in at the Federal Court in San Francisco. I'm in the unusual position of being a U.S. citizen by birth and also by application as an alien.[14]

MALCOLM HORMATS
Theatre: Canada, Great Britain,   Service: Air Force
      Mediterranean

I enlisted in the British Commonwealth Air Training Plan (BCATP) in April 1941. I had tried to join the U.S. Army Air Corps program in early 1939, but was turned down because of a "five diopter squint" in my right eye. The U.S. had not, of course, entered the war and their supply of cadets far exceeded the demand.

In 1939 I completed a civilian pilot training program which the

U.S. government established to
create a supply of flyers for possible future use. The government provided all instruction
leading to a private civilian
licence. We flew Luscombe
Silvairs and received about
eighty total hours of flying
time.

Joining the RCAF came
about naturally. Most of my
generation were deeply concerned about what had been
happening in Europe and felt
that American involvement
would only be a matter of time.
There were several groups
actively seeking American vol-

Sergeant Malcolm Hormats after
receiving his wings at Uplands
Airport, Ottawa, early 1942.
M. Hormats

unteers – the Clayton Knight group brought Americans directly
into the RAF. They were, of course, trained in Canada, as that had
become the locale for the BCATP for Canadians, South Africans,
Australians, New Zealanders and the RAF as well as a few who got
out of occupied Europe.

I drove to Montreal from my home in Troy, N.Y., with two
friends. They decided not to enlist so I went alone to 90 Bishop
Street in Montreal, the RCAF recruiting centre there, and took the
king's shilling. I returned home after being accepted and waited
several months before being asked to return. I do recall one item
that might be of interest: the U.S. constitution enjoins any U.S. citizen from swearing an oath of allegiance to a foreign government
so we crossed out the word "allegiance" in the RCAF paperwork
and entered "obedience" – it was accepted.

My initial tour was at the Manning Pool at St. Hubert, at that
time Montreal's only major airport. The basic purpose was to provide us with uniforms, teach us military basics such as the manual
of arms, and hold us until classes opened in the flying training program. We held the rank of aircraftman, second class (AC2, nicknamed "Acey Ducey") and pulled security guard at the field. It was
really interesting because St. Hubert was the terminus for the
Atlantic Ferry organization delivering Hudsons and Liberators to
Scotland.

We finally moved to Victoriaville, Quebec, for our preflight training. The facilities were a very old Catholic school and we had to mount guard continuously, as the building was a firetrap. As I recall it, Victoriaville was a solidly French Canadian town where nobody spoke English. We had no social life at all. At Victoriaville we were given some navigation training, Morse code and Link trainer screening. Then, on 1 September 1941, I reported to No. 3 Elementary Flight Training School (EFTS) at London, Ontario, where they flew the Fleet Finch. My instructor was an American who did not know that I was already a licensed pilot. My hope was to let him guess I had great talent so I could go to fighters rather than bombers and he did a great deal to help me. The training was excellent – much less formal than comparable U.S. training of the period. We had civilian instructors with one or two dreaded RCAF officers who conducted final flight checks. When I completed the course in six weeks, I had thirty hours of stick time plus thirty-five of dual instruction. I remember the people of London being very friendly – we had lots of invitations to dinners and dances.

A week after completing EFTS, I was flying at No. 2 Service Flying School at Uplands, Ontario. The trainer there was the Harvard, a North American AT-6. The course was completed in March 1942 and I logged another 120 hours at Uplands with another 35 in the Link. We flew through the winter which was quite an experience.

I received my wings in March. Uplands, in those days, was probably the best RCAF training station and the instruction was excellent – both ground school and flying training. Ottawa, during WW II, was an exciting city – but we spent a lot of free time in Hull. Every now and then one of us Americans would get lost and land at Watertown, N.Y., by accident. An instructor pilot would be sent to fly the plane back to Canada and both would return loaded with hard-to-get American cigarettes.

None of our training was actually designed to prepare us for combat – it was plain, fundamental airplane handling. Unlike the Army Air Corps, which trained in Texas, the BCATP operated in lousy weather and that really prepared us for flying in the U.K.

By the time we finished that winter at Uplands, I believe I was a pretty competent pilot with some real weather flying experience. I remember one time when, solo, I was practising aerobatics south of Ottawa. A blizzard came out of nowhere and we were all lost. There was no navigation equipment or radios in our Harvards. I got on the deck and flew north until I crossed the Ottawa River. I turned left until I found downtown Ottawa and then followed streets until I got to the airport. We all got into a left-hand traffic pattern. One American pilot panicked and flew a right-hand pattern. It was pretty scary when he came out of nowhere every half lap. As I recall, we all got down okay. Although combat flying was not on our syllabus, we would dogfight each other at the drop of a hat. I got caught around Xmas of '41 and that got me a sergeant pilot rank instead of pilot officer when the course ended.

Life during those days was great. We refought the American Revolution nightly, the French and Indian Wars hourly, and Germany all the time. When the Americans got together, alone, we'd reopen the Civil War and have at it. In between we'd find girls in Ottawa. I was twenty-two, unmarried and having a ball.

I reported to Halifax in late March and sailed to England on a Gydnia-American Line ship. It carried German POWs westward and troops east. We were put in the POW quarters. The sub menace was very real and I remember it was a very worrisome trip – but our convoy was untouched.

We were sent to Bournemouth to await flying assignments. Even as an American, I remember the total disgust of the Canadians, ANZACs and others when a RAF officer, welcoming us patronizingly, said, "I can't tell you how happy we are to have you colonials marching by our side." That was my first real inkling that the Commonwealth was heading into troubled waters.

From Bournemouth I was attached to RAF Fighter Command and posted to No. 5 Advanced Flying Unit at Tern Hill, Shropshire. There we flew the Miles Master and began to receive combat training. We received a lot of instrument flying, formation flying and night flying. The latter was practised in the daytime. We wore very dark yellow goggles, had a sodium vapour light in the cockpit to illuminate the instruments and there was a sodium vapour version of the regular nighttime flare path. It was like flying on a moonlit night and gave us a good feeling for the real thing. We also did some actual night flying.

By July, I had 200 hours and was posted to No. 61 Operational Training Unit at Rednal, Oswestry Salop. There we soloed the Spitfire 2 and began serious training – night, gunnery, formation, low level, aerobatics and, of course, radio techniques and aircraft recognition training. Instrument flying was particularly hairy – we went up in single-place Spits while people being trained as fighter controllers gave us vectors and kept us clear, we hoped, from other traffic. When you finished those sessions you were either an instrument pilot or dead.

My course finished at end September and I was supposed to be posted to a RAF squadron. I was told to report to Adastral House in London, where I found a number of other Americans. We were told we had to transfer to the army air corps or face possible loss of our citizenship. I later learned that the colonel passing that word was dead wrong – but none of us wanted to test it. So, I went back to Rednal, packed my kit and joined the U.S. Army Air Corp's 31st Fighter Group at Tangmere near Chichester. I had a total of 226 flying hours plus 52 in the Link. That, in a nutshell, is the story of my time with the RCAF. It was, in the main, a most enjoyable time and left me with a profound respect and admiration for Canadian flyers in particular and Canadians in general.

My U.S. career was even more interesting. I was involved in the North African invasion, Sicily and Salerno. Came back to the best job I've ever had as a ferry pilot flying everything everywhere all the time. For a number of years I was involved in long-range detection of U.S.S.R. nuclear bomb tests and flying cloud sampling missions in our own nuclear clouds (a harrowing experience). I ended up as the director of aerospace research at the Cape, where I retired in 1965. I had spent three years as managing director of Western Union's Advanced Communications Division. The USAF asked me to come back as a civilian and organize a computerized tracking system for all USAF flying. I ran that for the air force, national guard and reserves until three years ago, when I retired for good to Rockville, Maryland.[15]

ARCHIE MELVILLE COMPTON
Theatre: Northwest Europe   Service: RCAF

I am the widow of Archie Melville Compton. My husband was an American serving in the RCAF during World War II. He died in April of 1989 of lung cancer. Mel, born on 15 May 1916, was a native Virginian from Fredericksburg who flew out of the local small airport. He drove up to Toronto to the Manning Pool and joined the RCAF on 19 June 1941. He was stationed in Goderich, Trenton and Belleville and received his wings at Brantford in May of 1942.

I met Mel in the autumn of 1941 when his car broke down near my home in Westhill, Ontario. To his dismay, Mel was sent to instructors' school in Claresholm, Alberta, and then stationed in Dauphin, Manitoba, as an instructor from late September 1942 until June of 1943. We were married in early September of 1942.

Mel always longed to go on "ops" and was finally posted overseas in May of 1943. He wanted to fly fighters – Mosquitos, if possible. When he got to Bournemouth, in the south of England, the real need was for bomber pilots so he signed up for that rather than hang around waiting to fly. Since he had so much flying time, he was assigned to an experienced crew who had lost their pilot. He flew a Halifax

First Lieutenant A.M. Compton, USAAF, attached to 424 (Tiger) Squadron, RCAF. Skipton-on-Swale, Yorkshire, England, 1944.
B. Compton

bomber called *Oscar* out of Skipton-on-Swale with 424 (Tiger) Squadron. There were forty operations – the first, a flight to Berlin, the bulk of the others consisting of mine-laying ports and bombing railroad yards in France, mainly around Paris.

When Mel left his crew to return to the States, it was the saddest day of his life. He was stationed at Lockbourne Air Base in Columbus, Ohio, where he became qualified as an instructor for B-17s and, I think, B-24s. I was very anxious that we have our first child and the fact that our first baby was on the way may have deterred him from volunteering for Air Sea Rescue in the Pacific. Mel completed his career as a staff pilot at Boca Raton in Florida.

We settled in Richmond. The first couple of years he worked instructing at the small airport where he had learned to fly. After that he went back to construction as a carpenter, then aircraft parts salesman, and finally instrument making. He built one of the cameras that went to the moon.

At his funeral I stood up and said it was the privilege of my life to have been his bride and mother of his children. No one has to go to another country to offer their life for a cause greater than their own. Those Americans who enlisted in Canada were heroes. They fought to save our way of life – freedom versus tyranny.

J. Norman Clarke of Nanoose Bay, British Columbia, Mel's wireless operator, added his recollections:

I remember Mel Compton as a relatively frail, mustachioed and slightly bent figure with a certain hawk-like profile. His posture was not particularly military and he would not have been posted to any kind of guard of honour. He was also the most conscientious man I have ever known. Perhaps that attitude made it possible for the crew to complete its tour without casualties.

The following excerpts from Clarke's wartime diary offer some insight into the period and the men of the crew:

2 January 1944
Our new pilot is Archie Melville Compton from Richmond, Virginia.

23 January
Compton went to London to transfer into the U.S. Army Air Force but will return to do his tour with us. This is my third day at Skipton-on-Swale or, as the natives would have it, Skipton-in-Mud.

10 February
Our flight engineer is embroiled with a major problem as the result of some "hexperimenting" he did on some park bench with a Land Army woman in Ripon. The result of the experiments is that she is pregnant and he is the father. I was asked to accompany our flight engineer to Ripon to interview his erstwhile paramour. She says she wants to marry him. The marriage may be of a short duration at best considering the longevity of people in his present trade.

29 February
The target was Augsburg. We got airborne with 5,000 pounds of incendiaries. Half an hour out, the pilot's escape hatch blew away. The trip was a little breezier than we wanted particularly when the

month is February and the altitude is 18,000 feet. We got to the target right in the middle of the raid and the master bomber took control by directing the forces to drop their loads on designated target indicators. It could be determined that while we may have been cold the target was hot if the illumination meant anything. The enemy fighter flares illuminated as well as the searchlights and we were happy to get away from there.

16 March

On the night of the 16th we went to Trappes, a marshalling yard just out of Paris. It turned out to be a piece of cake. We dumped 11,500 pounds of explosives on the target. Some of the delayed-action bombs may not have gone off yet but as long as they lie there the station master will be on his toes.

Mel is a real motorcycle enthusiast as well as a mechanic, carpenter and anything else one might mention. He has purchased a 1938 Velocette motorcycle which he treasures.

20 March

Bomber Command suffered its greatest loss of the war to date. The morning news stated the loss at ninety-eight on Nuremberg. The operation had been scrubbed as far as our aircraft was concerned because the zipper of one of our crew's new flying suit had engaged with the jettison bar and the bombs which were not armed fell off the racks. The cause of the Nuremberg fiasco was partially attributed to high winds which were not forecast and which propelled the force to the target ahead of time. Aircraft then zig-zagged and orbited upon arrival, subjecting themselves to collisions, enemy fighters and flak.

The winds that sent them down made the return trip slow and there were losses due to fuel shortages. That evening we went to the Dog and Gun pub and drank their good ale and talked of old times. It seems that there are fewer of us left to talk about.

29 April

On 27 April we went to Aulnoye at 10,000 feet. We were lucky to walk away from that one. The weather was rough when we took off and as we passed out of the cloud at around 9,000 feet the aircraft had accumulated so much ice that it spun. We came out of it at around 4,000 feet and continued on to the target. Compton didn't give anyone permission to leave but had there been a convenient exit he could have counted on being short several of his crew members.

6 June
The BBC announced on the nine o'clock news that the invasion of Normandy had commenced. At 2330 we hit at Conde-sur-Noireaux on low level.

30 July
The last few days have been eventful beginning with a prang of Stuttgart on the 26th. Villers Bocage in Normandy was the target for today to open a way for an Allied breakout into France. The cloud held us down and therefore not far enough above ground level not to be hit by the muck churned up by thousand-pound bombs being dropped everywhere.

24 August
I returned to find Compton preparing to return to the United States. He has done forty missions and I have thirty-eight and therefore his reasons for being here have been vindicated. The House of Commons still stands by the Thames, and the Union Jack continues to fly.[16]

CLYDE EAST
Theatre: Northwest Europe   Service: RCAF

I was born in Pittsylvania County, Virginia, on 19 July 1921. I was raised on a tobacco farm and graduated from Chatham High School, Chatham, Virginia, in 1940.

I joined the RCAF for several reasons, but the primary one was that I wanted to learn to fly and get into the war. I didn't realize at the time that with the challenge facing Britain that I might end up as one of the casualties, but nineteen-year-old kids are not known for thinking things through. I thoroughly enjoyed my days as a trainee in the RCAF and never had a moment's regret for leaving home and country to enlist. I enjoyed meeting the hundreds of other youngsters and knew from the outset that we would make a name for ourselves.

I joined up at the recruiting depot at Hamilton, Ontario, June 1941, took manning depot training at Toronto and guard duty at

No. 31 Radio School, Clinton, Ontario. I took further training at Victoriaville, Quebec, and attended primary flying school at Windsor Mills, Quebec. I was washed out of elementary flying school on my fifty-hour check and spent almost four months at Trenton, Ontario. I was able to talk my way back into flying training and was assigned to the elementary flying training school at Goderich, Ontario, where I completed the course without difficulty in June 1942.

From Goderich I was assigned to No. 6 Service Flying Training School at Dunnville, Ontario, where I trained on Harvards and received my wings and a commission as a pilot officer on 6 November 1942. I think the RCAF training I received from start to finish was great. The instructions, both ground and air, were outstanding. I do not think there were any better flying training courses anywhere at the time.

Leading Aircraftman Clyde East on guard, Clinton, Ontario, August 1941.
C. East

From Dunnville I was sent overseas and spent the next four months at the RCAF replacement centre, Bournemouth, England, as well as several time-consuming intervals with the Canadian Army, another Tiger Moth elementary flying training school near Coventry, and finally a Miles Master Flying course near Norwich. The Miles Master was fairly close to the Hurricane in operating characteristics and I learned a lot about flying from it. By this time I knew I wanted to fly fighters and when a chance to go to the Mustang reconnaissance school at Hawarden, Cheshire, came up, I took it. It could well have been that I wanted to get into the

Mustang, rather than the Hurricane, where most of the assignments were. In any case I was elated at going to Mustangs.

The reconnaissance school at Hawarden had the early model Mustang, which had been selected by the RAF as the standard reconnaissance aircraft for army support. There were three Mustang tactical reconnaissance squadrons in the RCAF in England and probably five to seven in the RAF structure. After Hawarden, I was assigned in June 1943 to No. 414 Tactical/Reconnaissance Squadron RCAF stationed at Gatwick, Surrey. We moved about once every two to three weeks, so Gatwick was not a permanent base for us. For the several months I was with No. 414, we were at Dunsfield, Weston Zoyland, Ashford, Redhill and three times at Gatwick. I managed to accumulate about thirty operational sorties in the period of July 1943 upon assignment to No. 414 until early January 1944, when I transferred to the U.S. Army Air Force in England and eventually to the 15th Tactical Reconnaissance Squadron in the Ninth U.S. Air Force. These RCAF missions in flights of two into France, Belgium and Holland attacked trains, motor transports, canal barges and stray enemy aircraft.

By V-E Day I had flown over 200 combat missions with the USAF totalling over 350 hours, destroyed thirteen and a half enemy aircraft with them, and coordinated the destruction of numerous enemy tanks, motor transport and troop concentrations. I was awarded the Silver Star, the American Distinguished Flying Cross and Air Medal with thirty-six oak leaf clusters.

My primary reason for leaving the RCAF was that I wanted a permanent commission in the USAF. I would have stayed with the Canadians indefinitely if they could have promised a peacetime commission in the RCAF, but not being Canadian, I did not have a chance. At least in the U.S. service I could compete for a commission on an equal basis. My reasoning was good, and after the war I eventually got a regular commission and remained in the USAF until February 1965. I had a long series of combat in World War II, became a fighter ace with thirteen victories with the USAF, had two hours in Korea, participated in the overlights during the 1962 Cuban missile crisis, did a short tour in Vietnam, reached the grade of lieutenant-colonel, and always enjoyed my work. Following retirement in 1965, I was employed by the Rand corporation in Santa Monica, California.

I met my wife while training in Canada. She was the sister of a fellow I enlisted with at Hamilton. I met her the first time he took me to his home from the manning depot in Toronto. We married in 1944 while I was on a month's leave from England. By that time I was in the U.S. Air Force.

I've been back to Canada many times, since I make it a point to attend the Canadian aircrew reunion in Winnipeg every four years.[17]

DOUGLAS ALBERT MUNRO
Theatre: Pacific   Service: U.S. Coast Guard

Douglas Albert Munro was born in Vancouver, British Columbia, on 11 October 1919. Most of his life was spent in Cle Elum, Washington. In 1939 he enlisted in the Coast Guard. He was posthumously awarded the Medal of Honor

> as Petty Officer in charge of a group of 24 Higgins boats, engaged in the evacuation of a battalion of marines trapped by enemy Japanese forces at Point

Medal of Honor (Navy).
U.S. Coast Guard

Douglas A. Munro.
U.S. Coast Guard

Cruz, Guadalcanal, on 27 September 1942. After making preliminary plans for the evacuation of nearly 500 beleaguered marines, Munro, under constant strafing by enemy machine guns on the island, and at great risk of his life, daringly led five of his small craft toward the shore. As he closed the beach, he signalled the others to land, and then in order to draw the enemy's fire and protect the heavily loaded boats, he valiantly placed his craft with its two small guns as a shield between the beachhead and the Japanese. When the perilous task of evacuation was nearly completed, Munro was instantly killed by enemy fire, but his crew, two of whom were wounded, carried on until the last boat had loaded and cleared the beach. By his outstanding leadership, expert planning, and dauntless devotion to duty, he and his courageous comrades undoubtedly saved the lives of many who otherwise would have perished.[18]

Bernard D'Andrea's depiction of Munro earning the
Medal of Honor.
U.S. Coast Guard

THE REYNOLDS BROTHERS
– as told by John Reynolds

Both my brother, U.S. Army Air Corps First Lieutenant Arthur Joseph, and I, John, served in World War II. Both of us were born in Alberta, Canada, of Canadian parents. My brother was born in July 1919 at Hughenden and I was born five years later in Camrose. We moved to Camas, Washington, where Mom and Dad obtained employment at the paper mill. Our parents received U.S. naturalization papers in 1939. In the summer of 1941 my brother joined the Royal Canadian Air Force in Vancouver, where he was assigned to pilot training.

When the United States entered the war, it was agreed between the governments that persons training in Canada holding U.S. citizenship would be returned to the United States. In my case, I had to seek a waiver of citizenship requirements since I had not been a citizen (by virtue of our parents' naturalization) for ten years – the very first requirement for aviation cadet training. The waiver was granted the last day enlistments were open, 15 December 1942; after that date the draft board decided which branch of service you entered. I hitchhiked from Washington State College at Pullman to Geiger Field, Spokane, that day and was sworn in just before the deadline at midnight.

Arthur Joseph Reynolds
Theatre: Northwest Europe   Service: Air Force

Arthur was transferred to Lubbock Field, Texas, in June 1942. He received his pilot wings and was commissioned a second lieutenant in the U.S. Army Air Forces on 3 July 1942. Subsequently, he and other U.S. citizens similarly transferred were presented RCAF pilot wings. As a lieutenant Arthur went almost directly to a B-17 crew of the 91st Bombardment Group, 322nd Squadron, part of the Eighth Air Force, serving as the co-pilot. The group was deployed at Bassingbourn, England, in September 1942. The story of an incident involving Arthur and his crew on B-17 Chief Sly received wide publicity.

Rose O'Day, a B-17, and Chief Sly were part of a strong formation sent to bomb by day the big enemy air depot at Romilly-sur-Seine on 20 December 1942. The lead bomber, Rose O'Day, faltered on her way back due to flak damage. Chief Sly dropped back to protect Rose O'Day. The two aircraft staged a running battle against enemy aircraft from Paris to

First Lieutenant Arthur Reynolds (far right, standing on the
right-front jeep fender) in front of *Chief Sly II*,
Bassingbourn, Cambridgeshire,
9 June 1943.
J. Reynolds

the English Channel. Chief Sly *crash-landed at Fletching, Sussex,
England, with all safe (some wounded). Canadian medical personnel were
first on the scene to assist the crew.*

My brother went on to become captain of his own crew with 813
Bomber Squadron, 482nd Bombardment Group (Pathfinder). His
B-17 was the first to be equipped with H2S (British) pathfinding
radar equipment. The normal ten-man crew was increased by one
radar observer and two mechanics. All the crew were returning
from their advanced base, Thorpe Abbot, to their home base of
Alconbury when the aircraft crashed at about 10:40 a.m., 10
November 1943, at Brome, Suffolk, killing all aboard as well as two
civilians on the ground.

John Reynolds
Theatre: Pacific   Service: Air Force

Five years younger than my brother, I received my pilot wings and second lieutenant's commission in May 1944. I too went to B-17 pilot training and qualified as a first pilot. While awaiting assignment to a B-17 group, I was one of the first sixteen second lieutenants to be assigned to B-29 training. I became a co-pilot and was sent to Saipan, Marianas Islands (877th Squadron, 499th Group, 73 Bomber Wing) on the first replacement crew to reach that unit. I participated in many of the destructive fire raids over Japan and flew conventional-type bombing missions against most of the major targets in Japan. I returned briefly to California for a short Pathfinder course. We came back to Saipan and flew as a Pathfinder until war's end. I was demobilized in 1946 but recalled to active duty in 1948 at the time of the Berlin airlift crisis. C-54 (the military version of Douglas DC-4) crew training was full so I was sent to a year's training in communications. Based at Komaki Air Force Base, Nagoya, Japan, I flew wounded out of the forward

First Lieutenant John Reynolds (far left, rear row), Saipan, 1945.
J. Reynolds

areas in Korea on C-47 Dakota aircraft in October 1950. When it was discovered after a week I had a "Q" (atomic) clearance, I was restricted from flying to the mainland of Asia. I served a tour at Goose Bay, Labrador, often visited the Canadian DEW Line on communications matters, and also served in the U.S. Embassy in Ottawa. I retired in August 1972 after a thirty-year career.[19]

HUBERT LEWIS
Theatre: Northwest Europe   Service: Air Force

I am kept busy doing my bit in preventing a disaster for the human race. I am active in the anti-nuclear campaign. There has to be some point to risking one's life for a cause like halting a new dark age that would have appeared had the Nazis defeated us.

I was what one would call today a drop-out. I left school as soon as I could as I wanted to grow up and see what the world was all about. I got one good education, especially about the Great Depression.

I guess it was natural that when war broke out I would find some purpose to my life. To get into the flying branch of the RCAF I had to have a high school education. I was told if I enlisted in ground duties, I would be able to transfer to aircrew in a few months. That proved to be false. I then decided to desert. After my first leave back home in New York, I went to Halifax to see if I could work my way on a ship to England where, I was told correctly, the boys often left school at age fourteen, so I'd be accepted as aircrew there. No one likes the label "deserter" but as a young, unmarried, adventurous type, action seemed more important to me than safety. Many an old soldier in Canada had told me that I could survive the war if I kept my feet on the ground and let others be the fools. That philosophy didn't cut any ice with me.

I was almost found out in Halifax when someone noticed that despite the fact I was in "civvies," I had on an air force shirt. I managed, however, to get a job as a trimmer on a small Norwegian ship carrying timber to England. I had no papers, and since Norway had been overrun by June 1941, the Norwegians were desperate for seamen and were satisfied with just my New York driver's licence.

It was a very dangerous job being amidships below the water-line, shovelling coal. But luck was on my side, and although it was a slow-moving convoy and our ship was strung on the outside of the convoy, being more expendable I presumed, the crossing in July 1941 was without incident. That was how I spent my twenty-first birthday on 22 July. I discovered later that the previous month there had been record sinkings as well as the following month.

The month I went across was one of the quietest times. The convoy split when we arrived in the Hebrides. We sailed down the North Sea to London without incident. On a fine summer's day we finally sailed up the Thames. The masts of sunken ships were visibly sticking out of the water. It was an eye-opener for me in the fact that although the dock area (Surrey docks in the East End) was pretty flattened by bombing, the rest of London was surprisingly almost untouched. The dock workers were not interested in asking about my voyage, but only what kind of contraband like whisky, cigarettes or chocolates I had to sell. I had to disappoint them as I was really green. After a six-week voyage I was paid what at that time was a large sum of money, $175 (the average American manual worker's wage was $25 weekly). I had never received anything near that salary as a youth. Things seemed awfully inexpensive in London then and I booked into a moderate hotel for a week.

As an alien I was supposed to be indoors by 10 p.m. Late one night I was picked up off the streets by police who kept me in jail until next morning. The judge was very pleasant and gave me a lecture that in wartime they had to be careful as to who was on the streets at night.

After a strict medical examination and intelligence test, I was accepted by the Royal Air Force for aircrew and posted up to the well-known resort of Blackpool for training. It was interesting to hear lads my own age tell about their way of life. As I was an American, they were also curious to hear of my experiences. I had enjoyed the job aboard ship coming over and was tempted to stay on but didn't wish to get coal dust in my lungs. If I knew I would have had to wait two whole years before I saw action, I would have certainly stayed on as a seaman.

After the normal training routine I finally arrived – wings on a sergeant stripes – at an OTU (Operational Training Unit) where we were formed into crews. My crew, including two Canadians, were among the very few who were alive a year later. Out of our course of fifteen crews, two perished at this OTU; three crews were also lost in accidents on operations; and six crews were killed in action. Another crew was shot down and taken prisoner and another crew was shot down over France and made it back to England via the Resistance. One other crew had done twenty-five operations when I last saw them and I presume they survived. Our role was that of replacements.

My first mission was in midsummer 1943. I took the place of a wireless operator/air-gunner who was getting married. The bombing raid was against Mannheim and was what I would consider a normal and uneventful operation. That first time seeing shells exploding and flashing anti-aircraft guns from the ground made me realize that my life could come to an end. Seeing Mannheim on fire was an eye-opener too.

Here are details of several operations:

The usual route to Berlin was over Denmark, through the Baltic, crossing the enemy coast east of Rostock with a 150-mile dash to the target, thus avoiding the 600 miles of heavily defended areas. At the briefing on the night of 21 January 1944, it was revealed that we were to go through the Dutch coast straight to Berlin but turn off about eighty miles west and bomb Magdeburg. When we got over Magdeburg, there were almost no fighters to defend the city. We could hardly believe our good luck. But on the way home, all hell broke loose. Planes started to explode all around us and there were fights everywhere. We sighed with relief when we finally reached the coast. We lost a third of our squadron on that single operation. What went wrong was the fact that the enemy concentration of fighters just south of Hamburg was ordered to Leipzig. That route took the enemy fighters just west of our escape route and they ran right into the bomber stream. Out of 600 aircraft, we lost some 55.

On another operation on our way to Berlin, we iced up over Denmark and had to drop from over 20,000 feet to below 5,000. It looked for a time that we would perish in the Baltic. Luck was with us and we got out of the icy conditions. But by the time we crossed the enemy coast we were on our own. If we had made it to Berlin, we would have been easily picked off, so we dropped our bombs on a likely target over the coast and made for home.

On Christmas Eve of 1943 we were to do our first mine-laying operation. These were generally less risky than a main operation and were considered a perk. It felt peculiar leaving the sergeants' mess as they were getting ready for a Christmas party. Our two planes took only three and a half hours to get to the Dutch Frisian

Sergeant Hubert J. Lewis (left, front row) with the rest of the crew
of 102 Squadron, Pocklington, at the end of their tour, June 1944.
H. Lewis

Islands. We passed an enemy convoy but left them alone and they
held their fire too. We were told we should have broken radio
silence so others could have dealt with them. We were not sorry as
we wouldn't have liked to think we made them suffer on Christmas
Eve.

Our black spot was during three consecutive operations. We
lost about one-third of our squadron on each night. It came as a
relief when with the approach of D-Day we were put on to bombing
French railways, a "milk run" as the Yanks were to call such assignments. On D-Day we were to bomb a gun battery a few miles in
from Omaha Beach. Two days later we finished that mission, having done an extra ten more operations than normal. On the way
home from our final operation we flew low due to bad weather
depending on our radar to detect hills. By this time so many of our
aircraft had been lost hitting hills it was no joke. Our radar conked
out and everyone was in a sweat. When I fixed the fault, I felt really
good. The crew's gratitude was better than any Victoria Cross.

Afterthoughts

The negative side of my service was the some 50,000 people who were consumed, for example, in the fire storm that struck Hamburg. Reading about it after the war convinced me we must never have another war again, especially with nuclear bombs. A single one could kill 70,000 people as at Hiroshima. There is no excuse to use nuclear weapons. If wars have to be won by the massacre of so many civilians, better that we lose and take our chances.

I'll always remember one night when we were queuing for a bus back to Pocklington, Yorkshire. Older people, as usual, were congratulating us for our efforts. However, on this particular night one of our chaps said, "Thank you, but if you had done your bit before the war, we wouldn't have to be here." Never will anybody ever accuse me of not doing anything.

I remain an American citizen. During the McCarthy era I could have been prevented from returning to the U.S.A. if I had not retained my citizenship. Being married over here and my wife having a twin sister is why I chose to settle in England. I also get along quite well with the people here, having been with them through five years of war. I remain active in the Campaign for Nuclear Disarmament.[20]

DON VOGEL
Theatre: Northwest Europe   Service: Air Force

Don Vogel was born on 1 February 1921 in Standish, Michigan. Prior to enlisting in Canada he had been a member of the United States Marine Corps Reserve and had also done some civilian flying. First Lieutenant Vogel was shot down over France while a member of 362 Fighter Squadron, 357 Fighter Group, Eighth Air Force, USAAC. Upon his return to England, Don married. Following the war he returned to the United States, where he worked as an air traffic controller until retirement in February 1977. He now resides in Brandon, Vermont. Don recounts his war experiences:

I had just turned twenty, had a pilot's licence and the magnificent total of twenty-six hours of flying time to my credit. I took a train to Montreal to join the RCAF. I flew Fleets and Harvards and got my wings in November of '41. Pearl Harbor found me in Halifax about to ship out with the largest group of aircrew ever sent to England at one time.

We arrived in England on Christmas Day. Shortly thereafter we were told that there were no Operational Training Units for us and about a six-month wait for openings. Volunteers were needed for Africa. I was one of the volunteers. We went by boat, around the Cape and up to Suez. There we sat in the Middle East, a tent city by the canal. The story was a cable sent to England requested 2,000 airscrews and the first "s" was left out. So we became known as the airscrews of the Middle East. We were finally shipped back to England by way of the Cape. We took a refresher course in the Masters training aircraft then went to a Mustang Operational Training Unit. Finally, I received an operational post with 268 Squadron, RAF. Missions were short – channel patrols, photo reconnaissance into France. We never saw an enemy airplane, although there was a little flak here and there. In November of 1943, the squadron was sent to Scotland for a rest and I transferred to the USAAF. The group I was assigned to didn't have any airplanes so I didn't get back on operations again until March '44. I saw a lot of Europe from way up on escort duty, and got into a few dogfights.

Walking Back: Summer of '44
On 1 July 1944, our group's bomber escort mission was cancelled. Later in the day, however, our squadron was ordered out for a fighter sweep in an area north of Paris.

We tangled with a gaggle of German Messerschmitt (Me.) Bf. 109s near St. Quentin and I took a cannon shell in the engine of my P-51B. A belly landing was made in a wheat field near Laon. The front (between St. Lo and Caen) was about 200 miles away and since no enemy activity was visible, I commenced walking in a southwesterly direction. I had a date to be married on the 15th and decided it was feasible to get back somewhere near that date.

It darkened fast and began raining. A railroad track appeared and I followed it toward Laon. At dawn a line of railway coaches on a siding came into view and I crawled into one and fell asleep.

A slamming door woke me. A pair of German soldiers were coming down the line of cars looking in each compartment. One car short of mine, they broke off their search. When they disappeared, I ducked into the woods nearby.

With long days and short nights, civilian clothing seemed in order. I stopped some French farmers, told them my story and asked for help. About a dozen men and women came out and I had my pick of pants and jackets. I went on my way wearing a flat cap, a pair of brown pants, a dungaree jacket and a shirt off the back of one of the men. A bag containing bread, jam and fresh cherries hung from my shoulder.

I followed the railroad to Soissons and took a wrong turn to the north. In a small village railyard were a half-dozen Germans at work. Plodding along with head down and watching them out of a corner of my eye was a mistake. A pair of boots suddenly appeared directly in front of me and I stopped dead. There was a fence across the railyard and in front of it was a sentry with his rifle at port and a big grin on his face. I grinned back, shrugged and changed course. There was no challenge.

It was hot. With blisters on both feet and the cool water nearby, I stripped to my GI underwear and dove in. It felt good. My whole being relaxed and it became apparent that the journey was having an effect. It took quite an effort to get back to the river bank.

At Creil, the river was put behind and Vernon was selected for the Seine crossing. In the vicinity of Nucourt, bombs came down through the clouds. After the bombing, I got up off the dusty road and moved quickly through the area. There was a German camp nearby and there was the fear of being tagged for clean-up work.

The bridge across the Seine at Vernon was for foot traffic only, having been bent in the middle by some past bombing. There were no guards. Hunger called and a nearby bakery beckoned. A request for bread was met with a request for a ticket. I told him I was an American and was hungry. He chopped a two-foot loaf in half, gave it to me and shoved me out the door. With bread there should be wine.

A cafe down the street seemed appropriate but curtains blocked the view inside. I went in anyway. There were two German soldiers sitting at a table drinking beer. At the bar, "Beer si vous plait," got me a beer, and a bar rag was dropped on my 100-franc note. After the soldiers left, I negotiated a bottle of white wine. The bar lady held up my 100-franc note and said, "Non."

Westward ho and my feet were killing me. In Acquigny, on 11 July, a shed became my choice for a night's lodging. A couple of young Frenchmen came in. After a discussion, which included gestures and the use of my map, they concluded that the Germans were not in hot pursuit. They took me to a priest who organized my ID card and doctored my feet. A real bed was provided for the night.

The next day, Pierre (my new name) and another Frenchman rode bicycles to another village and from there we went by horse and buggy to yet another. There I was holed up on a farm until the end of August. Since we were in what was called the Falaise "Pocket," our liberation occurred about the same time as that of Paris.

Needless to say, I did not make my wedding date. We celebrate on September 11.[21]

False ID given to Don Vogel by the French underground.

D. Vogel

BRUCE BETCHER
Theatre: Northwest Europe   Service: RCAF

I was born 24 October 1921 in Ada, Minnesota. I eventually moved to Crookston, Minnesota, where I graduated from high school in 1940. I attended the University of Minnesota. I followed the war closely and at the end of the school year was ready to commit my life to stopping Adolf Hitler. During May of 1941, I journeyed to Winnipeg and took the physical for aircrew. I was informed that being partially colour-blind would not be an obstacle but a deviated septum and a heart abnormality would. I returned to Crookston, had an operation that opened my nose, obtained a statement from a heart specialist that my heart was normal and returned to Canada 6 September 1941 and enlisted. As I was an only child, this decision was not overly popular with my parents.

During that summer, I worked as a groundsman with an electric company line crew. I was digging a seven-foot hole in hardpan clay at Pembina, North Dakota, in the July heat when an Anson flew down the tracks at fifty feet trying to read the name of the elevator. I threw down the shovel and said, "That's the life for me." I knew the U.S. would soon be at war and I could not pass the U.S. Army Air Corps physical.

Thus, a friend and I enlisted at the Lindsay Building in Winnipeg, 16 September 1941. It was a Friday and we were told to come back Monday. We told them we had no money and if they wanted us they could take us now or forget about it. They solved the weekend problem by putting us on a train for the Manning Pool at Edmonton. We did guard duty at Fort Macleod and then returned to Edmonton for initial training school. At the completion of the course, I was re-examined for colour-blindness, washed out and sent to the Manning Pool at Trenton. There I received a colour-blind safe rating which was forever after endorsed in my logbook. My degree of colour-blindness did not present any problems during my ensuing flying career.

On 28 April 1942 eight washouts from Trenton, including three Americans, joined 36 RAF cadets at Goderich for Course 54. Americans Bob MacQuade, Clyde East and I requested that we be posted to the same service flying training school course. When the postings came in for three different schools, each of us went to a different flying training school. On 7 July I arrived at Brantford to form Course 59, which consisted of twenty-four Canadians, eighteen Australians, ten Americans and six RAF.

I was shipped overseas on the SS *Cavina*, a former banana boat, and after sixteen days disembarked at Avonmouth. Then it was on to Bournemouth, to No. 14 Advanced Flying Unit Ossington, No. 23 Operational Training Unit at Stratford on Avon, No. 1659 Heavy Conversion Unit at Topcliffe, and No. 419 Squadron at Middleton St. George, 5 May 1944, and subsequently at group headquarters as an accident investigator. From 13 April 1944 I was with No. 1666 Heavy Conversion Unit changing to Lancasters for a second tour. On 8 August 1945 I joined No. 419 at Yarmouth, Nova Scotia. The war ended and I was discharged at Winnipeg, 9 September 1945.

Some close calls: The night of 13 August we were over Munchen Gladbach in cloud. Fires in the target area coloured the cloud an eerie orange red. We could not see the ground nor anything else. As I looked forward, the head on silhouette of a Fw. 190 filled the windscreen. He was on a reciprocal course about ten feet above us. If I had blinked at that moment, I would never have been

Pilot Officer Bruce Betcher (third from left), Stratford-on-Avon, May 1943.
B. Betcher

aware of a very near miss. In 6 Group parlance, "Close doesn't count, except in horseshoes."

The next night we had just left Berlin and were settling down for a quiet trip home when a solid wall of flak erupted just off our starboard wing. It seemed as if we were flying along the face of Niagara Falls. The noise was deafening, spent flak rattled off the fuselage, the aircraft was being thrown about, and the odour of cordite permeated our oxygen masks. I figured the gunners would be correcting to port so I turned starboard, flew through the barrage and we eventually left them behind. A six-degree navigational error had taken us over Magdeburg.

On 22 October we were on the bomb run over Kassel when we were picked up by several searchlights. I asked the bomb aimer how long until drop. He said we should be at the release point in a minute, and I informed the crew we would remain on the run until the bombs were dropped. Meanwhile more searchlights joined the cone and I lowered the pilot's seat as far as I could to escape the blinding glare that filled the cockpit. The rear gunner advised "port go," but I stayed on course until the bomb aimer gave us "bombs away." I closed the bomb doors, put the nose down, and on reaching 250 mph hauled the nose up, did a wing over to port and lost the lights. We had not been in the cone long enough to attract flak or fighters. On the ground the rear gunner asked why I had not taken evasive action when he said, "port go." I told him there wasn't a fighter back there. He asked how I knew that and I told him because he wasn't screaming.

Coming out of Berlin we found ourselves flying loose formation with a Junkers 88 night fighter. He was visible in the light of the fires about a hundred feet and down to starboard. I thought of diving past him and giving him a blast, but the rear gunner was a bit shaky at this stage of the game and we continued on our way. At debriefing the intelligence officer asked why we didn't fire on him. I said, "Have you ever heard of the sheep chasing the wolves?" And he said, "No." I replied, "Neither have we." That was the end of that.

The citation for the Distinguished Flying Cross reads:

> This captain of aircraft has completed numerous operational sorties, including many night attacks on some of the enemy's most heavily defended industrial targets. His aircraft has twice been attacked by enemy night fighters, but although damage was sustained, the attacks were successfully evaded. On two occasions Flight Lieutenant Betcher's aircraft has been hit by anti-aircraft fire, nevertheless with determination he has pressed home his attack and successfully completed his mission.

Of the eight crews of our Operational Training Unit course, only one completed a tour of operations. Two perished in midair, two blew up over the target, one disappeared in the North Sea, two were shot down over Germany. Of the forty-nine crewmen involved, ten became POWs, one was an evader. Of our crew, Dave Turbitt, Bart Darney and I are left. I have often dreamed of being back in the RCAF, but when I taxi out on the runway and open the throttles, the subconscious says no more, and the dream ends.

I subsequently married First Lieutenant Elizabeth Anderson, a U.S. Army nurse. I graduated from the University of Minnesota with a B.A. and worked twenty-seven years at the Federal Aviation Administration. Our family consists of John Betcher, a geologist of Minneapolis; Ann Van Trump, a speech therapist of Sheridan,

Wyoming; and Barbara Malore, an occupational therapist of Vancouver, Washington. My wife and I are retired. I still keep in touch with former air force friends.[22]

HAROLD MAKINSON
Theatre: Great Britain   Service: Air Force

I was born in Oakland, California, on 9 November 1916. When I was three years old our family moved to San Anselmo in Marin County (across San Francisco Bay from Oakland). I had attempted to join the U.S. Army Air Corps but was turned down because I was fourteen pounds over what the tables said I should be. I was taking flying lessons at Oakland Municipal Airport at the time and my instructor, Gus Gustafson, suggested that I make contact with the Clayton Knight Committee. The latter was seeking American pilots for the RCAF or RAF at the Leamington Hotel in Oakland. Preliminary checks and tests were done in Oakland and those who passed were told to be ready to leave for Vancouver, Canada, when a draft was called. It was most strongly impressed on us that we must cross the border on our own, and at our own expense, lest we put the program in jeopardy.

On arrival in Vancouver, in the latter part of September 1941, we were fed and housed by the Clayton Knight group while we were taking various tests and physical exams. Those who did not pass were free to return home. A mixed group of Canadians and Americans enlisted at the same time. We were separated, however, when it came time for the oath of allegiance – the American group only had to agree to obey orders from a superior officer. We (the Americans) were enlisting to become pilot trainees and, should any of us be washed out as student pilots, we were to be given the option of re-mustering to another aircrew category for training or of being discharged.

Following my enlistment in Vancouver, my postings were from Edmonton as far east as Lachine. I met my wife while I was stationed at High River, Alberta. She was working as an RN [registered nurse] at the High River Hospital. We were introduced at the nurses' residence by one of the other nurses who had attended a flight graduation party.

I did not transfer to American air service when the United States entered the war after Pearl Harbor. I felt that Canada had given me a chance to earn my wings and that I had a moral obligation to return something to the RCAF. I was posted overseas to England in September 1944. I arrived at the RCAF reception centre at Bournemouth.

The U.S. Air Force had a rest and recreation base near Bournemouth and I met some other aircrew (Californians). One of them asked if I'd like to come to the American Red Cross club for "a real coke and hamburger." I was there for only a few minutes when I was informed in very cold tones that this club was for Americans only. Although the U.S.A. identification patches on my shoulders clearly indicated my nationality, my friend was told that I was "in the wrong uniform." I removed the patches in question shortly thereafter.

On V-E Day (8 May 1945) I was at No. 42 Operational Training Unit, RAF Station,

Flight Lieutenant and Mrs. Harold Makinson in Calgary, 9 September 1945. They are on their way to Banff, Alberta, where they will spend their honeymoon.
H. Makinson

Saltby (near Grantham). The *Duchess of Richmond*, on which I returned to Canada, arrived at Quebec City on the evening of V-J Day (15 August 1945). My friends and I were disappointed that the fireworks display was not for us but overjoyed to learn that the war was over. We docked at Lachine, Quebec, and then went on disembarkation leave. I was married at High River on 8 September during that leave. I was discharged in Calgary as a flight lieutenant.

I had hopes of attending the pre-med school at the University of Alberta but was deterred by the length of the application list and the fact that preference would be given to Canadians. My new wife and I returned home to California by rail in early November 1945.

I had been a licensed mortician before the war and decided to return to that field. I retired in 1979 and reside in San Rafael.

My wife and I have visited High River several times since the war. On one occasion I did go out to the old military base and learned that you shouldn't go back to those well-remembered places. Only one hangar remained and it had been converted into a cattle auction shed. Along the weed-grown streets were empty rows of old foundations. There was nothing of the life and activity I so fondly remembered.[23]

H.P. MILLIGAN
Theatre: Mediterranean   Service: RCAF

I joined the RCAF in the fall of 1941 and did basic training in Toronto and flight training at Dunnville, Ontario. I departed for England from Halifax on New Year's Eve, 1941, on a Swedish freighter in a convoy. The North Atlantic in February was something I'll always remember – forty-foot waves and the ship laden with ice, including the rope handholds. There were just six of us who were passengers on this freighter. One of the chaps, after hearing how cherished chocolate was in England, took twenty pounds of Hershey chocolate kisses with him. He stowed them under his berth for safekeeping. When we arrived in England this chap's package was twenty pounds lighter and the rest of us were all a few pounds heavier. It was a mean thing to do, but war is hell.

About ten days later I arrived in Liverpool. Training followed at No. 9 Advanced Flying Unit, Hullavington, England, in March 1942, then at No. 61 Operational Training Unit in April, where I was trained on Spitfires. Assigned to 243 Squadron RAF in June at Ouston, England, I was next posted to Newcastle to do submarine patrol in the North Sea. Submarine patrol was good practice but, being young, I found it rather routine; so in July 1942, when they asked for volunteers to go to Malta, I volunteered with one or two others.

We arrived at Gibraltar on 14 July. After we had disembarked, we saw many badly wounded being taken off another ship. I asked, "What in the world happened, was there an accident at sea?" I was told that these poor devils were pilots returning from Malta.

We reached Malta three days after leaving Gibraltar. There was an air raid in progress upon our arrival. We left the carrier with thirty Spitfires and after the air raid we had about twenty-five left.

Pilot Officer H.P. Milligan holding a frisky mare he and several friends purchased. The top of the carriage was damaged when it overturned. Dunnville, Ontario, July 1944.

H.P. Milligan

I was assigned to 249 Squadron at Ta Qali Airfield, where I gained experience very quickly. We were kept busy protecting the island and occasionally being able to be aggressive, bombing and shooting up air bases in Sicily.

We were kept at the ready to "scramble." The weather in Malta is very hot, and we would sit under the wing of the aircraft, fully dressed with a Mae West inflatable life jacket. After take-off, and reaching 25,000 feet, where the temperature was approximately minus twenty degrees Fahrenheit, we would relax a little and lean back in our seats. It was then that you could feel the ice crystals cracking in your frozen clothing.

The food on Malta was not gourmet, but after watching the local Maltese cutting and eating grass, our daily ration of "bully" (corned) beef and one two-ounce slice of bread seemed plentiful. Needless to say, I lost considerable weight, going from 175 to 128 pounds during my stay there.

Buzz Beurling, the Canadian ace, flew with our squadron. The thing I remember best about him was his exceptional eyesight and perception. He could see airplanes in the distance minutes before anyone else could spot them.

I was shot down at Malta on 24 October 1942. I managed to get the Spitfire back to the airport. The rest of the time was spent in the hospital on Malta. When I was well enough to travel, I was flown along with other wounded pilots to Cairo on a Liberator aircraft. From Cairo we went to South Africa, and from there to Toronto. After I recuperated I was sent back to Dunnville, where I ended the war as an instructor.

After the war I worked as a test pilot for Bell Aircraft Company in Niagara Falls, New York, as a commercial pilot in Latin America, and then with Standard Airlines of the United States until 1967. I ended my flying career in 1985 as an instructor pilot with Douglas Aircraft.

I was married in 1952 and have one daughter, who is a flight instructor in Santa Ana, California.[24]

BILLY HOPKINS
Theatre: North America   Service: RCAF

I was born on 28 October 1918. My real name was Billy. I was named after "Billy" Bishop, the war hero at the time.

I left Seattle to join the Royal Canadian Air Force in Vancouver on 3 December 1941. We Yanks came to Canada for various reasons; most commonly it was a burning desire to fly, supported by an enthusiastic attitude about crushing the Axis, and a great deal of compassion for the folks in the United Kingdom. The United States was not yet at war, and to become an air force cadet, one had to be single with two years of college.

The Canadian civilian population treated the kids with U.S.A. identification patches

Sergeant Billy Hopkins while home on leave at Seattle, December 1942.
B. Hopkins

on our uniforms like visiting royalty. We couldn't buy a beer at the taverns (we were always treated), were frequently asked to dine in their homes, were invited to parties and even given gifts. The people made us welcome and proud to be wearing RCAF blue.

Through the entire training program I was fortunate to have the experience of staying with a small group of friends formed in the dismal days in Manning Pool. We became bonded like blood brothers. This closeness has endured these fifty years. Our ranks have been thinned by casualties on operations and life. Our most illustrious survivor is Squadron Leader J.T. "Johnny" Caine, DFC and two bars. We keep in touch and see each other when we can.

As a result of a low flying incident, I ended up as a staff pilot on Fairey Battles at No. 3 Bombing and Gunnery School, MacDonald, Manitoba. The brass decided to keep the Yanks at their tasks in Canada, where we remained until 3 June 1944. I then transferred to the USAAF on P-47s. I never did make it overseas.

Canada and the RCAF have had a profound effect on my life. I still have to fight back the tears when I hear "Oh Canada." I don't care much for the new flag, and I miss seeing the RCAF uniforms. My most impressive memory from that period, apart from the people, was the *esprit de corps* prevalent – even among the lowly staff pilots at bombing and gunnery school. I honestly don't know if this resulted from an inherent trait among Canadians or the fact that it was a 100 percent volunteer outfit. My lasting impression is that for some reason Canadians living during that era were deadly serious and had very high moral and ethical standards. One could leave valuables lying around – they would never be touched. I had a billfold of a couple of months' pay fall out of my flight jacket in a snowstorm. It was returned to me in barracks a few hours later.

On 21 April 1944, I married Joan Hughes of Winnipeg. We had four children. I graduated from Washington University (St. Louis) Dental School in 1950. I served with the U.S. Army Dental Corps in Korea and Japan. I entered private practice in 1954 in the San Francisco Bay area. After six years, I was fed up living in a densely populated area and moved to a small town in the Sierra Nevada Mountains where the family could enjoy fishing, skiing and outdoor life. In 1983, I retired and moved to Rancho Murieta, near Sacramento, to enjoy year-round golf.[25]

JOHN WRIGHT
Theatre: Italy   Service: Army

I was born in Great Yarmouth, Norfolk, England, on 25 February 1925. The following year my mother and I followed my dad overseas to settle in Milwaukee, Wisconsin. In my early teens I developed a wanderlust. I spent my sixteenth birthday farming out west and working in a lumber camp in Wisconsin. At age seventeen, I became obsessed with joining the military and going to war. I was under age, so I changed the 1925 year of birth to 1923. I entered Canada at Sault Ste. Marie, Ontario, found a recruiting office and was in. I had to wait a day or so until they had more recruits. We were taken by automobile over some primitive roads from the "Soo" to Sudbury then by train to Toronto. I ended up at the Exhibition Grounds and was billeted in the old Horse Palace. I did my basic training at a new tent camp at Brampton, Ontario. We were the first troops there.

Private John Wright, Milwaukee, autumn of 1942, while home on embarkation leave.
J. Wright

My original request on enlistment was to join a marine-type unit. I did my advanced training at Kingston, Ontario, but much to my dismay, was assigned to the Ordnance Corps. Late in 1942 we were shipped out to Halifax en route overseas. I believe we were among the first to use the *Queen Elizabeth* as a troopship.

I spent my first Christmas overseas at Aldershot. I kept after the commanding officer for a transfer out of the Ordnance Corps. I was eventually sent to No. 5 Canadian Infantry Reinforcement Unit. After more training we were shipped up to Scotland and joined a convoy for North Africa. We landed at Philippeville, Algeria, and travelled overland to Sousse. We landed at Syracuse, Sicily, in late July 1943 as reinforcements. I was assigned to 7 Platoon, A Company, Princess Patricia's Canadian Light Infantry. We went through central Sicily to just below Mount Etna. On 3 September 1943 we crossed the strait of Messina and entered Italy at Reggio Calabria. We worked our way up in the mountains. The Germans blew up the bridges and we were on foot for the first month or so with occasional rearguard skirmishes. We commandeered mules, donkeys, whatever, to haul our supplies. We encountered stiff fighting at the Moro River. The action around the city of Ortona was rough. Beyond Ortona there was a winter line across Italy to a little south of Rome. We changed positions several times in the Adriatic area. Most of the action in early 1944 consisted of night patrols, which were either fighting, reconnaissance or ambush. On fighting patrols we were out to get prisoners. Always the same routine. Move up to a certain point and hold. At a specified time our 25-pounders would lay in a barrage and then we would rush in. I think the Germans knew the routine as well as us.

In the middle of May 1944 we moved westward to the Cassino area. It was a terrible place, completely devastated. The German dead lay where they had fallen. On the night of 22 May we moved into a position just before the Hitler Line. At daybreak we got out of our slit trenches and some tanks moved up behind us. We were told that we were to follow a creeping barrage moving up a hundred yards every ten minutes. Soon pandemonium broke loose. Some of our tanks were blown up before we even started. Our first obstacle was barbed wire and minefields. The artillery was so intense that it was impossible to tell where the hundred-yard points were. We thinned ranks in a hurry. After getting through the German minefield, the next defences were small-arms fire from slit trenches. I still recall one incident where I was so dazed from what was going on that I didn't even fall or take cover as I came up on a paratrooper firing at me and next thing I knew he was staring up at me from the bottom of his trench with a terrified look on his face. I didn't shoot him. I didn't even stop. Shortly afterwards I got knocked down twice in a row from what must have been our shells.

The second time I thought I had been hit as my back was all wet. It turned out that shrapnel had torn my water bottle apart. Up again and I suddenly realized there were fortifications just ahead of me. There was a wounded comrade lying there wanting me to bandage his leg which was really torn up. As I finished bandaging his leg, the German paratroopers began firing intensely from everywhere. They must have realized we were through to their main positions. I dived into a bomb crater with some others. We were pinned down by very heavy fire. As I was returning fire with a Bren gun, something hit the gas port, shattering it and blinding my best friend from around North Bay, Joe Voldock.

One memory that still keeps recurring to me is that of the small New Testament I had received as a kid in Sunday school. I always thought of it as watching over me. One of the other guys in the crater had a terrible face wound. Part of his chin or jaw was missing. As he was cold, I gave him my jacket which contained the Bible. I became worried that my protection might be jeopardized. It was. Eventually, the Germans overwhelmed us and we were taken prisoner.

This was a hectic period to be taken POW (prisoner of war). The German defences were crumbling and they were falling back. At first we were always being strafed by our own aircraft. After about two weeks, we were placed in a large POW camp. Most of the prisoners had been captured during the North African campaign. On 19 and 20 June 1944, the Germans took us on a brutal march. We were told that due to a shortage of equipment only the very sick could ride and that anyone who fell out would be shot.

I chose to hide under the old straw mattress of our bunk-style beds. Soon all was quiet, although I was being eaten by fleas from the straw sack. Some guards were left behind to check for stragglers. They raised the mattress and then proceeded to kick the hell out of me. Fortunately they didn't shoot me. They also found two others who were hiding. We were placed on a truck and caught up with the others. Then we were put at the rear. If the group slowed down, the guards would strike us and the dogs would snap at our legs. Most of the guys had dysentery. Any who asked permission of a guard to step aside in a ditch to relieve themselves were shot by another guard further back. While passing through a small town, there was a lot of shooting up ahead. The guards had shot six or seven of us. They were lying there wounded as we passed by. We couldn't help them. The guards would shoot anyone who stopped to help.

The Germans' strategy had been to take us to a railhead and place us on a train to Germany. Their plans fell through, however, as the line had been heavily bombed. We spent a rainy night on the ground. The guards were drunk and kept firing over us. The next morning they chose to march us back to the camp. It was then that we saw the bodies of our comrades lying where they had been shot in the middle of the road. Trucks had run over them during the night.

After some more delay, we were shipped out by rail. We were loaded into boxcars so crowded there was only sitting room. There was a hole in the floor for sanitary purposes. We were each given a loaf of bread and a piece of sausage. They would hand in drinking water through an opening near the top front of each car where a guard would ride. This trip took us five days. We spent part of one day hiding in a tunnel after the train had been strafed by our planes. We went through the Brenner Pass and finally got out of the boxcars at Innsbruck. What a beautiful sight!

We were taken to Stalag VIIA at Moosburg, where I spent the majority of the duration of the war. Due to a shortage of manpower by mid-1944, the Germans took Canadians whom they figured were more likely to be from a rural background and placed us on farms in order to complete the harvest. This proved to be a good break for me as I was put on a farm where I was treated well and fed exceptionally good under the circumstances. When I was returned to Stalag VIIA, I was in pretty good shape. This helped me through the winter of 1944 when food was scarce and we worked mostly in Munich.

We were taken daily from camp to Munich by train. We repaired the railway tracks and bomb damage. When we would arrive at Munich, the buildings would still be burning from night air raids. As time wore on, the raids were switched to day raids by U.S. Flying Fortresses and night raids by British Lancasters. We would sometimes be taken to shelters and other times remain in the street and the ack-ack would fall all around us. We often used to work alongside political prisoners from Dachau. Then we realized how fortunate we were.

In early April 1945 the Germans thought they could perhaps get some sort of favourable peace terms if they had control of a large group of U.S., Canadian and British POWs. As a result, we spent the last days of the war on a march trying to evade capture by our forces. One day in late April an American tank force cut us off and I regained my freedom at last. Five of us took two German cars and made our way to a repatriation in Epinal, France.

After the war, I went to work for the Chicago and Northwestern Railway, which helped fulfil my wanderlust. I put in forty-three years and am now happily retired. My wife and I have been married forty-six years and have three daughters. In spite of the some fifty years that have passed, those few years so long ago with the Canadians still remain one of the major memories of my life.[26]

GERALD CAMERON CLOUGH

Theatre: Northwest Europe   Service: Air Force

I was born in North Dighton, Massachusetts, on 3 July 1921. This is a suburb of Taunton. In 1939, the year I graduated from high school in Springfield, the seeds of World War II were sprouting in Europe. I enrolled in early September as a freshman at American International College in Springfield about the time the United Kingdom declared war on Germany. To assist the U.K., the United States gave one hundred World War I destroyers to their friends, and one of the quid pro quos my country received was a ninety-nine-year lease on a U.S. naval base in Bermuda. The general contractor for building this base in Sandys was the F.H. McGraw Company of Hartford. My father, a civil engineer, received the job as project manager. In 1940, my mother and sister and I went to Bermuda for a three-week vacation visit. About the time we arrived, my father had a contract disagreement and was replaced as project manager. We enjoyed our visit anyway. I developed an infatuation with an Alabama cutie named Patsy McKibbon whose stepfather was an engineer on the naval project.

Shortly after I returned home, I learned that the Bermuda Flying School, which taught Bermuda boys to fly prior to sending them to join the Royal Air Force, was planning to accept Americans. To me this was a good excuse to drop out of college and possibly renew my young love affair with Patsy. If we were to join the fight against the Nazis, I wanted to fly airplanes against them.

I spent almost the entire year of 1941 in Bermuda and I believe it was early January 1942 that I, along with four others, left on the *Queen of Bermuda*, which was then camouflaged as an armed merchant cruiser in the Royal Navy. We were going to pick up 200

Royal Canadian Navy Officers in Halifax before proceeding to England, where we had orders to report to the Air Ministry for enrolment in the Royal Air Force.

After we picked up the naval officers, we left the dock only to run aground on Mars Rock at the mouth of Halifax harbour. At the next high tide we were towed off this rock by a couple of sea-going tugs and returned to the dock. That night, a Royal Navy lieutenant named Doug Knight and I went to visit the LeMoine family at 262 Gottingen Street in Halifax. Doug had heard that they held nightly parties for servicemen and merchant seamen. I began a small romance with their daughter, Mary, and she sent me food parcels and love letters until I married a British WAAF (Women's Auxiliary Air Force) in December 1943. They certainly were gracious hosts.

RCAF, Canada

After the *Queen of Bermuda* returned to the Halifax docks, we Bermuda Flying School fledgling pilot graduates were sent to an embarkation depot in Debert, Nova Scotia, to await ship passage to England. While at Debert, I met several recent aircrew graduates of the British Commonwealth Air Training Plan who were also awaiting ship passage to England and all were eager to join the fight. A couple of the pilot officers asked why I was going to join the RAF instead of the RCAF, as I would, in all likelihood, be sent back to Canada for training and would get paid 50 cents a day as a leading aircraftman 2 during training. The RCAF paid much more. That made sense to me and I told the officer in charge I wanted to join the RCAF. He couldn't care less so I took a bus to Halifax and enrolled in the RCAF in January 1942. Since I had some college background, which was more education than the other recruits, I was put in charge of the group taking the long CNR train ride to Toronto's Manning Pool. All I remember about this train ride is playing cards and losing a good share of my immediate funds.

An influential factor in my decision to join the RCAF was the fact that my mother was Canadian, born in Kingston, Ontario. My dad's first job upon graduating from Yale had been a surveyor for the CPR in British Columbia. My parents were married in Nelson, where my mother lived at the time. This should help explain my close connection to Canada.

Manning Pool at the Toronto Exhibition Grounds was quite pleasant even if I slept on an upper bunk in the sheep pen. We learned how to clean a Lee-Enfield rifle and did some guard duty. Paul Hutsell, who hailed from Athens, Tennessee, and I went all the way through RCAF training together. As "Hut" was a good-looking chap with a nice smile and a way with the ladies, we managed to use up our share of the free condoms handed out by the medical officer when we went out at night on weekend passes. We both were sent to ITS (Initial Training School) at the Eglinton Hunt Club in Toronto, next to No. 12 EFTS (Elementary Flying Training School) at Goderich, Ontario, and then to No. 14 SFTS (Service Flying Training School) at Aylmer, Ontario, where we got our RCAF pilot wings on 1 March 1943. Only one-third of RCAF graduate pilots received commissions (or at least that was the way it was in 1943) and I was proud that I received one but sad that my pal, Paul Hutsell, did not. He transferred to the U.S. Army Air Forces (USAAF) from a sergeant pilot RCAF to a warrant officer USAAF and became a bomber pilot. I later learned from his mother that he was killed in the China-Burma theatre of operations.

Nothing much out of the ordinary happened during my RCAF flight training. A couple of my classmates killed themselves on night training solo flights in North American Harvards. I think the fact that a lot of my advanced training in Ontario was in the winter of 1942 when we had to think about snow, sleet, ice and hoarfrost made me a better pilot. I received above-average ratings from all my flight instructors. I have always felt that my RCAF training, with its emphasis on aerobatics, navigation and Link trainer, was superior to the training received by Americans – at least as judged by the performances of P-51 pilots. I later joined in the U.S. Ninth Air Force.

England

After I arrived in England in March 1943 in a sixty-ship convoy, I was sent to Bournemouth. I believe all RCAF personnel went to Bournemouth in 1943, but later on the Yanks took it over. There followed more training and familiarization flights in England.

The first part of September I was posted to No. 53 Spitfire Operational Training Unit in Kirton Lindsey, Lincolnshire, which was a permanent RAF base with brick buildings and brick cottages for the staff officers. The officers' mess was quite nice and the food very good. There I met a WAAF corporal named Anne Everson and I married her on 9 December. Anne and I spent our one-week honeymoon at the Spa Hotel in Tunbridge Wells, Kent.

Although I was really happy in the RCAF and had been promoted to flying officer when posted to Kirton Lindsey, I heard about a deadline for Americans to transfer to American forces and a board was set up in London to interview those who desired to do so. It was a purely selfish move, as I was thinking of the greater pay and allowances and the promised post-war benefits.

I was assigned to the Ninth Air Force. I was appointed first lieutenant as I had been in an equivalent flying officer RCAF grade for six months or so. I regret that I transferred before being posted to a Spitfire squadron, as I have always been prouder of my white RCAF wings than my American silver wings. I had looked forward to flying Spitfires against the Luftwaffe but it was not to be.

I was assigned to the 380th Fighter Squadron, 363rd Group, which had just arrived at Rivenhall, Essex, from Tonopah, Nevada. We flew a variety of missions, mostly bomber escort. The bombers would generally fly at 25,000 feet and would cover them at 4,000 feet above. We would go on oxygen at 10,000 feet. We also did a lot of dive-bombing in March and April of railroad yards in France and Belgium and some fighter sweeps looking for targets of opportunity.

First Lieutenant Gerald Clough, U.S. Army Air Corps, April 1944, Staplehurst, Kent, England.
G. Clough

We received P-51D Mustangs to replace P-51Bs. The newer model with bubble canopy and Rolls Royce Merlin engines was a vast improvement over the earlier model. When we got 75-gallon external gasoline tanks hooked up to our bomb-release switch, our range was vastly improved. We could then escort the bombers all the way to Berlin and beyond, much to their relief, as bomber flights had been devastated by the Luftwaffe after the fighter escort had had to turn back. My first escort mission to Berlin was on 7 May 1944. The Berlin missions lasted from five to six hours, which is a long time to be strapped into a cockpit with only a candy bar to eat.

The only Luftwaffe aircraft that I received credit for shooting down was on 28 May on a five-hour, ten-minute mission to Dessau and Magdeburg, and return to our base at Staplehurst, Kent, where we had moved to on 22 April. We were just making a rendezvous with the B-17s when we met a lot of bandits (enemy aircraft). There were Messerschmidt (Me.) 109s, Junkers 88s, Me 410s and Focke-Wulf 190s all over the place but heading straight for the Flying Fortresses. I latched on to a Me. 410, a twin-engine fighter bomber with remote backward firing 29-mm cannon. I stayed on his tail all the way from 25,000 feet to less than 1,000 feet before he crashed into the ground. I damaged two others on other missions and destroyed two or three on the ground but I only got credit for the one 410. For that action, I was awarded the Distinguished Flying Cross.

The only combat mission on which I took off in the dark was for the 6 June invasion of Normandy. We saw no enemy planes that day but plenty of Allied ships, planes and gliders. Our fighter group moved from Staplehurst, Kent, to Maupertus Airdrome at Cherbourg on 4 July.

In mid-September, while the war was still going on, a point system was devised and if sufficient points were accrued based upon missions and months overseas, a pilot could return to the States. Believing my wife Anne would get discharged shortly, I elected to return to the States. My wife joined me – but eight months later! I had flown ninety missions overseas with a total flying time of 212 hours.

I was sent to Venice Air Base, Florida, to instruct in P-40s and later P-51Ds. This was an Operational Training Unit and all the students were experienced pilots. On 3 March 1945 a first lieutenant made a foolish manoeuvre over Fort Myers, Florida, at 10,000 feet.

He managed to slice the tail section off my plane with his prop. Then, I had a nice five-minute float down by parachute to the swamp boondocks. I still have two screws in my right ankle from the landing. Shortly thereafter, my air force career came to an end.[27]

CRAIG SMITH
Theatre: Northwest Europe   Service: Army

I was born in Ottawa on 1 August 1918. My father was a physician, having graduated from Northwestern University Medical School in Chicago. He started practice in Gracefield, Quebec, near Ottawa, but when I was two years old we moved back to Chicago. I was an American citizen by virtue of both parents being Americans and have lived in the U.S. almost all my life.

My story really begins in 1941 when I graduated from the University of Virginia and then came to Montreal to enter McGill University Medical College. After enrolling and seeing Canada at war, I felt that medical school could wait. I joined the Canadian Army on 8 June 1942 hoping to be assigned to the Canadian

Lieutenant C. Smith, London, England, just prior to D-Day.
C. Smith

Grenadier Guards. As a boy in Chicago, I had remembered hearing over WJZ Radio the Canadian Grenadier Guards' Band under the direction of J.J. Gagnier. I was sent for officer training at Brockville, was commissioned second lieutenant, and posted to the Armoured Corps school at Camp Borden, Ontario. I left Camp Borden after Christmas in 1942 and was put on a troop train to Halifax. The train stopped at Campbellton, New Brunswick, on

New Year's Eve. We all went across the road from the station to a dance at the hotel there, clad only in pyjamas and great coats. We all had a great time.

I joined the Grenadier Guards in Brighton as a full lieutenant. After extensive training in England with the Canadians and the British, I took part in the Normandy operations as leader of No. 3 Troop of No. 1 Squadron. Our landing in Normandy was uneventful, as the beaches and some ten miles inland had already been secured. There were only a few skirmishes and shots until we crossed over the Orne at Caen. There then was a holding of high ground prior to the drive to Falaise in an attempt to encircle the German Seventh Army.

The actual attack (Operation "Totalize") began on the night of 7 August. Searchlights were aimed up at the clouds to simulate moonlight and 40-mm Bofors guns were aimed south with tracers to give the infantry a centre line for direction. It was eerie. At first light we led the armoured attack. No. 1 Squadron was in the lead. Lieutenant Doug MacDonald led off with No. 4 Troop and the squadron followed, spread out in a diamond formation. After several miles we passed through the infantry. Major E.A.C. Amy told

Artillery and armour move forward along the Caen-Falaise road during Operation "Totalize," August 1944.
National Archives of Canada, PA-116536

me to take the point with No. 3 Troop. We passed through a barrage of heavy explosives and phosphorous shells which did us little harm, and approached a ridge in a wheat field. We first took a "turret down" then a "hull down" position with three tanks in reserve. I went over the crest and received fire from an 88-mm gun. There was no cover so we discharged smoke and fired all our guns at their position. Two of my other tanks came over the brow of the hill to support me, but they were immediately hit.

I kept going down the hill and was holed twice, once through the turret that killed my gunner and wireless operator-loader. I was wounded. We were apparently hit again by a German Panther tank in the right sponson, which was full of ammunition, and I was blown out with my driver and co-driver. Four hours later, after crawling about one mile, we were picked up by the Argyll and Sutherland Highlanders of Canada who had fired on us with a Bren gun and rifles thinking we were Germans. I was taken to their regimental aid post, in a barn. The barn was hit by mortar fire and I was pulled under a cement horse trough and eventually evacuated by half-track to No. 121 British General Hospital in Bayeux. There I was operated on and evacuated to Portsmouth. After I had lost my troop on 8 August, the advance was resumed, now led by the British Columbia Regiment, who were practically annihilated on 9 August. The next officers who took over my troop were killed and I consider myself most fortunate to have been spared. On 10 August I was sent to No. 22 Canadian General Hospital at Bramshott. I was hospitalized for three months, then posted to a Canadian Army recovery unit, from which I returned to Camp Borden with the rank of captain as a gunnery instructor.

Prior to the invasion my mother in New York City forwarded a draft notice from the U.S. Selective Service and I went down to Grosvenor Square, the American Embassy, and was told I could transfer to the U.S. Army, keep my present rank, and would be assigned to Camp Gordon, Georgia, for armoured training. I chose, however, to stay with the Canadian Army and especially the Grenadier Guards, to which I felt privileged to belong. The war in Europe ended and I was discharged and returned home. I reported to my draft board but the Far East war was ending and my service was deferred.

I entered medical school at Cornell University College of Medicine in New York City and graduated four years later in 1950. Following that I did one year internship and three years of residency at St. Luke's Hospital in New York City. I was drafted in 1951 in the "Doctors Draft, Public Law 9." I wrote Dewey Short, secretary of the armed forces, stating that I had served, was wounded and was receiving a disability of 25 percent. As a result, the law was changed to include all those who had been wounded serving in Allied forces, so I went from 1A to priority IV.

I have practised medicine in the City of New York for thirty-one years and retired in 1985 but still return to periodic reunions and get-togethers in Montreal. I have many friends in the regiment and keep in close touch. I would not trade being a member of the Grenadier Guards for anything and am very proud of my association with them.[28]

DAVID LEWIS

Theatre: Canada   Service: Air Force

I was born in Llantrisant, Wales, Great Britain, on 1 March 1920. My mother died while I was an infant. My father and I emigrated to the U.S. in May 1929 and began our life there in Ferndale, a suburb of Detroit. I was a college senior in the academic year 1941–42. My temporary exemption from the draft was to end upon my graduation in June of 1942.

Since I wanted to be a pilot and was denied the opportunity to enlist in the U.S. Air Force because I was not yet an American citizen, I got permission from my draft board to visit Canada and rode a bus from Detroit over the bridge to Windsor, Ontario, where I promptly passed my physical and mental exams. I joined the RCAF on the spot. When I was

Pilot Officer David Lewis,
Moncton, New Brunswick,
November 1943.
D. Lewis

released in the fall of 1945 I was a flying officer.

I had about 1,200–1,400 hours on the Harvard and about 700–800 hours on the Avro Anson. I got my wings at No. 6 Service Flying Training School, Dunnville, Ontario. After instructors' training I went to Moncton, New Brunswick, for a few months before the whole station was moved to Weyburn, Saskatchewan. After a few months there, they sent a few of us to Hagersville, Ontario. I was still at Hagersville at the end of the war.

My very first assignment as an instructor at Moncton was to take a student, Kane, who was near graduation, on his final three-hour instrument cross-country test in an area with which I was unfamiliar. That day all of the flying instructors in the flight I belonged to were going on instrument cross-countries. During those exercises the student pilot remained under a hood the whole way. The planes were Harvards – the advanced single-engine trainers which could easily do 175 mph straight and level and were a lot of fun to do aerobatics and dogfighting in with other pilots.

After flying rather uneventfully for about five minutes on this first sixty-minute leg, we began to pop in and out of small cumulus clouds. But each time we went into a cloud we stayed in a little longer than we did in the one before. After a while we were in clouds more than we were out of them. Of course Kane didn't know this because he was under the hood. All of his flying must be done by instruments. There was an "artificial horizon" which showed him what the plane's altitude was with respect to the actual horizon – climbing, diving, banking to the left or to the right, etc. He could also see his air speed, his altimeter (which told him how high he was off the ground), and his rate of climb indicator, which told him whether or not he was climbing or descending and, if he were going up or down, it told him how many feet per second he was climbing or falling.

Finally, after about ten minutes of flying time from the airport, we got into a cloud and didn't leave it – it was solid cloud and I could barely see our wing tips. It is really spooky to fly in clouds. I kept a close watch on the instruments in my cockpit to see that Kane was flying in the right direction, at the right air speed, and at the right altitude. By looking at my instruments I could see that he was doing well. Whenever our left wing would drop a little on the artificial horizon, he would correctly move the stick over to the right slightly until the wing came up, and then he would take off the stick and hold the wings level. And whenever our rate of climb indicator began to show we were going down, he would very calmly pull back the stick a little until the plane was once again flying straight and level as it should. In fact, Kane was doing an excellent job, and he was doing it all by watching the instruments in front of him. He didn't know we were in solid cloud. Neither did he know I couldn't see much more than he could.

After we had been in the cloud for a few minutes and it looked as though we wouldn't be out of it for a while, I began thinking, "What should I do? Turn back?" Turning back seemed to be the sensible thing to do. In 1943 we didn't have very complete weather reports, so I didn't know what the weather was like in the direction we were going, or what it would be like when we returned nearly three hours from now. I was scared and wanted to get back to the airport as soon as I could. Remember, just south of the airport were mountains which went up five to ten thousand feet, and just beyond the airport to the east was the Atlantic Ocean. Everywhere else, except for a few lakes that aren't very good to land on with wheels, were solid woods. But, I wasn't going back. I was a new instructor, and the others surely wouldn't let a few clouds stop them. We didn't have any radios in our planes, but we used to say a good pilot didn't need radios, all he needed was a map, skill in picking out landmarks, guts, and some sense. I didn't want to chicken out on my first assignment as an instructor.

When we reached the calculated destination of the first leg, I took control, climbed into the clear blue sky above the clouds, and asked Kane to plot a direct return route and ETA (estimated time of arrival). I set the plane on a course about ten degrees north of the course he gave me in order to avoid the mountains to the south. We flew over the clouds on the way back until about fifteen minutes before our ETA in the hope of seeing land before the ocean. I began our slow let-down. With considerable trepidation we passed 1,000 feet. Finally at around 300 feet we broke through the clouds into a heavy rain, but we could see ground. I found a railroad track and followed it to a station and read the name of the town off the station sign. Fortunately for us we were on a track leading to Moncton.

We took a longer time on the trip than you might imagine. We had used up the fuel in the left wing and were nearing the end of the fuel in the right wing tank. Shortly afterwards the engine began to sputter so I quickly threw the lever to "emergency" gas – enough for ten minutes in the air – barely enough to get home even if nothing happened in the meantime. Seven minutes after we had gone to the emergency gas tank I began to recognize landmarks around the airport. I turned on both my landing lights to signal emergency because if I didn't land the first time around, I probably wouldn't have gas for a second try. Still flying at 500 feet in pouring rain, I entered the airport pattern. I came in, made a normal landing, and taxied up to our hangar. When we got out of the plane, I found out that everybody else had turned around and come back as soon as the weather closed in, within fifteen minutes of take-off. They all thought we had cracked up and they were waiting for the weather to clear enough so that they could begin a search for us. The veterans, the men with thousands of flying hours, had turned back. But I didn't want to chicken out. I was a lucky fool!

While I was in the service I knew one had to have been overseas in order to get anywhere in the permanent force after the war and, therefore, much as I loved flying, I left the service after the war. I have not really regretted that decision, as I have made a good life for myself and my family as a university professor until retirement in 1985.[29]

JOHN C. TATE
Theatre: Northwest Europe   Service: Air Force

I was born 7 October 1918 in Ardmore, Oklahoma, where I was raised. I graduated from high school and came to Alice, Texas, to visit my cousin. I stayed in Alice about a month looking for work. Then I decided to go to Corpus Christi and found a job digging telephone pole holes and did that for perhaps five months. I ran across a friend from Ardmore, Oklahoma. His uncle had a drilling rig just east of Corpus so I went down and applied for and got the job. One of the men living in the same boarding house was very talkative. He was perhaps thirty years older than I and an explosives expert. He told me he was going to Canada to join the military to handle unexploded bombs. That led me to think that if he could do that, I could go to Canada and get into the air force. Soon after that I quit my job. I went home to Ardmore and told my parents I was going to Canada to enlist in the RCAF. My father said, "Son, if that's what you want to do, your mother and I are behind you all the way."

Pilot Officer John Tate (second row, eighth from left), Class 22,
No. 10 Service Flying Training School, Dauphin, Manitoba, 28
May 1941.
Sylvia Tate

I had little money from my job so I hitchhiked in September
1940 to Windsor, Ontario. The RCAF recruiting officer said that
they were rather heavy on recruits and if I would come back in thirty days they would have a place for me and that it would be pilot
training. So I hitchhiked back to Ardmore and then back up to
Regina. There I went through four weeks of basic training. I was
sent to the elementary flying school on Tiger Moths, and after
training I went to advanced training on Harvards. Then I went to
advanced flying school which included AT-6s and Hurricanes. After
we had finished our Hurricane and Harvard training and hadn't
received our new assignments, we were told we could fly anytime
we wanted in the Harvards.

One morning I took a Harvard up and went into the northern
part of Canada as far as I could go and come back. I saw a school-
yard full of children and I thought it would be nice if I buzzed
them and gave them a thrill. I could see that the children and
adults liked it, so I buzzed them three or four times and decided I
would show them what a hot rock pilot is. There were two outhouses about ten feet or twelve feet apart so I was going to show them
how I could put the wings down between the two outhouses. My
judgment wasn't as good as I thought it was and I hit one outhouse
and took six and half feet of wing off the Harvard. I really thought
I had done myself in. I did steady the aircraft and said to myself, "If
I get to 1,000 feet I will bail out." The aircraft still climbed very
slowly at full throttle so I told myself I would climb until I stalled
out, then bail out. I didn't stall so I started back to the base at

8,000 feet. When I got back to the base I felt a little bit better about the airplane and I thought I'd better make an effort to land the plane. So I buzzed the tower to show them my problem (missing wing) and came for a landing but I let the air speed bleed off too much and had to give her full throttle and the wing just didn't want to come up. At this point I was below the pilot-housing building, which was two stories high. I thought I would dump the plane into the ground rather than hit the building. As I got ready, the broken wing started coming up and I knew that was a good sign so I stayed with it and cleared the building by at least twenty feet. My next landing was faster and I had no problems and didn't hurt the aircraft further.

The wing commander met me on the ground and said, "That was good flying, but you are going to be court-martialled." During an RCAF court-martial all activity except military police, fire, and other essential people ceases. All others form a large circle and the commander and his deputy are in the centre of this circle. The accused is marched into this circle with military policemen in front and in back. There the sentence was read. I was fined $75, my officer's commission was revoked, and I was made a sergeant pilot. Then I was marched off the field.

The entire class was scheduled to go to instructors' school and they all did except for me. I was sent to England. I've always thought that breaking off the wing was the best thing that ever happened to me in my flying career.

In England, I was assigned to 253 Squadron of Hurricane night fighters. The Hurricane would take off from our field (Hibaldstow) and just as we left the ground the Douglas Havoc bomber would get into position for take-off and we would come around to the take-off direction of the Havoc as he got airborne and we could come in formation together. The Havoc had a three-inch stripe of white on the trailing edge of the wings and small lights shining on the back of the wing to illuminate the white. The Havoc had radar. Its bomb bay was loaded with batteries and on the nose was a searchlight. The controllers who had a bigger radar would vector the Havoc to the vicinity of the enemy aircraft. When the Havoc came into contact with the enemy they would give a code word by radio to the Hurricane, and at that point the Hurricane would give full throttle and dive about fifteen feet below the Havoc. Then the Havoc would turn on the searchlight in the nose and the Hurricane would pull up in front of the Havoc and shoot the enemy aircraft down. All of this was theory. We never shot anyone down.

A memorable incident occurred when the weather was very low. An Eagle Squadron which was thirty to thirty-five miles north of us was responsible for the enemy aircraft in that area of The Wash of the North Sea. However, there was some high ground between us. I was put on alert with another pilot. We were fortunate to have a canal right beside the flying field leading to The Wash, which gave us the opportunity to get out into the North Sea. When we got over the sea the ceiling had lifted to 1,500 feet and we scrambled because a Dornier 217 was molesting a convoy. I was fortunate to be in the right position to get behind him (in a Hurricane). I shot him down – the first Dornier 217 brought down in the war. In the British way, I got credit for a fraction of the Dornier destruction and the convoy got the other fraction.

Being night fighters we were on alert every night. However, at times when the weather was bad or the ground fog was thick, we would be excused from flying and would always go to a little pub about a half mile from the airfield. When the pub owner said, "Drinks, gentlemen," that meant one more drink and the pub would close. Everyone was drunk and the squadron commander (Stick) would climb on the roof of the pub which was connected to four or five houses. He would say, "Follow me, gentlemen," and take a roof tile and throw it in the street. Everyone else (maybe twelve people) would do the same. We would get a bill for damage and all chip in. The pub owner and the people in the houses never said a word about it. I believe perhaps they felt this was a tension reliever for us. We always replaced all the tiles.

John Stitt (a Canadian) and I went to London in a truck to bring back rations. We left London about 9 a.m. and started home. When we got to the outskirts of London we ran into the densest fog I have ever seen. John was driving. We stopped, so I got out in front of the truck with a flashlight, feeling as well as at times seeing the edge of the road. John could see the light so we travelled about as fast as I could walk on my knees and one hand. We did this for about two hours before the fog lifted enough for us to see our way home.

Each RAF base was given a certain amount of food to distribute to the squadrons. Our squadron (and I suspect, many more) would also buy food from local farmers, which was not allowed. All farm products went to the several distribution centres by law to be distributed to the military. We found that the local farmers would sell to us, onions being one food. It must have been a good year for onions because our farmer had a wonderful crop. I asked him if we could buy some for our mess. He said, "How many do you want?" and I said "Whatever you can spare." That was a lot of onions. The onions still had their tops on and I brought them back to the mess hall and proudly displayed them. The squadron commander chewed me out royally for buying them but he told me to tie them in bunches of eight or ten and hang them underneath the mess hall. So I did. I also got a lot of eggs and Ovaltine. The eggs were appreciated even though I got bawled out again. I had two cases of Ovaltine and no one but me would drink it. Shortly thereafter I was transferred to the USAF and I have no idea what happened to all the Ovaltine.

Everyone in the squadron got along. Sometimes, on a night when we couldn't fly because of fog, pilots would get on a bus. We would start out and at the first pub we saw we would stop and go in and have a drink. We would continue down the road to each pub until about midnight. By that time we were all drunk except the driver. These were always happy occasions because the English people thought the world of all pilots and it was a good feeling when they were all so friendly. Frequently the pub owner would not charge us (twenty-two people maybe) for our drinks. The squadron had three Canadians, two Norwegians, two men from New Zealand, one South African, Aussie, Scot, English and Irish. I was the only American.

One Norwegian (P.O. Christie) was in his fifties and the other was in his twenties. They were inseparable. Both spoke fluent English. After I left the squadron to go to the USAF, the two Norwegians were on patrol over the North Sea. The younger man's engine quit and he parachuted down and the older man climbed up to 8,000 or 9,000 feet and gave the Mayday and circled where the young man went down. He stayed there until he ran out of gas and then gave the Mayday that he was also bailing out. Search parties never found either one.

A Dance

We had a Christmas dance during the holidays. Someone went to town and arranged for a city bus and gathered up a bunch of girls to be brought out to the dance. By English law during the war the city bus could only go a number of miles outside the city limit, so those arranging the dance also made an arrangement to meet the city bus with a military bus at some point between the town and the air base to bring the girls to the dance and again at 1 a.m. to take them home.

I really didn't care to dance so I stayed in the bar most of the evening and finally wandered into the dance hall to watch and noticed a girl sitting in a chair by herself. I asked her to dance. She said she didn't dance so I sat down and talked with her and found her to be a very interesting young lady. However, I ran out of things to say and, of course, by this time I was drunk. I asked her if she would like to see one of our airplanes. This thrilled her beyond words. I hoisted her up into the cockpit and explained all the instruments and everything I could for her. I looked at my watch and it was about 1:10 or 1:15 so I said we better get back before the bus leaves. When we got there the bus was gone and a jeep was sitting there so I told her to get in and we'd try to meet the city bus at the appointed place.

When we got on the road I pushed the accelerator to the floor and left it there and at some point I knew I was having a hard time holding the jeep on the road. We went into a ditch and the next thing I knew I was about fifteen feet from the jeep and it was standing on its wheels. At that point I knew I had a bit of a wreck and wondered where the girl was.

Across the road I saw a house and there was a light on. I went over, knocked on the door and entered and, lo and behold, the girl was there. Apparently she was not hurt at all but her clothes were torn a little. I now know that the other person in the room besides the owners of the house was John "Sandy" Sandstead. The lady of the house was upset with me and would have had me put in jail if it was possible. I felt very sorry for the girl and pulled out my wallet. I had no idea how much money it was – didn't count it – and gave it to the girl and asked her if that was enough. She said it was more than enough for her clothing and a taxi ride home. I often wondered how much it was. The lady of the house was satisfied but still not happy with me.

Sandy and I went out to the jeep. (I never knew he was asleep in the back of the jeep until I saw him in the house.) We started the jeep, the motor ran, it moved forward. The windshield was gone but we didn't need it. Sandy got in the back seat and went to sleep again and I drove back to the base.

I drove up to Stick's (the squadron commander's) quarters to put his jeep there for him. The parking area was butted up against the building. Stick was sleeping in. As the jeep was moving toward the side of the building, I couldn't think what to do and the jeep crashed into the side of the building. Unfortunately (I was told later) that was Stick's room and he was asleep and I knocked him out of bed. I got out of the jeep, went around the building and went to bed. As Stick, now out of bed, rounded the building, Sandy was getting out of the jeep and, as I learned the next day, was to be court-martialled. Sandy didn't think he was driving the jeep but he was too drunk to deny it.

Next day I went to the squadron doctor. I didn't remember whether there was a hospital or dispensary at the base but I know they took me to a temporary civilian emergency building. Then they moved me the next day to a British Air Force Hospital to be checked for internal injuries.

John Tate
Sylvia Tate

At some time while I was gone, Stick was at the bar and the squadron doctor was there. Stick hadn't seen me for a day or two and asked the doctor if he knew where I was. The doctor said – don't you know? He was hurt in the jeep and he's in the hospital.

When I reported to Stick he said if you will accept my punishment I will not court-martial you. I said I accept your punishment – which was confinement to whatever base we would be in for three or four months – I didn't remember exactly how long. The group commander was in Africa at that time and when he heard about me and the jeep and my punishment he sent word back that he did not accept the punishment and said he would court-martial me when I got to Africa. He was shot down a day or two later and for all practical purposes that ended the whole affair.

I was discharged from the RAF on 28 September 1942 for the purpose of joining the American air force. In total, I flew 150 combat missions, shot down one Fw. 190, two 109s and the previously mentioned Dornier. I was awarded the U.S. Distinguished Flying Cross and Air Medal with twenty-four oak leaf clusters.

I married Marilyn Freeman in 1946 and have two sons and six grandchildren. My wife died in 1981 and I remarried in 1982. I am retired and live in San Antonio, Texas.[30]

WILLIAM FOSSEY
Theatre: Europe   Service: Air Force

I was born in St. Prudentienne, Quebec, in 1922. My parents, who were both Canadian-born, moved to Woburn, Massachusetts, in 1924. My oldest brother, Donald (now deceased), and I were born in Canada and my two younger brothers and sister were born in the United States. My mother became an American citizen, but my father retained his Canadian citizenship.

When the Second World War broke out in 1939, I received some sort of recruitment information from the Canadian government. As I had lived all of my adult life in the U.S.A. I did not respond. Eventually I was drafted in the States.

I was sent to the USAAF for basic training, radio school and the gunnery school. After this initial phase of training, I was assigned as a radio operator/gunner on a B-17 bomber with the 463rd Bomber Group, 775 Squadron at MacDill Airfield, Florida.

Several times during training, at various bases, the question would be asked, "Who is not a citizen of the U.S.?" In each instance I was told it would be taken care of at the next base. It never was. In fact, I went overseas with the group to Foggia, Italy, and flew twenty-three and a half missions before being shot down by fighters over Yugoslavia, on a mission to Austria on 24 May 1944. I had attained the rank of technical sergeant.

As for my experiences as a POW, I can still recall some incidents vividly, while others have faded. I injured my back during the bail-out. While in a cell at an airfield in Graz, Austria, I was lying on the floor. The guard brought in an officer who I thought was a doctor to examine me. He examined me by poking the toe of his boot into my back!

Another memorable incident happened when we were transported by train to Frankfurt. When we arrived at the station the guards had to point their rifles and shout at the crowd to keep them from attacking us. We heard at the interrogation camp, where I was kept in solitary confinement for five days, that some Allied flyers had been hanged by civilians at the station.

I was shipped by boxcar from Frankfurt to Stalag Luft IV at Gross Tychow in East Pomerania, arriving there on D-Day. The guards at the camp made no secret of the invasion. I stayed at Luft IV until late January and was shipped by boxcar (fifty men to a car) to

William H. Fossey on leave at home before going overseas.
W.H. Fossey

Nuremberg, a trip which took nine days. We stopped several times while the engine was detached during air raids in the area and hidden – one of the times being at night in Berlin. I stayed at Stalag XIIID in Nuremberg until the end of March 1945 and then was forced to march to Stalag VIIA at Moosburg in Bavaria, which took about two weeks.

I was liberated on 29 April 1945 by units of Patton's Third Army, then flown to Camp "Lucky Strike" in Reims, France, and after a couple of weeks shipped home. I was discharged at Mitchell

Field, New York, on 20 September 1945. At that time the question was asked "Who is not a citizen of the U.S.?" I thought it was finally going to be taken care of, but it was not to be. I was given a form to fill out with instructions to take it to the Naturalization Service in Boston and it would be done. When I presented the piece of paper I was told that the form was obsolete and that I would be issued the proper ones with which to apply. Eventually in 1946, I was sworn in as a U.S. citizen.

I was married in 1947 and had three boys and a daughter. For the first few years after leaving the service I worked as a watchmaker in Boston. I eventually entered the U.S. Postal Service as a letter carrier, later becoming safety manager, the position I had until retirement in 1985.[31]

HAROLD WILSON
Theatre: England, Northwest Europe   Service: RCAF

I was born in Vancouver on 6 November 1922. When I was fourteen months of age our family moved to Seattle, where I have resided ever since. In November 1942, while attending Washington State University at Pullman, my draft number came up. Not wishing to be drafted in the U.S. Army, I received a release from my draft board and I believe it was in December 1942 that I joined the RCAF at Vancouver and was sent home for Christmas.

In January 1943 I was posted to the Manning Depot in Edmonton. From the Manning Depot I was sent to Regina, in sort of a "holding pattern" waiting to go to the University of Alberta. In the spring of 1943 I was posted to Pearce, Alberta, EFTS (Elementary Flying Training School), for tarmac duty. In the spring of 1943 I attended the University of Alberta at Edmonton and was designated to go to wireless school, which I refused. In the summer of 1943 I was at the Manning Depot at Toronto. In the fall I was posted to Laval University, Quebec City, for pre-gunnery instruction. About 15 October 1943 I was posted to Mont-Joli, Quebec, for aerial gunnery training. Upon graduation I was offered a commission, which I refused. I would have had to stay at Mont-Joli and instruct.

In January 1944 I was posted overseas and arrived at Bournemouth, England. On 10 March 1944 I was posted to No. 22

OTU (Operational Training Unit) at Wellesbourne near Stratford-on-Avon for training as a rear gunner on Wellingtons. While at No. 22 OTU, I did leaflet trips to France as a rear gunner on a Wellington. In May 1944 I was posted to No. 1666 Heavy Conversion Unit at Wombleton, Yorkshire, and at that time was interviewed to join the U.S. Army Air Forces. I refused and in November 1944 commenced training at No. 1659 Heavy Conversion Unit at Topcliffe, Yorkshire. I trained there until 13 December 1944, and was posted to 429 Squadron RCAF at Leeming, Yorkshire.

I flew on bombing missions in 1944–45, including two daylight mine-laying sorties at Wangerooge on 22 April 1945 in which we had a close call. Six of the seven bombers lost there were involved in collisions.

No. 429 Squadron, Leeming, Yorkshire, May 1945. Back row, left to right: WO2 Harry Wilson, RCAF (Seattle), mid-upper gunner; S/L McKay, RAF (Scotland), rear gunner; F/O Don MacNeil, RCAF (Newfoundland), bomb aimer; F/L Reg Seale, RCAF (Vancouver), navigator. Front row, left to right: WO2 René Lamanque, RCAF (Montreal), wireless operator; Sgt. Frank Brazier, RAF (West Drayton, London), flight engineer; F/L Matt Ages, RCAF (Ottawa), pilot.
H. Wilson

On a typical night mission we would leave (never in formation) and arrive at the target through an indirect course to avert German fighters and ack-ack. We had to be at the target at a given time, with the navigator using the "Gee box" (navigation aid). There were several close calls. One of the more memorable missions was the attack on an oil refinery at Hemmingstadt, Germany.

On 7 March 1945 at 1850 hours we took off from Leeming in our Halifax nicknamed "Queenie." We climbed to 18,000 feet, headed north towards Copenhagen and then turned south over northern Germany. I advised the skipper that every time we made a turn horizontal searchlights on the ground moved in our direction (we did not know it, but our bomb aimer evidently had caught his canvas bag on the "Gee" switch, which meant the German night fighters would be homing in on us).

We arrived at Henningstadt and missed the target, and Matt, our pilot, advised us that he was going around again. In the meantime all the other aircraft had headed home. We had just dropped our blockbuster, which I think was a 20,000-pounder, were closing the bomb bay doors, and a German night fighter, either an Me. 210 or a 410, came up under us on the lower rear port. The rear gunner commenced firing but his guns froze (evidently he had too much oil on the breech block). We commenced evasive action, going into what we call a "corkscrew," which means the aircraft dives 1,500 feet to port, then at the bottom ascends 1,500 feet to starboard.

As we went into our dive I put 600 rounds into the night fighter and he was so close I could see the pilot's face. I got a "probable."

Cannon shells exploded under my turret and the wireless compartment, and the skipper's windscreen was blown out. It was pouring rain and Frank, the engineer, held his canvas sack in the hole of the windscreen. As I recall, we were losing altitude continuously.

We received the emergency flares when we arrived at Leeming; everyone had been debriefed and evidently they had given us up as a lost cause. It so happened that the RAF brass from headquarters were at Leeming that evening and I was recommended for a Distinguished Flying Medal; instead I received a commission.

To conclude, the Halifax was a total wreck and could not be repaired, and at that point in time we were given a new Lancaster in which we finished the war.

Between 8 May (V-E Day) and 7 June 1945 we flew prisoners of war back from Belgium and France and did bomb disposal work (clearing out the bombs at the 429 Squadron and jettisoning them in the North Sea). I volunteered for "Tiger Force" (Pacific) against Japan and was posted home immediately, with thirty days' leave, to report back to Debert, Nova Scotia, where we commenced training on Lincolns, the equivalent of the English Lancaster.

Of course the rest is history – MacKenzie King announced on 15 August 1945, V-J Day. I was discharged on 27 September 1945, and used my Canadian veterans' benefits to attend the University of Washington in Seattle. I got a B.A. in business administration, doctor of jurisprudence from Georgetown Law Center in Washington, D.C., in 1951, and have been in continuous law practice since then.

After the war I returned several times to Leeming where I planted a maple tree alongside a monument to honour our comrades of 429 and 427 Squadrons. As a result of the war and our experiences together the members of the crew became good friends. Those friendships have continued long after the war.[32]

BERYL DIAMOND (née CAKE)
Theatre: Europe, Pacific   Service: Army

I was born 17 January 1917 in St. John's, Newfoundland. I moved to Boston in August 1937. I graduated as an RN from Faulkner Hospital, Jamaica Plain, Massachusetts, in October 1940. I joined the U.S. Army Nursing Corps in 1943, as I was by then an American citizen. I began as a second lieutenant and at war's end I was a captain.

I served in England (1943), France (1944), and the Philippines (1945). In England I treated casualties from France after D-Day. This included an active hospital for wounded German POWs. Doctors, nurses and patients there functioned in a restricted area. In France, I received a decoration for participating in the Battle of the Bulge, operating near Reims. This was followed by a rest period in the south of France at Cap D'Antibes in luxurious surroundings which were especially welcomed after the mud. What the French chefs could do with army rations was unbelievable.

After the cease-fire in Europe, we proceeded to the Philippines to await the invasion of Japan. We stopped at Luzon to prepare, and helped at an existing hospital. The work here was mostly on local inhabitants who had obtained explosives and were throwing them into the fishing grounds to surface the fish. The locals were doing as much damage to themselves as their food supply, requiring repair work in surgery. At this point the atom bombs were dropped and we turned our thoughts to home.

Following the war, I worked as office and surgical nurse to an orthopedic specialist, Dr. A.P. Aitken, in Boston. I met my husband in St. John's while visiting my parents. Following my marriage in 1949 to Maxwell Diamond, I returned to the land of my birth. It was the opinion of friends and relatives that as I was returning to Canada, there was no further need to reapply and become a Canadian citizen. So I did nothing further. Eventually, I returned my American citizenship to the American government, and in time, applied for and received a Canadian passport. In 1952 we moved for business reasons to St. Catharines, where we still reside.[33]

Seated in a sleeping hut that was built in one day is
Captain Beryl Cake (left). Luzon, the Philippines, 1945.
B. Diamond

MALCUS HORTON
Theatre: North America, England   Service: Air Force

I was born on 8 March 1920 at Richmond, Virginia. I graduated from Christ Church Preparatory School for boys in Urbana, Virginia, and then attended the University of North Carolina. I had a lot of personal reasons to go to Canada and join the RCAF. I had learned to fly in my freshman year at university – my roommate had two light planes. I talked to my father. He was a country doctor and had been in the U.S. Navy in World War I. He was sure that the U.S. would join the U.K. in a short spell, so advised that I get a head start.

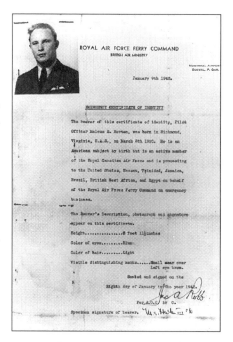

Pilot Officer M.S. Horton.
M.S. Horton

At Toronto I slept in a gym with hundreds of other recruits and passed medicals. Then there was guard duty for one month, more selection boards, and I was assigned to elementary pilot training at Prince Albert, Saskatchewan, from 16 November 1941 to 27 December 1941. I trained on bi-wing Tiger Moths open cockpits with great instruction by a U.S. bush pilot. We shot an occasional woodland caribou and with a hindquarter on each ski made our way to the local butcher. Meat was rationed.

Next there was primary flight training at Saskatoon, Saskatchewan, on the two-engined Crane. The last night before graduation I took on the class bully (a Yank) but broke my right hand. I was given an admonishment and a commission, and I was assigned to RAF Ferry Command from May 1942 to March 1943 at Dorval, Quebec. It was not what I wanted at all. I did get to fly first-line aircraft. I would pick them up at a U.S. factory, fly to Montreal and then across the North Atlantic. However, it was not combat. Most pilots were Americans and Canadian civilians.

In April 1943, I was sent to the U.K. for training. The ten-day blind flying course I attended at Banff, Scotland, I passed the first day. I also had great salmon fishing there with the local laird. In the system I was a round peg with no hole so I transferred to the U.S. Army Air Forces in June 1943. I later returned to the U.K. and flew 36 bombing missions on the B-24 Liberator.

Since my retirement in 1974, my wife and I have divided our time between homes here in Kailua-Kona, Hawaii, Taupo, New Zealand and Oregon.[34]

CHARLES MacGILLIVARY
Theatre: Northwest Europe   Service: Army

Charles MacGillivary was the second Canadian-born recipient of the Medal of Honor during the Second World War. Born in Charlottetown, Prince Edward Island, he had joined the U.S. Army in Boston in January 1941. MacGillivary was assigned to Company I, 71st Regiment. On 16 December 1944 the Germans launched a counter-offensive in the Ardennes. MacGillivary's unit was involved in the American counterattacks. The citation for his Medal of Honor reads:

President Harry S. Truman congratulates Medal of Honor recipient Charles A. MacGillivary.

C.A. MacGillivary

Sergeant MacGillivary led a squad near Woelfling, France, on 1 January 1945 when his unit moved forward in darkness to meet the threat of a breakthrough by elements of the 17th German Panzer Grenadier Division. Assigned to protect the left flank, he discovered hostile troops digging in. As he reported this information, several German machine guns opened fire, stopping the American advance. Knowing the position of the enemy, Sergeant MacGillivary volunteered to knock out one of the guns while another company closed in from the right to assault the remaining strongpoints. He circled to the left through woods and snow, carefully worked his way to the emplacement and shot the two camouflaged gunners at a range of three feet, as other enemy forces withdrew. Early in the afternoon of the same day, Sergeant MacGillivary was dispatched on reconnaissance and found that Company I was being opposed by about six machine guns reinforcing a company of fanatically fighting Germans. His unit began an attack but was pinned down by furious automatic and small arms fire. With a clear idea of where the enemy guns were placed, he voluntarily embarked on a lone combat patrol. Skilfully taking advantage of all available cover, he stalked the enemy, reached a hostile machine gun and blasted its crew with a grenade. He picked up a sub-machine gun from the battlefield and pressed on to within ten yards of another machine gun, where the enemy crew discovered him and feverishly tried to swing their weapons into line to cut him down. He charged ahead, jumped into the midst of the Germans and killed them with several bursts. Without hesitation, he moved on to still another machine gun, creeping, crawling and rushing from tree to tree, until close enough to toss a grenade into the emplacement and close with its defenders. He dispatched this crew also, but was himself seriously wounded. Through his indomitable fighting spirit, great initiative and utter disregard for personal safety in the face of powerful enemy resistance, Sergeant MacGillivary destroyed four hostile machine guns, and immeasurably helped his company to continue on its mission with minimum casualties.

MacGillivary served in the U.S. Customs Service from 1950 to 1975 as a criminal investigator. Since retired, he lives near Boston. He has three married daughters and eight grandchildren.[35]

LUCIEN THOMAS
Theatre: Northwest Europe   Service: RCAF

I was born in Kingston, England, of American parents. I attended private schools in Virginia and left the University of Virginia to go to Canada because of the war.

Second World War
I came to Canada in the early summer of 1940. I was unable to join the RCAF and ended up serving with the Black Watch for almost a year before being released to join the RCAF in March 1941. I was washed out of pilot training and ended up as a gunner. I flew a tour with Bomber Command during the period May 1942 to March 1943 with 405 Squadron. I was awarded the Distinguished Flying Medal for shooting down three Ju. 88s, one in the summer of 1942 and two in the winter of 1943 over the Ruhr.

Sergeant Lucien Thomas, 1943, after receiving the Distinguished Flying Medal.
L. Thomas

I can truthfully say that during my time with 405 Squadron, I earned a solid respect for Canada and Canadians which has remained with me as a distinct part of my character. I cannot speak too highly of the Canadians I knew at the time.

The Americans who crossed the border to join the Canadian forces were very special. Once crossing that international border, they rolled the dice, and to most there was no turning back. A few disgraced themselves by deserting or committing criminal acts. The acts of this minority were overshadowed by those who served gallantly or made the supreme sacrifice.

At this late date the names of many Americans I knew have slipped away. There were a number of people – members of the "Eagle Squadron" (71, 121 and 133 Squadrons) – whom I knew well such as Gussie Damon, Don Gentile and Chesley Peterson. George Harsh was an air-gunner who was shot down in 1942 and was responsible for security on the "Great Escape." He was a close friend of Walter Floddy, who engineered the tunnel. George died several years ago.

Another friend was Billy Orndorff. He was shot down while flying with 419 Squadron in the summer of 1942. Bill told me that the underground hid him in a French whorehouse and that he stayed there for three months as a sort of pet. He finally came out through Spain.

On the pilot side there was Dambuster J.C. McCarthy, DSO, DFC and Bar, from Long Island, New York. He flew with 617 Squadron. McCarthy and an American friend joined the RCAF in Ottawa in the summer of 1941. There followed training in Canada and England. With No. 97 Squadron McCarthy flew out of Woodhall Spa in Lincolnshire. At nearby Conningsby he met Wing Commander Guy Gibson, who persuaded all but one of the crew to join his squadron. Although the crew had completed their tour of thirty-four operations on 22 March 1943, they continued to fly even more dangerous pathfinding missions, including the attack on 16–17 May 1943 on the Sorpe Dam. In all, McCarthy flew sixty-seven operational sorties.

Harold "Whitey" Dahl was an American who flew in the Spanish Civil War. He was shot down. Franco pardoned him after receiving a letter containing the nude photo of a New York City stripteaser who wrote: "Please spare the man I love." Dahl served in the RCAF during World War II.

There was a marked similarity among those Americans in the RCAF. Many came from relatively well-to-do families. Those of us on the east coast all seemed to have known the same girls. Most flew bombers. Many were killed. I was in the first draft of air-gunners who left Trenton in 1941. Seventy-two were involved. We were sent to six gunnery schools (twelve per class). By December

1942 overseas I learned in London that less than six were still alive. These included one who walked out and another who had lost both legs in a crash. At least three had found an excuse not to fly. As far as I could determine, only Flight Sergeant Wayne Merrick and I were still on operations. I later transferred from the RCAF and flew with the USAAF. I ended the Second World War with more than 100 missions. I went to Korea and flew three tours on B-26 Invaders and part of a tour on B-29s.

Early days in England were depressing. We were initially posted to Bournemouth with no duties other than answer roll call twice a day. (This would have been great if we had money.) Then we went to Hastings. I finally ended up at Mamby. This was a thoroughly depressing and demoralizing place. We were supposed to be attending an advanced gunnery school. We were denied access to the sergeants' mess, and as students were given a small dining room where they served the worst food I ever ate. After the dining room was cleaned we were allowed to drink beer there on a limited basis. The bright spot were a few WAAFs, who were sympathetic, friendly and fun.

Then it was the 22nd OTU (Operational Training Unit) at Wellesbourne, near Stratford. I recall going to a large hangar on the second day. A squadron leader stood on a table, pointed at two or three barrels of beer and told us to wander around and get acquainted. He informed us that after five of us had agreed to fly together to give him our names. Needless to say, there were a few idiots. One guy asked what he should do if he could not find a crew. The reply was: "Don't worry about that. I'll handle that detail."

I wandered around until I met someone who had been trained as a Hurricane pilot and then sent there. He was as disillusioned as I was. We found a bomb aimer, formerly an observer, then picked up a navigator who had majored in mathematics, and found a WOP (wireless operator). Although the training was filled with crashes, etc., we survived and ended up at Pocklington. As I recall, the pilot who had asked about a crew ended up with an airborne awkward squad. They bombed a chicken farm by mistake, came to 405, and were shot down shortly after arrival. I remember the rear gunner well because he was a wonderful piano player who loved attention and could play any song. As a matter of fact, he was having a hot affair before being shot down.

The HCU (Heavy Conversion Unit) at Pocklington was a

refreshing sight. Leonard Cheshire, a squadron leader at the time, was the CO. He was the first genuine British officer I had ever met. He knew all of us by our first names shortly after our arrival. (How he managed this was and still is a mystery to me.) In those formative days I had never met a person like him before. He already had two DFCs and was a sharp contrast to those who I had met at Mamby and OTU. To digress, it was already apparent to us that the instructors we had encountered were arrogant, overbearing and just plain phoney. It was obvious that most had no intention of flying ops again and were out for a free ride. They detested us and the feeling was mutual.

I flew my first three trips on the thousand-bomber raids while in the HCU. The first was with Squadron Leader Leonard Cheshire as the member of a scratch crew. As I recall, only one other member had flown ops before. Although I never served with him after Pocklington, a friendship grew. I saw him infrequently after that time and was always delighted at his quick wit, his deep compassion for those who did not return from ops, and his dedication. When I read of the award of the VC in 1944, I sent a brief note of congratulation. The award did not come as a surprise to me.

405 Squadron was the best experience of my RCAF career. Everything else fell by the wayside. This squadron was international by any measure. It always seemed to me that in 1942 the Canadians were the minority. Johnny Fauquier was the CO, soon to be replaced by Len Fraser. Both were wonderful leaders. Fraser was replaced by Wing Commander A.C. Pitt-Clayton.

Charlie Palmer, Bill Sweatman, Bob Turnbull and Howie Hill were sergeant pilots in 405 who were awarded battlefield commissions. They were superb people. Then there was Lloyd Logan – a wonderful person by any measure. All made up the legend of Bomber Command and somehow contributed to a legacy.

As far as the air-gunners were concerned, we had Gerry Witherick, who became the most celebrated air-gunner with the RAF. He was a close friend. Then there was Taffy Thomas, Red O'Neill, Fred Sipple and many more. They were good people to have around.

This takes me to reflection. I am amazed that anyone survived. Imagine turning loose a bunch of twenty-year-old kids, whose idea of a joke was to pull a chap's pants down and throw a pint of beer on his bare ass, onto a four-engine bomber containing 8,000–10,000 pounds of explosives. The navigational equipment was seriously lacking and the skill level of the crew was marginal.

My first trip was an unbelievable experience. I stared at the city of Cologne some 15,000 feet below. It was burning and since we were one of the last aircraft over the target, the searchlights were wavering around. It looked like the Fourth of July, a giant forest fire and the best of Hollywood all rolled into one.

Our losses during this time were very heavy. I cannot remember a night that we did not lose at least one aircraft, and often two of the eight or ten we sent out. People came and went. In many cases, we never knew their names. There were lucky and unlucky rooms. I remember the room next to ours at Topcliffe where three crews went for the chop in less than two weeks. White pigeons (which some idiot decided we should carry) were bad luck and we always turned them loose before take-off.

Death drifted through the quarters and we listened to Lord Haw Haw to determine who had become a POW. It was about this time that I discovered through some strange set of circumstances that I enjoyed operational flying. Perhaps it was because one could make an agreement to place his life on the line a couple of times a week and then do as he pleased. This only made matters worse, however, because a dismal reputation/record had followed me from ITS (Initial Training School). I knew that any hope of promotion was out and only became more bitter when I realized that most of my contemporaries had been commissioned. I learned one thing. I considered myself already dead and after that stopped worrying about it. Perhaps this attitude was my salvation for the next several years. It also helps explain why I transferred to the American air force.

When I was awarded the DFM, an NCO could only earn it or the Victoria Cross. The powers to be were parsimonious at best in awarding these medals. A DFM under a pair of gunner wings in 1943 was sort of like a Ph.D. It distinctly showed that one had earned a post-graduate degree.

I was sitting in my room at Leeming, waiting for the sergeants' mess bar to open. The senior warrant officer knocked on the door and informed me that the squadron's commanding officer wanted to see me now. I asked what this was about, but received no reply. As I recall, I walked to the hangar in an awful Yorkshire rainstorm. Ignoring the rain, I tried in vain to figure out what Wing Commander Pitt-Clayton wanted to see me about, speculating as to what I had been caught doing. I was ushered into his office and he immediately started in on me, saying that in addition to looking like a mess, I was out of uniform. Then he broke out laughing, told me to sit down and pulled a message out of the drawer. He read the message to me concerning the immediate award, handed me the lone ribbon of a DFM and told me to pin it on. He shook hands and a group of us, consisting of the flight commanders (Charlie Palmer was one and I think that Lloyd Logan could have been the other), went to the sergeants' mess.

The squadron was standing down that night due to weather and the party which ensued generally followed that of a normal gong party. Drinks in profusion, WAAFs all over the place and the senior warrant officers standing around like a bantam rooster. (The old sweats loved those gong parties, not because they admired the twenty-year-old NCOs and officers, but because there was so much booze in circulation.) The award of the DFM made a great deal of difference. Despite the company one was in, a sergeant AG (air-gunner) wearing a DFM stood out in a crowd. The diagonal stripes of that medal demanded respect. A recipient did not stand in the pay line. He just ambled over to the paymaster at his convenience and drew his pay when it was convenient to him. Any gunner wearing a DFM had magic. Girls who scorned me only days earlier became available, sprogs (new recruits) looked at you in awe. It was a wonderful feeling.

As I look back on those days in 405 Squadron, the best comparison I can make is asking a guy who had never played baseball to save the game in the bottom of the ninth inning. We did the best we could, but at this late date I am amazed that anyone survived.

The people in 405 were superb. I cannot recall the names of the ground crew at this late date, but do recall the friendship that existed at the time. The aircrews were superb. Although almost none completed a tour, they went forth willingly, knowing their chance of survival was almost nil. The parties were legend. They sprang up spontaneously when we stood down or when ops were cancelled after it was too late to do anything else.

I was never very impressed with the wingless wonders who also seemed to be around. I am sure that they resented us and that the feeling was mutual. We had a disciplinary sergeant at Pocklington who had an enormous red moustache. He wore pyjamas with a pair of wings sewn on. He got drunk one night and a couple of aircrews went into his room and shaved half his mustache off.

I have only seen one member of my crew since those days. I ran into Nat Daggett, who was a flight lieutenant, in London. I have never seen the others since. Too bad because we were not only a fairly good crew but a very lucky one. To the best of my knowledge we were one of the few Halifax crews to complete a tour.

I learned one thing from 405. I swore that if ever I was placed in a position of responsibility I would set an example by flying frequently and only going on the most dangerous missions where the unexpected could happen. It would take ten years for this to become a reality.

I would like to say in summation that all rode white horses and were gallant knights riding to the rescue of a besieged empire. Not so. Some were outright bums, others were criminals escaping the authorities, and others disgraced themselves by going LMF (lack of moral fibre). The fact remains that the casualties were so terribly high that some took the easy way out.

I flew some 400 combat missions. Many people have asked my views in comparing these missions. It is difficult to form an impression on the first tour because everything is new. In most cases, experiences range form amazement through ignorance to sheer terror. At this late date I must say I got more satisfaction from night intruder operations than any other kind. Although I flew about 175 daylight missions (in WW II and Korea), I never enjoyed them. I found them restricted and regimented – this was especially true of heavy bombers and formations. I liked night intruder missions because once the wheels cleared the ground, every crew was on its own. These reflected the truest form of combat flying because a pilot could do as little or as much as he wished.

I will not bore you with details regarding medals other than to say that I received the Silver Star, five DFCs, seventeen Air Medals, the Bronze Star and five USAF Commendation Medals. Foreign decorations included the British Distinguished Flying Medal, French Croix de Guerre, Czech War Cross and Polish Cross of Valour. In addition, I have the usual campaign and theatre medals awarded with the commissary supplies.

After service in Korea with the USAF, I lost all interest in flying. I went into the munitions business and drove racing cars as a hobby. I am retired and now reside in Scottsdale, Arizona.[36]

PART THREE
From Korea and Vietnam to the Persian Gulf

B Company, 2nd Battalion, Princess Patricia's Canadian Light
Infantry crossing log bridge, North Korea, c. February 1951.
National Archives of Canada, PA-115034

THE KOREAN WAR, 1950-1953

A few Americans served with the Canadian forces in Korea. In most cases they had been previously working in Canada. Many more Canadians ended up with the American forces in Korea. Some of them were already serving, while many others were living and working in the United States and either volunteered or were drafted. Other Canadians crossed the border to join special services such as the U.S. Navy as a means of employment.

In August 1950 the Canadian government moved to raise a brigade group for Korea. One battalion, the 2nd Princess Patricia's Canadian Light Infantry, took its place in the front line in February 1951. In April, for defending a completely surrounded height (Kapyong), the Patricias received the U.S. Presidential Citation. The rest of the brigade arrived in May, in time to participate in the final United Nations advance to and beyond the boundary between North and South Korea. For the next two years the front was relatively static, although shelling and occasional raids resulted in higher casualties. The original battalions of the brigade were replaced by new ones from Canada. In addition to 21,940 troops who were in Korea during hostilities, another 7,000 served in the theatre between the cease-fire and the end of 1955, during which period the UN troops were progressively withdrawn.

As part of the U.S. Military Air Transport Service, No. 426 (Thunderbird) Squadron RCAF helped operate a Pacific airlift for nearly four years. As well, some twenty RCAF fighter pilots were attached to the U.S. Fifth Air Force and flew with Sabre-equipped fighter interceptor squadrons. The RCN assigned eight destroyers, three at a time in rotation, to the United Nations fleet in the Far East. While the fighting continued, they helped to blockade the enemy coast, defended friendly islands and provided gunfire in support of the UN and South Korean ground forces.

A little-known aspect of Canadian-American cooperation during the Korean conflict was the use of Canadian Army members who were in Korea, as well as members of other countries' forces, as spotters with the 6147th Tactical Control Squadron and Group, part of the U.S. Fifth Air Force. They would assist in locating suitable targets for air strikes.

Lieutenant G.B. Meynell of Lebanon, New Jersey, a member of the 3rd Battalion, the Royal Canadian Regiment, led a fighting patrol of fifteen men from A Company on the night of 2-3 May 1953 to deal with an enemy wiring party on the northern flank of C Company. In a clash with an enemy patrol, Meynell was killed. He was the only American in the Canadian forces known to have been killed in Korea.

Many of the Canadians who fought in the American forces in Korea have much more in common with Canadians who served in Vietnam than with their counterparts in the Second World War. A significant number of young men in both cases had moved to the United States for economic reasons and were drafted. However, while the United Nations operations in Korea resulted in a limited victory, the Vietnam War was an American defeat. Thus, the public perception of a Canadian who served with the U.S. forces in Korea is likely to be much more positive than the public perception of a Canadian Vietnam veteran.

KOREAN WAR EXPERIENCES

FRANK CASSIDY
Theatre: Korea   Service: Army

My service in Korea with the U.S. Army was very brief. Most of my
Far East service was in Japan. I was in Korea for less than three
months, mainly in the Pusan area.

I was born in Montreal on 13 March 1926. Since June 1938
when I joined the sea cadets I had been connected with the military. After the sea cadets I went to army cadets – No. 4 Highland
Cadet Battalion and then to the Reserve Force, 2nd Battalion
Victoria Rifles of Canada, ending up with the 3rd (Reserve)
Divisional Column, Royal Canadian Army Service Corps. While
with the Reserves I tried a number of times between 1943 and 1945
to go active. Each time I was turned down because I was fifteen
pounds underweight. I thought this was unfair but there was nothing I could do about it. I took my release from the Reserves 25
October 1945.

While I was working at CP Express, I thought about trying the
U.S. forces. I took a leave of absence and went to Plattsburgh, New
York, and inquired. On a return trip, I passed the written test and
signed a paper stating that I intended to become an American citizen. The medical was fine but I was still fifteen or so pounds underweight. The recruiting sergeant told the doctor, "Don't worry, we'll
put that on him in basic training." They did that and some. The
United States gave me the chance the Canadians had denied me.

I enlisted in the U.S. Army 10 June 1948, took my basic training
with the 9th Infantry Division at Fort Dix, New Jersey. I took a leadership course before being shipped out to the newly activated 17th
Airborne (Training) Division then being formed at Camp Pickett,
Virginia. In May 1949, I was warned for overseas duty and in early
June I was on a train heading west to Camp Stoneman, California. I
left on a large draft for the Far East, arriving in time to see my first
big parade of American troops on 4 July 1949, held on the grounds

of the Imperial Palace in Tokyo. I became part of the Army of Occupation of Japan and taken on strength of the Quartermaster Corps, Eighth U.S. Army, Far East. I was in C Company and we were stationed at Shinagawa, located right on Tokyo Bay. I remained with this unit until rotated home in May 1952 with the exception of a detached posting to Pusan.

I was in Tokyo when war broke out in Korea in June 1950. When ground forces were eventually committed to Korea in August, I believe, things began to move quickly. Eventually, for a time, all the combat occupation forces in Japan were transferred to Korea.

The Tokyo quartermaster depot was the largest of its kind in the world, supplying all U.S. forces in the Far East. No large

Wedding of Frank Cassidy and Rosita Mitsuhasha, 29 May 1954, Tokyo.
F. Cassidy

group left our unit until the fall of 1950. In October about forty or so left for Korea to assist in setting up a quartermaster depot at the port of Pusan pending the arrival of a quartermaster company from the United States. I was one of the group, arriving in Pusan in October 1950. Pusan was not only a very busy place around this time but also a dirty place. We helped to unload and stockpile a steady stream of supplies arriving from Japan and the United States. Although we saw no action, we were not far from the fighting. The North Koreans never did enter Pusan itself, being stopped at the Naktong River, close enough for anybody in Pusan. By late December a quartermaster company had arrived from the States and those of us who were only attached were returned to our parent unit in Japan.

When the whole of the Eighth Army had moved to Korea to set

up its headquarters at Taegu, troops remaining in Japan became the main supply base, assuming the same position England had during World War II in Europe. Not long after my return to Japan I was promoted to the rank of sergeant and given a new assignment – command of the railhead of the depot, plus train three officers of the newly formed Japanese Self-Defense Force in our methods. President Truman extended everyone in the service one year, so on a three-year enlistment, I actually spent three years and eleven months before discharge, which came for me on 7 May 1952.

While serving in Japan, I met a local girl. We dated until it was time for me to return to the United States. We didn't have time to get married and I knew that when I returned to the United States the chances of being posted back to the Far East at least for a while were slim. I took my discharge at Camp Kilmer, New Jersey, with the option of going back in should I change my mind.

While on leave, I applied for enlistment in the Canadian Army and was accepted on 16 June 1952. That night I was on my way to the Royal Canadian Army Service Corps school at Camp Borden. After basic training yet again, trades training and advance training, I was posted to the Korea-bound 56 Transport Company, RCASC. We left Borden in February 1953, arriving in Korea in March, and I served until posted to Japan the following January 1954. I received permission to marry and on 29 May 1954, I married Rosita Mitsuhashi in Tokyo. We have celebrated our fortieth wedding anniversary. I met her as an American sergeant and married her as a Canadian private.

We were occupation troops and were not trained for war but occupation duty. When the Korean conflict broke out, we could not believe our troops would be sent in so fast. I witnessed a sergeant in training only weeks before he was sent into combat cut all four fingers trying to take the bayonet off his rifle. He had never seen a bayonet before and did not know there was a catch you had to press. Casualties were high in those first few months until things got organized.

I was in the Far East when the Korean conflict broke out and was there when it ended, returning to Canada in July 1955. I retired from the Canadian forces in 1977 as a master corporal and now reside in Toronto.[1]

F.W. DEMARA, JR (alias JOSEPH C. CYR)
Theatre: Korea   Service: Navy

Peter Chance shares here his memories of F.W. Demara, alias Joseph Cyr. Chance, originally from Ottawa, is now retired in Sidney, British Columbia. He served in the Royal Canadian Navy during the Second World War and aboard HMCS Cayuga *as a senior lieutenant during the Korean conflict. Demara (Cyr) was that ship's new doctor.*

An Ingrown Toenail
I joined my ship in April 1951, having been to a Royal Canadian Navy Hospital (RCNH), the one in Esquimalt, for treatment of a badly infected ingrown toenail. I was advised to see our new surgeon lieutenant who, by the way, was said to be an American from the Boston area. If he could deal with my problem, then I could sail with the ship. The alternative, totally unacceptable to me for the sake of my family, would be a three-week stint in the RCNH and a catch-up with my ship in Japan. I was in luck to find Surgeon Lieutenant Joseph C. Cyr still on board and having looked at my swollen foot he said, "No problem. We'll deal

Lieutenant Peter Chance, spring 1952.
P. Chance

with this first thing in the morning. Can you be here at eight o'clock?" It all seemed straightforward to me. As he was certain that I would be able to sail with the ship, I was much relieved, all the more so as this was an emotionally charged moment for me and my family with the ship due to leave for a year's absence in a war zone in two days. True to his word, the deed was done in jig time. The needle seemed enormous as I was frozen in three well-placed jabs. Next, the scalpel, skilfully handled, removed the offensive nail and surrounding tissue. In a trice I was wrapped like an

Italian tomato, outfitted with crutches and a cane for later, and provided with Darvon pills. "You'll need these later when the anaesthetic wears off," and he sent me on my way.

Dentistry by Proxy

HMCS *Cayuga*, commanded by Commander James Plomer, DSC and Bar, was on a routine patrol behind the enemy lines in the North Korean portion of the Yellow Sea off the Gulf of Chinnampo. It was some considerable distance to the normal operating base at Sasebo in southwest Japan and unless there was some very urgent reason, the ship would be normally expected to remain on patrol for approximately twenty-one days. In this instance, the ship had been less than ten days on station. It was not the normal practice for a single warship the size of a destroyer to carry a dentist; however, because of the nature of the duties, most ships in Korean waters, including this one, were provided with a doctor.

A gun crew stands by as personnel of HMCS *Cayuga* inspect a junk with refugees off the coast of Korea, 9 July 1950.
National Archives of Canada, PA-151993

Ship's company of HMCS *Cayuga,* spring 1952. Senior Lieutenant
Peter Chance is fifth from left, front row.
Peter Chance

During the evening, our commanding officer began to feel the
onset of a serious toothache. As the hours went by, it was obvious
that there was something very seriously wrong with Commander
Plomer's jaw. Throughout the following day the pain became more
acute. Was Plomer to stoically bear his pain, and with the assistance
of available medicine to hope for a sufficient reduction of the
swelling to allow the ship to remain on duty? Towards evening, the
pain became quite unbearable, and upon the advice of the doctor
it was decided that an emergency operation was necessary. Not at
once, but first thing next morning, for, as the doctor explained,
"although I have my degree in medicine, you will surely recognize
my experience in dentistry is extremely limited." With words of
encouragement after this rejoinder the doctor, having provided a
local pain reliever, went away to study his available textbooks. It
would appear that he did this throughout most of the night. In the
meantime, the captain's day cabin was readied as for major surgery
before an imminent major battle. The emergency operating table
was draped in pristine white tablecloths and from one end to the
other, in dramatic display, was equipment in varying sizes apparently adequate for operating needs from the eye of a mosquito to the

leg of a horse. Surely this hardware was more than sufficient to put the unsuspecting patient into a state of abject terror. To heighten the drama of the moment, the noble doctor appeared fully capped and gowned. The gown, somewhat off-size, reached nearly to the floor but did not quite match at the back and so the bows took on a prominent position from the rear. With arms upraised in a beckoning fashion and with his face wreathed in a confident smile, he gaily invited the captain to sit in his favourite chair. By now the patient was feeling truly seedy to say the least, and in a dejected and resigned fashion he eased himself into position ready for the "doctor's worst." The acting dentist armed himself with needles and pliers and went to his work with a will. From here on our story tends to be anticlimactic because not only did the doctor do the job, which is for certain, he pulled the right tooth.

The Unmasking
It was one of these night efforts, with a lot of Republic of Korea troops. We poured in enfilading fire when they went ashore and they did their thing and came back with sacks of rice and cattle and God knows what else and a couple of other guys that had been casualties. We had people dead on arrival and we had people who were very wracked up and Joe paraded up and down rather like the fellow Horatio at the bridge, in his whites, looking every inch the most cool customer going. Anyway, he patched some people. There was one guy very badly wounded. He had a big hole in his chest and Joe tended the wound and the chap lived. And so Don Saxon and I, in particular, were very keen about this and so was everybody else. We were so gung-ho for Joe. We said that something had to be done to get Joe a medal. So our public relations fellow was on board at the time, nice fellow. He cooked up a message and he sent it off to Canadian Press and everybody else and sure enough, the real Doctor Joseph Cyr, somewhere in New Brunswick, stood up and said, "Hey that's me, that fellow you've got out there is an impostor."

We had a message that came to the ship from naval headquarters and John Waters and I showed this to the old man. It said, "to captain's eyes only. Have reason to believe your Medical Officer is an impostor. Investigating report." "Those bloody idiots, they've done it again. Here's Joe, a first-rate doctor and those desk-bound captains back there haven't got a clue what we are doing back here." Afterwards Joe was sent for and he said, "You don't believe

me, you don't believe me." And
he blew up and he was very
upset. Well, the end of it was
that he locked himself in his
cabin and filled himself full of
barbiturates despite our protes-
tations prior saying, "Look we
believe in you, Joe. You're
great and you're doing a great
job and what the hell." Finally
our chummy ship *Ceylon* came
along and we went alongside
and transferred Joe to *Ceylon*
and he was in terrible shape.
He didn't kill himself but he
said before he left and I'll
never forget this, "I'm so sorry.
I had hoped that we could have
got home and then I could
have just left." So we lost a
great member of our ship's
company.[2]

F.W. Demara, Jr., alias Surgeon
Lieutenant Joseph Cyr, 1951.
Department of National Defence

*This American who had served in the Canadian forces in 1951 as Surgeon
Lieutenant Joseph C. Cyr, medical officer of HMCS* Cayuga, *was in fact
Ferdinand Waldo Demara, Jr. of Lawrence, Massachusetts. He was quietly
discharged. Demara became known as "The Great Impostor," which was
also the title of the book and the 1961 film starring Tony Curtis that told
his story. He had been Brother John in 1950 at a monastery at Grand
Falls, where he had borrowed the real Dr. Cyr's credentials. He was also a
psychology instructor at a college in Pennsylvania. Demara served legiti-
mately around 1970 as a pastor at Friday Harbor on the Island of San
Juan, Washington State. There he used his real name. Demara last worked
as himself as a religious counsellor at the Good Samaritan Hospital in
Anaheim, California,[3] from 1974 until his death in June 1982.[4]*

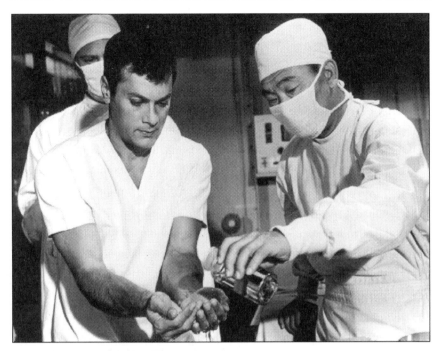

Tony Curtis as "The Great Impostor" about to undertake surgery.
National Archives of Canada, 16053

LEWIS MILLETT
Theatre: Korea   Service: Army

I am an American who served in the Canadian Army. I was born 15 December 1920 in Mechanic Falls, Maine. As a high school student, I joined the regular army air corps but deserted in October 1941 in order to fight. I enlisted in November at Saint John, New Brunswick. I took my basic training at Edmundston, many miles from Saint John. I was originally posted to the 8th Princess Louise's (New Brunswick) Hussars, but was transferred to the artillery. I served for a time in Ottawa at the National Research Council for a "briefing" on radar. I was sent to a Royal Canadian Artillery replacement training centre in southeast England (I don't remember the name of the place) but I transferred to the U.S. Army in England after the attack on Pearl Harbor. I was ordered to the 1st Armored Division in Northern Ireland. After basic training I was assigned to the 27th Armored Field Artillery Battalion.

We embarked for North Africa in October. I fought at Oran, against the Afrika Korps in the desert. At Medjez el Bob in Tunisia as a private with B Battery, I was awarded the Silver Star for driving a half-track loaded with ammunition out of haystack camouflage that had been set afire by enemy shellfire. I fought at Salerno, Cassino, Anzio, the Appenines, Rome, Venafro, and the valley of the Po. I received a Bronze Star in Germany for calling an artillery barrage down on my position in order to break up a German infantry attack.

After World War II, I left the army and joined the National Guard at Lewiston, Maine. I attended Bates College in New England for

Captain Lewis Millett in Korea. The photo was taken on the day of the action for which he won the Medal of Honor.
L. Millett

three years after the war. I requested active duty and on 1 January 1949 was ordered to the 25th Infantry Division, stationed in peacetime garrison in Japan. I was assigned to the 8th Field Artillery, the support battalion of the 27th Infantry (Wolfhounds). I became a forward observer and subsequently took over Company E, 2nd Battalion, after Captain R.B. Desiderio had been killed.

The action for which I received the Medal of Honor took place on Hill 180 in early February 1951. It followed part of a well-coordinated tank-and-infantry attack which began in early February 1951. E Company's fight was one small piece of the offensive.

With Company E, 2nd Battalion, 27th Infantry Regiment, Captain Millett was awarded the Medal of Honor for valour in the vicinity of Soam-Ni, Korea on 7 February 1951.

While personally leading his company in an attack against a strongly held position he noted that the 1st Platoon was pinned down by small-arms, automatic, and anti-tank fire. Captain Millett ordered the 3rd Platoon forward, placed himself at the head of the two platoons, and, with fixed bayonet, led the assault up the fireswept hill. In the fierce charge Captain Millett bayoneted two enemy soldiers and boldly continued on, throwing grenades, clubbing and bayoneting the enemy, while urging his men forward by shouting encouragement. Despite vicious opposing fire, the whirlwind hand-to-hand assault carried to the crest of the hill. His dauntless leadership and personal courage so inspired his men that they stormed into the hostile position and used their bayonets with such lethal effect that the enemy fled in wild disorder. During this fierce onslaught Capt. Millett was wounded by grenade fragments but refused evacuation until the objective was taken and firmly secured. The superb leadership, conspicuous courage, and consummate devotion to duty demonstrated by Capt. Millett were directly responsible for the successful accomplishment of a hazardous mission and reflect the highest credit on himself and the heroic traditions of the military service.

At the White House ceremony in which Millett was presented the Medal of Honor, he met his future wife. They have been married some forty years and have had four children. They live in Idyllwild, California.[5]

VIETNAM

A significant number of Canadians crossed the border to fight in the Vietnam War. It was the first time since the American Civil War that so many Canadians had volunteered to serve in an American war in which Canada was officially neutral. This conflict proved a more difficult and drawn-out war than expected. The experience left many veterans with serious physical and psychological problems. The war also exacted a considerable emotional toll on their families. Estimates of Canadians involved have ranged between 12,000 and 40,000.

Many of the Canadian volunteers were motivated by a desire for adventure. Some joined because they had strong anti-communist feelings. Of that group some had come with their families from countries under communist rule; others objected to communism on religious grounds. About a third who served were those residing and working in the United States. They could have moved back to Canada but chose to obey the laws of the country in which they were living. They decided to fight because they believed it the proper thing to do.

Americans who were drafted to serve in their country's forces reacted in different ways to the Canadians who volunteered to fight. Some initially thought the Canadians were crazy; others welcomed them; some even thought Canada was in the war as an ally of the United States. Most Americans were indifferent.

Would those Canadians who served in Vietnam do it again? A good number said no. They felt used and then abandoned by the American government. This includes particularly those who contracted disabilities as a result of exposure to "Agent Orange," a defoliant, or suffer from post-traumatic stress disorder (PTSD). A higher proportion of Canadian Vietnam veterans are affected by PTSD than Americans. This is due to their isolation from other veterans and to the absence of support groups and programs in Canada to help them. A lack of public support or sympathy in Canada has also made their readjustment more difficult.

The Canadian Vietnam Veterans Coalition was organized in 1986 to provide the sort of support network developed in the

Marines of the 2nd Battalion, 9th Regiment, 3rd Division, on patrol
during Operation "Carol," 1966.
United States Marine Corps / K. McVeigh

Marines of the 3rd Division on patrol, 1966.
United States Marine Corps / K. McVeigh

United States to cope with the needs of veterans. Up to that point, Canadian Vietnam veterans had been on their own.

The construction of the Wall in Washington has helped the healing process for Vietnam veterans and the public. Other memorials to remember those killed in Vietnam have been built throughout the United States. To remember those who were killed and all who served, the Canadian Vietnam Veterans wanted a permanent national site in Canada where family, friends and others could go to pay their respects and reflect.

After having published *Unknown Warriors*, I thought that feelings in Canada against Canadian Vietnam veterans would have ameliorated. Although there is generally much more understanding of their case than before the book's appearance, there remains a degree of hostility. The chairman of the National Capital Commission, Marcel Beaudry, and the Honourable Michel Dupuy, secretary of state, have refused the Canadian Vietnam Veterans Coalition permission to use federal land in Ottawa for a memorial. In contrast, the Senate, led by Senator Jack Marshall, passed a resolution in favour of federal land being made available.

As for Remembrance Day ceremonies, only some Royal Canadian Legion branches have permitted the Vietnam veterans organization to march with them and lay wreaths. This has not happened at the national level. In most areas, branches have forbidden them to take any part whatsoever in Remembrance Day ceremonies. The Royal Canadian Legion National Command, however, has voted to allow Canadian Vietnam veterans to join the Legion as full members as of 10 October 1994.

The structure for this memorial consists of one main centre panel extending eleven feet high by four feet wide and held in suspension by two four-foot square panels, one on each side, standing on odd-height pedestals. The three panels are faced on both sides with the same black granite as was used in the design of the Vietnam Veterans Memorial in Washington, D.C. The main centre panel facing the approach path contains the names of Canadians killed or missing in action while serving in the United States forces. The side panels contain a bilingual poem composed by a Canadian Vietnam veteran, the crests of the branches of U.S. armed forces, and a map of Vietnam, all on the granite surface. The entire structure is fifteen feet wide and is centred upon a decorative, circular masonry pad containing the coat of arms of each of the Canadian provinces and territories. At the back of the memorial, three flag-

Drawing of the Canadian Vietnam Veterans Memorial.
Michigan Association of Concerned Veterans

poles present the Canadian, American and POW/MIA (prisoner of war/missing in action) flags. A memorial to Canada's Vietnam veterans is to be just that. It is not intended to praise or condemn, just to remember those Canadians killed in that war. Although this memorial has been built, its site has not as yet been determined.

Many of the Canadians who joined the U.S. military and volunteered for Vietnam did so with a mistaken concept of war. They viewed war as an opportunity for glory, adventure and heroism. They believed it was the other fellow who would be killed. Few seriously imagined being casualties themselves, killed or maimed, their bodies poisoned by chemical defoliants or their minds damaged by the trauma they endured. They were wrong. And there was no glory. When they returned home, there would be no cheering crowds welcoming them back.

POWS IN VIETNAM

Are American POWs still alive and being held in Southeast Asia? In spite of numerous photos, media reports, articles and books alleging their existence, none have successfully escaped since the end of the war and only one has been returned home. That exception was Private, First Class, Robert Garwood, a marine captured in Vietnam on 28 September 1965.

Garwood approached a Finnish businessman in Hanoi in the winter of 1979 and dropped a note in his lap identifying himself. The United States State Department was informed and asked the Vietnamese for an exit visa, which was granted. On 25 March 1979 Garwood headed home.

Upon returning, Garwood was charged with four violations of the Uniform Code of Military Justice. On 5 February 1981 he was found guilty on two charges – aiding enemy forces within POW camps and of assault. He was acquitted of soliciting American troops to refuse to fight and of desertion. Garwood sought over $140,000 in back pay and benefits. On 13 February 1981 he was sentenced to reduction to private, forfeiture of all pay and allowances, and a dishonourable discharge. A United States Marine Corps court of military review affirmed his conviction on 29 July 1983. The case has been pronounced closed.

Some of the media seem to think that the louder the chorus of belief in the existence of POWs in Vietnam the more seriously the issue is taken. A rumoured sighting or the publication of a murky photo can be chalked up as evidence. The profitability of the issue has led to books and articles on both sides of the question. The victims of all this ill-founded speculation are the unfortunate families of the missing servicemen. They deserve the complete truth from both the American and Vietnamese governments.

There are those who say that Canada was an indifferent bystander in the Vietnam War. However, although this country was officially neutral and served as a member of the International Control Commission, it provided training areas for American bomber pilots going to Vietnam, allowed the manufacture and testing of Agent Orange, and sold $2.5 billion worth of war materiel. The war had a significant impact on Canada – socially, economically and culturally. Americans who moved to Canada to avoid the draft had a significant influence at all three levels.

VIETNAM WAR EXPERIENCES

GEORGE ODOM
Theatre: North Africa, Italy,
Service: Army
France, Germany, Korea,
Laos, Vietnam

I was born in Albany, Georgia, 4 September 1923. My father died in St. Petersburg, Florida, in 1926. My mother passed away in 1929. I went to the orphanage at age six and nine years later hitchhiked across the country. As Canada was at war, I joined the Canadian Army in Montreal on 16 May 1941. I trained at Camp Borden until November 1941 with the 6th Duke of Connaught's Royal Canadian Hussars. I was subsequently shipped out of Halifax to Liverpool and stationed at Aldershot. I was seeing no combat, so on July 1942 I joined the 135th Regiment of the 34th Infantry Division of the U.S. Army to fight. In late 1942 I landed with the 34th in Oran after the initial invasion forces went ashore. Despondent at not having yet participated in the fighting, in January 1943 I went absent without leave to the 1st Infantry Division, which was then the only American infantry unit engaging the Germans. I was assigned to Company I, 26th Infantry Regiment.

With the "Big One" (1st Infantry Division), I knocked out a machine-gun nest at El Guettar about 20 March 1943. I also saw action in the second battle of the Kasserine Pass and at the Foundouk Gap. I fought at Hill 609 (Djebel Tahent), Tunisia, April–May 1943 with the 34th Division, to which I was returned.

I went to Italy with Company C, 135th Regiment, 34th Division, and was assigned to Company K, 179th Infantry Regiment, 45th Division. I saw action with them through France and Germany. I was discharged in August of 1945 but re-enlisted in December.

In 1950 I went to Korea as a member of Company A, 27th Regiment, 25th Division. I got slightly hit the day I arrived. Twenty-one days later, 16 August 1950, I was more severely wounded in action and was sent back to the United States.

In 1961 as a sergeant major I went to Vientiane, Laos, with the Special Forces. While there I met Canadian members of the International Control Commission. We got along splendidly. In 1963 I first went to Vietnam on a six-month tour and saw some combat. On my last tour in Vietnam from June 1968 to 31 May 1969, I was command sergeant major of the 5th Special Forces. In 1971 I retired. I tried to re-enlist in the army to fight against Iraq but was told I was too old.

I will always be thankful for the training I got in the Canadian Army. It helped me to survive World War II, Korea and Vietnam. I wear a tattoo of the old Canadian flag, the Red Ensign, to always remind me of my early training and experi-

Command Sergeant Major George Odom, Nha Trang, Vietnam, July 1969.
G. Odom

ences. Only some 275 American servicemen had been awarded the Combat Infantrymen Badge three times. More Medals of Honor have been awarded than the third Combat Badge. I am the only ex-Canadian in that category.

In response to your questions, I still recall being told by a superior in 1941, "You go where the King sends you, you fight where the King tells you and you had better damn well win. When you see the enemy, shoot."[6]

KEITH DANIELS
Theatre: Vietnam   Service: Marines

Having been born during an air raid on 1 August 1943 in London, I was born for war. My father died in 1946 from war wounds. I left England in 1947 with my mother and brother to come to Sudbury, Ontario. My mother married shortly after arriving in Canada. I grew up and went to school in the Sudbury area.

When I was old enough I joined the RCAF in February 1962 to become an air force policeman. I was stationed at Rockcliffe, Ottawa. After a little more than a year, I could see little chance for advancement in the near future. In mid-1963, I requested, and received, an honourable discharge and went across the border to try to join the marines.

It took about six months to process. Finally, in January 1964, I was told to report for duty. My first station was Parris Island, South Carolina, for recruit training. We arrived in the early hours of the morning by bus. When the bus stopped, a raving marine entered telling us in not too polite terms to exit the bus. We lined up on the sidewalk where he ranted and raved some more. Finally, we entered a building, where we took one test after another. We broke for breakfast at about 6 a.m., after which we received haircuts and were issued clothing. With all our hair gone, we all looked similar. I couldn't even recognize the friends I had made during the trip.

We had three drill instructors. They could be described as mean, meaner, and meanest or medium, large and wow. They were with us from 6 a.m. until 10 p.m. The training never ceased. We had been there for three days before I realized I hadn't had a cigarette since arriving. (All cigarettes and lighters were confiscated upon arrival.) The aim was to break us down and then build us up to be marines. They started by calling us maggots. As time wore on, we were girls then ladies. We had plenty of physical training along with self-defence, weapons and marine corps history.

We went through obstacle courses. I didn't complete it the very first time. After some personal "hands on" counselling, I never failed to complete it again. I learned a new meaning to the "laying on of hands." Our training lasted from 14 January 1964 to 3 April 1964. When we graduated we were finally called marines by our drill instructors. We were told we had joined the brotherhood of marines and once a marine, always a marine.

After recruit training, the U.S. Marine Corps decided to send me to infantry school in North Carolina for more training, six weeks of it, to learn how to use flame throwers, rocket launchers, machine guns, grenades and anything else they thought we might need to use. After infantry training we got thirty days' leave. I went back to Sudbury to show off my new muscles and uniform. Nobody even recognized the uniform or had any idea what a marine was.

Upon my arrival back to North Carolina I was sent to join Headquarters and Services Company, 1st Battalion, 7th Regiment, 1st Marine Division, in Camp Pendleton, California. I was assigned to 81-mm mortar platoon. In August I met a girl on the beach in Oceanside. Five months later we were married. As time wore on, I heard more and more about Vietnam. Our field training was stepped up. By February 1965 we knew we would be going to Vietnam.

On 23 May 1965 the regiment boarded ships, mine was the USS *Renville*. The "Rusty *Renville*" we called it. We left San Diego on the 24th. We stopped off in Hawaii for a couple of days and were allowed to go ashore. Then it was on to Okinawa on 18 June. In Okinawa, there was more training for jungle warfare. At 8 August it was back to the ships. This time it was the USS *Bayfield*. We slept below decks in hammocks stacked six high. I had learned by now not to take a bottom bunk. It was hot down there so we would try to find a place on deck to sleep.

We arrived somewhere off Vietnam on 14 August 1965. We were issued live ammunition and got into the landing boats. The aircraft flew overhead strafing and bombing. Was I scared? You bet. Then the landing craft stopped going in circles and lined up to hit the beach. While running up the beach I almost ran over a guy laying on a beach chair holding a can of beer. Above him was a sign, "Welcome to Chu Lai Acres." The guys from the 3rd Battalion, 3rd Marine Regiment, 3rd Marine Division, had come down to the beach to watch the show. The planes had bombed the beach further away. Was it a mock assault landing or a screw-up? I still don't know.

Anyone stationed at Chu Lai became very familiar with the sands of Chu Lai. It was in our beds, our food and our clothes. I have spent many hours walking on the sandy beach on guard duty. Once during a typhoon it rained so hard I had to cup my hands over my nose and mouth just to breathe. You couldn't see an arm's length away.

While at Chu Lai I managed to go to Da Nang, fifty miles north, on a beer run. What impressed me was the French influence on the buildings, especially the restaurants. In our bathroom was a bidet, the first I had ever seen. After a shower, our second priority was food. I ordered a Chateaubriand steak. Bread was brought with our meal. Ants were crawling all over. I told the waiter to take the bread back and bring us fresh bread without ants. He came back with the same bread. I know it was the same bread; I recognized some of the ants. I ate the bread anyway.

I went to a museum and was awe-struck at the age of everything. Coming from Sudbury, where 40 was considered old for a building, I was surrounded by buildings at least 500 years old.

Booby-traps were quite common in our area of operations. We were dealing with North Vietnamese Army as well as Viet Cong troops. Both knew how to make booby-traps. Members of the North Vietnamese Army were usually dressed up in green uniforms and pith helmets, while the Viet Cong wore black peasant-style pyjamas with cone-type hats. Their traps could be anything ranging from *pungi* stakes (made out of steel or bamboo) buried in a straw-covered hole attached to grenades or unexploded shells, usually our own.

Private, First Class, K.C.L. Daniels.
K. Daniels

Marines from the 2nd Battalion, 7th Marine Regiment, move along
a dike across a flooded rice paddy during Operation
"Harvest Moon."
United States Marine Corps

Our booby-traps were Claymore mines or grenades with the
pins pulled out stuck in an old "C" ration can with a string across
the trail. We got more inventive as time wore on. Some of the guys
from Texas would catch poison snakes and tie them by their tails
along suspected trails.

Both the enemy and ourselves would lay ambushes. In these we
had the upper hand because we could usually call in air support.
Choppers or jets would come in minutes of our getting hit. A week
later we were involved in Operation "Starlite" in the Chu Lai area
against enemy forces. Then from 7 to 10 September we were on
Operation "Piranha," then Operation "Neptune" in October,
"Black Ferret" in November, and "Blue Moon" in December.

All the operations seem blended together. I remember once we
hit the beach in typical Marine Corps fashion. When I came ashore
I saw a woman on the beach holding a baby whose arm was held on
by a piece of skin. I heard the baby died after being taken aboard
ship for medical attention. Later, I was assigned to remove enemy
bodies from a chopper and bury them. Later, I guarded POWs. I
still remember one in particular who was a doctor. He had come
from a cave hospital. We, of course, did not know at the time how
big the cave was nor that it was a hospital. The doctor had a wound

behind his knee. It did not appear to be a severe wound but as the day wore on he slowly died.

In January 1966 half of my group was traded to the 1st Battalion, 3rd Regiment, 3rd Marine Division, the other half to the 1st Battalion, 7th Marine Regiment, 3rd Marine Division. I was with the first group. We arrived on 22 January and I went to the 81-mm mortar platoon in Headquarters and Service Company, just north of Da Nang. We were assigned to guard an Esso plant at a little village. Within a week we had cleared a hill of elephant grass and fire ants to set up camp. We had a good view of the village and Highway 1 going to Da Nang. By the end of the second week we were established. Our days were spent going down to the beach and filling sandbags. Because I had a military licence to drive a mule (wheeled transport vehicle), I made all the trips.

By the start of the third week, the people in the village made use of free enterprise. They sold us Coca-Cola for 100 piastres or one dollar. The woman vendor would open the bottle of coke with her teeth. This was in the days before twist-off or pull tabs. Mirrors and other items were sold. "Cycle" girls (prostitutes) came in from Da Nang and charged 500 piastres or $5.00.

The days here were good. If you weren't on guard duty, you were allowed to go to the beach which was only half a mile away and could be seen from our hill. Nighttime was another story. The only ones to leave camp at night were patrols. These patrols were no picnic. No smoking, no noise, just follow the leader. If that meant going through swamps, you went. Once you left base camp there was no turning back. Sitting in ambush letting the mosquitoes have their fill is not fun. On the other hand, if your duty was to stand watch on the mortar, that was better. You could sleep until it was your turn, then if any of the patrols got into a fire fight you would aim the mortar in that direction and send off illumination rounds. Usually you could have three in the air before the first one lit up the night. As well as patrols and night duty on the mortar, there was guard duty at an outpost. While out there, you would be too scared to sleep. We would take two-hour shifts with a partner. The duty sergeant would check on you several times a night.

While at this village, I was happy to have several other Canadians in our group. They were mostly from Montreal. They even had the new Canadian flag up in their bunker. They told me there were twenty-one Canadians in our battalion. Every one I met not only did as required but added a little more because they knew they were not only a marine, but that they represented Canada. We were generally treated with respect because the U.S. Marine Corps was an all-volunteer force at that time and we had come from another country to enlist.

By June 1966 it was time to go home. About a week after leaving Vietnam, I was walking the streets of Oceanside, California. There was no debriefing, just some money and orders to report to Camp Lejeune, North Carolina, in thirty days. It was difficult getting used to the regimentation of stateside bases again. Some could not, so they got into trouble or signed up for another tour back to Vietnam.

At that point I had no idea of how much my tour had affected me both physically and mentally. Physically I had aged considerably. The only emotion which I could display was rage. I would go from calm to rage in an instant. I didn't understand why I acted like that.

On the positive side, when I saw indecision around me, I would take charge and make decisions. Consequently, I made sergeant (E-6) and when I left the U.S. Marines in January 1968, I was a platoon sergeant. I was not prepared for civilian life. I found it confusing. There seemed to be no leadership and no chain of command like in the military. I became a service station attendant. I had a wife and two kids to support so I worked 105 hours a week for $100 pay. There was no time for family life; a year later we split up. Life was a roller coaster.

Finally, I came home to Canada. I started work with the Correctional Service of Canada as a prison guard. I remarried in 1981. In 1988 I found I was not the only Vietnam veteran in Kingston. I have since found seven. No one was aware of any benefits to which we were entitled. I decided to become a service officer. After two weeks' training in Washington, D.C., I was accredited by the Vietnam Veterans of America. Now I am authorized to help Canadian Vietnam veterans acquire benefits to which they were entitled. In January 1994 I became the first Canadian resident to be appointed to the Board of Directors of the Vietnam Veterans of America. I hope I may be of benefit to all Vietnam veterans across Canada and represent them and their needs to our American brothers.

Although there were 58,000 Americans killed in Vietnam, people fail to see the suicides of another 125,000 who have died since and of the thousands of homeless vets who cannot hold a job. War is sometimes necessary but before it starts you must look at the whole cost of war.[7]

DENNIS RICHARD SCHMIDT
Theatre: Vietnam   Service: Marines

Dennis Schmidt was born on 6 June 1945 in East Chester, Nova Scotia. He attended high school in Kentville and later joined his parents and three younger sisters who had moved in 1964 to North Plainfield, New Jersey. His father's employer had transferred him to the company's head office in New York City. Dennis enlisted in the U.S. Marines shortly after his nineteenth birthday. He completed basic training at Parris Island, South Carolina, and served at Camp Lejeune, North Carolina. Two of his letters have survived:

May 1966

Dear Aunt Jean, Uncle Clancy, and family (Halifax)
    Yes, I am in Vietnam. I got here in early April. Right now I am working with my platoon of twenty-eight men in and around the Da Nang area close to the border. We are moving further north to Phu Bai the 1st of June. We are rumoured to be going on a twenty-one-day operation to meet a new VC regiment. A lot of good men are lost on operations. I've been lucky several times already – sniper fire and mines on two patrols killed my sergeant and four other marines with us.

    Love,
    Denny

Private, First Class, Dennis Schmidt, 1965.
B. Schmidt

June 1966

Dear Uncle Clancy, Jean and kids,

It's three months since I arrived in Vietnam and it has truly been the longest three months of my entire life. Things are rough and I cannot foresee any slack in the future. I have counted twelve times so far where I've been damn lucky to be writing this letter. It's not very nice seeing your buddies falling all around you.

In one operation, my sergeant got three machine-gun bullets in the stomach. I saw him fall and crawled fast to him. I then poured some of my water on a dressing and tied it to his stomach. Then I began to loosen his belt when his arms and hands dug with tremendous force into my shoulder blades. He stretched with a groan and then died in my arms. Tears ran down my cheeks in silence cutting through the twenty-one days of filth over my face. I have never told my parents about this and I won't till the day I am safe home again. It is because of the many experiences I am going through that make me realize my chances of making it home – nil. I think of you often.

Love,
Dennis

On 8 August 1966 in Quang Tri Province, an ambush of Company E, 2nd Battalion, 4th Regiment, 3rd Marine Division ended the life of Corporal Dennis Richard Schmidt. He had only recently celebrated his twenty-first birthday.

Richard was buried in St. Margaret's Bay Cemetery, near Halifax. A joint contingent of U.S. Marines and Canadian servicemen participated in the funeral service. His parents now reside in Tillsonburg, Ontario.[8]

JAMES M. MACKAY
Theatre: Vietnam   Service: Army

I was born on 22 October 1945 in New Waterford, Nova Scotia, and enlisted in the U.S. Army on 4 October 1965. I took my basic training at Fort Dix, New Jersey. After basic training I was assigned to Fort Knox, Kentucky, for advanced individual training as a personnel clerk. I then volunteered for airborne training and was assigned to Fort Benning, Georgia. I completed jump school March 1966. I was assigned to the 82nd Airborne Division at Fort Bragg, North Carolina. I worked as a clerk until February 1967, when I volunteered for Vietnam. I arrived in Vietnam in March 1967 and was assigned to the 5th Special Forces Group in Nha Trang. After completing my twelve-month tour I extended my tour and was assigned to Ho Ngoc Tao, located about seven miles from Long Binh, as an assistant reconnaissance team leader in early March 1968. On 25 March I became reconnaissance team leader. In September 1968 I was discharged. In February 1969 I re-enlisted in the army in Boston and was assigned to the 7th Special Forces Group, Fort Bragg, North Carolina. I again volunteered for Vietnam and was assigned to IV Corps

J.M. MacKay calling in an air strike, IV Corps, 1969.
J.M. MacKay

Mobile Strike Force from October 1969 to November 1970 during which time I was reconnaissance team leader.

I worked most of my time in Vietnam and Cambodia in long- and short-range reconnaissance. The tasks were small raids as well as finding and fixing on enemy targets for artillery and air strikes. I worked inside territory dominated by enemy forces. I also conducted ambush operations and had an air boat section (5th Mobile Strike Forces Airboat Company) on the Mekong Delta at Cao Lanh during the rainy season of 1970. I received four Purple Hearts for wounds received in these operations. I was also awarded four Bronze Stars, three with V device for combat service.

The following excerpts from MacKay's Bronze Star citations testify to his bravery:

16 May 1968
Specialist MacKay distinguished himself by valorous actions on 25 to 29 March 1968 while serving as an acting platoon leader whose platoon was part of a

two-company sized unit on a search and destroy operation deep in enemy held territory. They became engaged in a prolonged and fierce fire fight with a North Vietnamese Army battalion ... Throughout the intense battle Specialist MacKay moved outside the perimeter to obtain sorely needed water which was in containers outside the perimeter. Specialist MacKay provided aggressive and positive leadership when his CIDG (Civilian Irregular Defense Group) soldiers were overpowered and a breach of the perimeter appeared imminent. Because of his actions and personal bravery in the heat of battle, his soldiers continued to resist a far superior sized enemy.

12 July 1970

Staff Sergeant MacKay distinguished himself by heroism on 29 April 1970 while serving as a senior advisor to the 2d Company, 3d Battalion, IV Corps Mobile Strike Force in the vicinity of Nha Bang, Chau Doc Province, Republic of Vietnam. The 3d Battalion ... had set up a night perimeter on the eastern edge of Nha Bang. Shortly after 2000 hours Staff Sergeant MacKay's element on the eastern perimeter received a heavy enemy probe, supported by 60 mm and 82 mm mortar fire, and B-40 rocket fire. Staff Sergeant MacKay, ignoring his own personal safety, ran from position to position, continuously exposing himself to the extremely heavy hostile fire, encouraging his exhausted and battle-worn troops. The MSF troop's morale was greatly boosted by Staff Sergeant MacKay's presence and returned a murderous volume of fire, temporarily halting the enemy's ground probe on Staff Sergeant MacKay's eastern perimeter ... Later on during the night his southern perimeter began to run low on ammunition due to the extent of the enemy probes. Realizing the danger of the situation Staff Sergeant MacKay ... helped devise a plan using air strikes as a cover, to enable two resupply ships to come in allowing them to continue to ward off the enemy attacks until dawn.

10 September 1970

Staff Sergeant MacKay distinguished himself by heroism on 29 March 1970 ... when he saw and heard a fellow soldier just forward of the enemy's position wounded and staggering toward him crying for help. Displaying high personal courage and complete disregard for his own safety, Sergeant MacKay rushed forward to aid his comrade. The enemy, observing this action directed heavy fire at both men ... Sergeant MacKay was severely wounded by enemy fire, but continued to drag his fellow soldier with him until both reached a friendly position.

There were many interesting experiences and close calls. However, for some reason I didn't get killed. There were lots of times I should have been. After seeing all the useless killing, hurting and hatred, I still was able to return with a somewhat stable mind. There were also a lot of good things done. I have seen people change and do things they would never have done to another human back in the world as we called it. We could do almost any-

MacKay relaxes at a party with his team.
J.M. MacKay

thing. There were no laws in the jungle. Torture was an everyday occurrence. One day while on an operation we captured three Viet Cong wounded in the fighting. Their wounds were not serious. I was giving them some of my water and checking their wounds when one of my South Vietnamese counterparts starting poking one of the prisoners with the end of his rifle. I told him to stop. He just laughed and continued. I stopped him by knocking him to the ground. He had the gun and we were in the middle of the jungle in Cambodia. I thought I was soon going to be dead. However, I had the radio and knew how to operate it. They couldn't get extracted without me. After returning to the operational base in Vietnam, I turned the prisoners over to the South Vietnamese interrogators. I was told later that the three Viet Cong had died from their wounds. When I asked to see the bodies I was told that they had been dropped from a helicopter – so that their friends could bury them.

Why did the U.S. fail in Vietnam? Maybe because they shouldn't have been there in the first place. The French tried and were unable to win there because they lacked the support of the Vietnamese people. It was the same case with the U.S.

I was on patrol one day when we came across an old Vietnamese man gathering firewood. I had my interpreter ask the man what he thought about us being there protecting him from the Viet Cong. His answer was: "I wish you all would go away and have your war some place else and just leave me to my rice paddy." It didn't matter to the people who won. They still would be working in the same fields.

I served overseas in Thailand training Laotian and Thais for combat in Laos in 1971. I next served in Panama (1972–73), Korea (1975–76), Panama (1980) and El Salvador (1981). I retired from the U.S. Army in April 1986 and moved to Cape Breton Island.[9]

GUY DOUGLAS DICKIE

Theatre: Vietnam   Service: Marines

The following account is by David Ford, one of Guy Dickie's friends who survived. Dickie, from Hamilton, Ontario, was killed in combat on 8 February 1968.

Until three years ago, I avoided everything that had to do with the Vietnam War, including books, movies and veterans' organizations. I tried not to think or talk about it. Guy Dickie was a member of the squad in which I was a fire-team leader and we'd been through enough that I knew Guy was one of those marines you could trust in any situation. He was friendly, outgoing and liked by everyone. He was also very intelligent and capable under the extreme pressure of combat. He had a great sense of humour. I can still picture his face as if I'd seen him yesterday.

Although he was only a private, Guy could have had an outstanding career in the Marine Corps. He was a rifleman with the 1st platoon of Alpha Company, 1st Battalion, 9th Regiment, 3rd Marine Division. The 1/9 was nicknamed "the Walking Dead" because of the extremely high casualty rate it suffered during its time in the country. When 1/9 was flown into the Khe Sanh in January 1968 to reinforce the 26th Marines, all of the battalion was set in on the northwest perimeter of the Khe Sanh Combat Base near the Rock Quarry, except our platoon which was sent out to

Guy Douglas Dickie (left).
D. Ford

occupy a small rise called Hill 64. Our platoon-size outpost was located near the Rock Quarry a few hundred metres outside the perimeter with its mission being to protect one of the avenues of approach. Its military designation was Alpha One Outpost.

On 7 February 1968 the Special Forces camp at Lang Vei was overrun. The following day our platoon was attacked by what some believe was a reinforced battalion of North Vietnamese Army regulars. The attack lasted for many hours in the early morning darkness, preventing any help from Khe Sanh from attempting to reach the hill for fear of a major ambush. The fighting was hand to hand at times, and before it was over the few marines who could still fight actually threw rocks at the enemy out of desperation when the supply of grenades and ammunition was nearly exhausted. Of the sixty-four marines on the hill, twenty-four were killed and twenty-nine wounded, leaving eleven men to rebuild the platoon, which would remain at Khe Sanh throughout the remainder of the siege during the Tet Offensive of '68.

It appears that Guy was killed instantly when his bunker either took a direct hit from a rocket-propelled grenade or more likely from a satchel charge which was thrown inside his bunker by the enemy, who controlled most of the hill and trench-line. The bunker collapsed after the explosion and fell in on Guy, James Scott and another marine whose name I do not know. I helped dig their bodies out on the 11th.

I'd like his family and his country to know what our platoon accomplished. We fought an overwhelming force to a standstill and kept the outpost in marine control. It is possible that Guy's actions that night before he was killed were worthy of the Medal of Honor but anyone who witnessed these actions was also killed. His family and his country can be proud that he lived up to the finest traditions of the U.S. Marine Corps.

We rested for two or three days at Khe Sanh while receiving occasional incoming shells and were told one morning that we were going back to Hill 64 with one of the platoons from A Company to look for four missing in action. I do not remember much about the patrol except that before we climbed the hill and started searching through the bunkers, I noticed the body of the dead North Vietnamese soldier I had seen a couple of days before. We could smell him long before we saw him.

When I reached the top of the hill I went to the bunker where Private Dickie had been, the one I had seen destroyed. Some marines began digging it out. They had been digging a few minutes when we heard tubes popping on the ridge line across from us. We all took cover in the trenches and bunkers just before the mortar rounds hit the hill. After the first rounds hit, we looked for the mortars, which were spotted with binoculars. Air strikes were called in and as the jets attacked, we continued digging. It wasn't long before we found the first body. It was Guy Dickie. His head was blown apart from the base of his skull to his forehead. Even though his face was distorted, I could still recognize him. The smell was sickening. We then dug out a black marine, Lance Corporal James Scott. After we put their bodies in bags we sat on the edge of the trench while the hill was searched again. We did not stay long and the patrol made a direct route back.[10]

ALEXANDER KANDIC
Theatre: Vietnam   Service: Marines

I was born in Innsbruck, Austria, on 2 November 1946. My parents moved to Canada and settled in a small community north of Quebec City. I was about two and a half years old. Our house in the resort community of Lake Beauport was my home for many years until 1 September 1966, when at age nineteen, I enlisted in the U.S. Marine Corps. This came about after having made several trips across the U.S. border to gain recruiting information, take pre-induction tests and generally fulfil all the requirements to getting the necessary papers to enable me to join the American military while still being a Canadian citizen.

I was always intrigued by things military, loved hunting and shooting of weapons as a youngster, and enjoyed reading books and seeing combat films. I met, while living in the Quebec City area, a number of people older than me who had fought in wars in Europe, North Africa and so forth. I had the romantic notion of life in a select military unit, wearing an elite uniform, travel and adventure, enjoying a rather special way of life with none of the tedium of the normal nine-to-five routine of civilian employment.

It was fantasy to go back to Europe and try to join the French Foreign Legion. As things would have it, I found another route to adventure, and joined what to me was another elite military unit, namely the U.S. Marines.

Marine basic training started for me on 5 September 1966 at

Parris Island, South Carolina, and terminated with graduation on 28 October 1966. I began advanced combat infantry training on 29 October near Camp Lejeune, North Carolina, and completed this course around 12 January 1967. I then spent some time on leave with my family and friends back home and prepared myself to bid them all farewell and embark on the grand adventure which was going to change my life forever or even possibly end it prematurely.

It should be noted that I could at this time have chosen to stay in Canada and go AWOL from the marines and the U.S. military could not have done a thing about it as long as I never set foot back in the U.S.A. However, I had decided on this adventure of my own free will and I felt that the war in Vietnam was going to be a part of history and I wanted to be a part of this.

So I flew from Quebec City to San Diego, California, and spent some weeks' additional training at Camp Pendleton, which is the marine base on the west coast. There I had plenty of experience climbing the mountains and doing patrols in the valleys and simulated combat in mock-up Vietnamese villages.

When it came time for my group of marines to ship out to Vietnam, I was rather lucky, because instead of going by military or commercial aircraft and landing in Vietnam within say forty-eight hours, I embarked upon a navy troop transport, the USNS *Upshur*, and sailed from San Diego on 9 March 1967 and arrived and disembarked at Da Nang harbour, Republic of Vietnam, on 28 March 1967.

While aboard ship, about twenty-four hours prior to arrival in Vietnam, we had a general meeting on deck and received our unit assignments. Mine was with two or three other marines to report as replacements to Company F, 2nd Battalion, 5th Marine Regiment, 1st Marine Division. We flew from Da Nang air base by first available military aircraft (in this case a C-130 resupply flight) to the combat base set up at An Hoa, Vietnam.

Now started three days of local familiarization, consisting of touring the combat base, receiving combat gear and weapons, test-firing of these weapons and getting used to the heat, dust, smells and noises of the military mission. It was soon to be an actual combat situation and no longer a training situation as before.

I then joined my company for the first time and was assigned to the weapons platoon (with specialization in anti-tank weapons and machine guns) and started combat operations with local patrols, road security during mine-clearing sweeps, security details protect-

Private, First Class, Alexander Kandic, near An Hoa, summer
1967. A coal mine is located near the mountain in the background.
An enemy attack took place here on 4 July 1967.

A. Kandic

ing vital bridges and other important installations. While on one
such local patrol several kilometres out from our combat base, our
fifteen-man patrol came under intense enemy fire and we had to
try and manoeuvre out from this tense situation. I was assistant
machine-gunner and when the gunner got hit in the gut, I was
rapidly appointed to gunner. In the course of treating this wounded marine, our corpsman was shot in the upper thigh and we had
to call for a medevac helicopter to come pick up this wounded
marine. The corpsman stayed with the patrol because he knew the
situation to be serious and that his services would probably be
required. In our pull-back to safer and higher ground, we used all
the combat skills learned to fire and manoeuvre ourselves out of
this crossfire. With the M-60 machine gun in my arms I had to run
a zig-zag course up a hill, and rounds from various arms were
cracking and snapping all around me. All of a sudden the machine
gun flew from my hands and I hit the dirt as a reflex, thinking my
gun had been hit, when a few seconds later I felt a burning pain in
my left forearm and only then saw that I had been hit. Meanwhile

the rounds were still aimed at me, and with my right arm I grabbed the handle of the M-60 and ran those several yards over the top of the hill and relative safety.

We finally walked the several miles back through the rice paddies and returned to our base. The doc and I waited about thirty minutes for a marine helicopter to come pick us up and fly us both to the field hospital in Da Nang. While we were en route this helicopter was asked to go in and pick up other wounded marines in a hot landing zone, and I hugged the steel floor of the copter while the door gunner peppered the landing zone and rounds outgoing and incoming seemed everywhere. We continued onwards to Da Nang and after treatment there I was flown for a short convalescence to Cam Ranh Bay. I then rejoined my unit and company and the months of my tour went on. I spent one week of leave in Hong Kong about September of 1967. As to my rank in Vietnam, started as PFC (private first class) and was promoted 1 October 1967 to lance corporal.

The most memorable event of my tour of duty with the marines in Vietnam came to pass almost at the normal end of tour with the events of Tet 1968. My company was withdrawn from an operation in the mountains around Phu Bai and taken to the marine base located there [Phu Bai] where we spent the night on 100 percent alert. The base was rocketed by incoming mortars, rockets, etc. Around dawn of the 2nd or 3rd of February 1968 my company loaded onto CH-46 and CH-53 helicopters and made a heliborne combat assault towards Hué City. We landed in a city park near the River of Perfumes and fought our way towards the MACV (Military Assistance Compound Vietnam) compound, which was one of only two military installations to have not fallen to enemy forces during the takeover of Hué City. I participated in the retake and clearing out of enemy forces (both Viet Cong and NVA units) from the modern section of Hué City and we retook that portion of the city on or about 9 February.

It has to be understood that for the average marine grunt our combat experience was mainly jungle fighting in Vietnam. Now within a matter of hours we found ourselves lightly armed and with no heavy guns nor air support fighting in the streets of Hué in a classic infantry battle in an urban setting. We had to fight house to house, street by street, and suffered setbacks as well as advances and took many wounded and several killed. We really had on-the-job training in a big way, and had to improvise as we went along. The

Hué City, 1968.
A. Kandic

enemy had plenty of time to set in and dig fighting holes and defensive positions throughout the city. Because of the natural beauty and historical importance of Hué, it was ordered that we would fight and retake the city only with light infantry weapons. When the real scope of the battle became apparent and the size and determination of the enemy forces was determined, we then were allowed to use heavier weapons. They were anti-tank recoilless rifles, heavy 4.2-inch mortars, some artillery support, some naval gunfire support and, to a limited amount, some air bombardment. It must be noted that the monsoon rains were here and the heavy and low clouds prevented much of the needed air cover or bombardment.

While the events of Tet occurred throughout South Vietnam and just about every major city and town was attacked, including major military installations, it was Hué City that involved the greatest number of crack NVA (North Vietnamese Army) and VC (Viet Cong) units, who took part in the attack and takeover of the city. Approximately 5,000 NVA and VC soldiers under the direct leadership of the commanding general of the Communist Tri-Thien-Hué Military Region participated in the assault. This seems to have comprised the 4th, 5th, 6th NVA Battalions, 12th NVA Sapper Battalion, one NVA rocket battalion, and local VC combat and sapper units. It was my impression that the NVA soldiers fought bravely but lacked proper military leadership and were defeated by tough, young marines who, like me, were scared by events happening around us but at the same time had a mission to complete and also continued to uphold the traditions and esprit de corps of the marines.

During the last days of fighting to clear the modern section of Hué City, my company had trapped a group of the enemy in an old bunker built by the French. I was one of those marines in the second floor and I had to stand on top of a chair to see and direct fire from my gunners' M-60 through the narrow window at the enemy troops breaking out of the bunker. I was knocked from this chair onto the ground by a fragment of grenade or rocket which hit me literally between the eyes on the bridge of my nose and lodged down beside my right eye. Had it hit less than an inch left or right, I would have lost sight in any eye. I was treated by the combat corpsman and continued combat operations until our unit had secured the heart of modern Hué bounded by Highway 1, the Perfume River and the Phu Cam Canal. This took place around the 10th of February. I was sent out of Hué back to Phu Bai for medical treatment and did not participate further in the ongoing battle for the old historical section of Hué and the fight for the Citadel, which continued until about the 25th of the month with the final assault and retaking of all areas of the Hué City region. The results of the Tet Offensive show NVA/VC dead in Hué at 5,113 with another 59 captured, and no account of the number of wounded or those who died of injuries. The U.S. Marines reported 147 men killed in action and 857 seriously wounded. Somewhere close to half of the marine infantrymen committed to the battle were killed or wounded.

After a thirteen-month tour of duty I left Vietnam on 15 March 1968 with a stopover on Okinawa, and then left on 17 March for a flight to Travis AFB, California, where I was processed at the navy installation near San Francisco and went on one month's leave. I flew back to Canada and visited family and friends in Montreal and Quebec City.

I was then scheduled to report to the marine base Camp Lejeune and joined the H&SCo, 2nd Battalion, 2nd Marine Regiment, 2nd Marine Division. Our unit was rumoured to be getting ready to relieve a unit guarding the U.S. navy base Guantanamo Bay, Cuba. As luck would have it, my unit was part of a marine amphibious group which went to replace such a group already on station in the Mediterranean. This was from about July 1968 to mid-December 1968. I was promoted to corporal during November of that year.

When I returned to the U.S.A., I continued to serve at Camp Lejeune. Due to an understanding that under normal circumstances marine infantry would not be sent back to Vietnam until two years after a tour of duty had been completed, and since I had enlisted for a basic three-year period, the marine corps asked many of us if we wanted early release from service. I was honourably discharged from the marines on 9 April 1969.

I went to live, work and study in Philadelphia and in the summer of 1971 I moved back to Canada and settled in Montreal.

Looking back at the events during those years, I now know that even if I joined the U.S. military out of a sense of adventure and felt that in some ways I was helping fight communism, once there in Vietnam it basically became a personal goal to just do the right thing and serve with honour and get back home alive. I have to still live with the visible scars, but also the emotional scars which haunt me still. I suffered hearing loss during my tour of duty caused by the combat environment and this bothers me today. While I do not suffer from PTSD (post-traumatic stress disorder) as portrayed by Hollywood movies – that is, the crazed drug dependent and violent Vietnam veteran – nonetheless I do suffer from its effects but have managed to get on with my life. I now work for the large multinational corporation Matsushita Electric/Panasonic Division, and enjoy married life and travel and gourmet food and wine.

Today I am a director of the Canadian Vietnam Veterans Quebec group and try to meet other veterans groups here in Canada and the U.S.A. We hope to one day win the respect of Canadian veterans from other wars, win the respect of the Canadian public at large, and let them know that Canadians did serve with honour in the Vietnam conflict. I have met veterans groups of former South Vietnamese Army fighters living here in Quebec. They think of us as freedom fighters and not as mercenary troops and seem in awe that we as Canadians chose to come fight as volunteers in that conflict. I have never regretted my own time spent in-country. I did my job well and with military discipline, and I was proud to have worn the uniform of a U.S. Marine.[11]

KENNETH H. LEWIS
Theatre: Vietnam   Service: Army

The Lewis, formerly Otowad-
juwan, family was originally
from Manitoulin Island,
Ontario. We moved in the early
1940s to Sault Ste. Marie,
Ontario, in search of better
economic opportunities. I was
born there on 12 October
1945. From 1963 to 1965 I was
a Junior A hockey player with
the Soo Michigan Indians.

I was going to join the
Marine Corps upon graduation
from high school in 1966 when
Vietnam came into my con-
sciousness. A local veteran, a
fellow hockey player, had
returned from Vietnam minus
a leg. The town gave him a
warm welcome. When I
expressed sympathy about the
loss of his leg, the veteran told
me that he was just happy to

SP-4 (Specialist 4) Kenny Lewis,
South Vietnam, 1969.
K. Lewis

come home alive. The reality of war suddenly set in. I decided to
join only if they came after me.

The army did draft me on 29 August 1967. I did basic training
at Fort Bragg, North Carolina, and AIT (advanced individual training) at Fort Leonard Wood, Missouri. I was trained as a combat
engineer and demolition expert. After AIT in 1968, I was sent to
Hawaii for jungle warfare training. Because of the Tet Offensive,
large numbers of military personnel were being deployed from
there to Vietnam. I remember on Easter Sunday in April being sent
on a Trans-World Airlines flight to Chu Lai. Two days of training
ensued. There followed patrols out of Duc Pho as a private with C
Company of the 4th Battalion, 21st Light Infantry Brigade. But
there wasn't anything light about a seventy-pound pack.

I served for a short time as a member of the 11th Brigade Long
Range Reconnaissance Patrol unit but found their tasks quite risky.

I got reassigned to D Company, 2nd Battalion, 196th Light Infantry Brigade for the remaining five months. I finished my full tour of duty after serving under the "Southern Cross" symbol of the 23rd Infantry Division (Americal).

After Vietnam I returned to Fort Lewis, Washington, then on to Virginia where I was reunited with my wife, Joan. My final assignment was to Fort Hood, Texas. I received an honourable discharge in August 1969.

I played semi-pro hockey for a few years in the Washington area. I now work as a high-rigger ironworker and have been active in the National Indians Veterans Association, the Americal* Division Association, the Indian Veterans Vietnam Association, the 196th Light Infantry Brigade Association, the Vietnam Veterans of America, the Canadian Vietnam Veterans Association, the American Legion and the Veterans of Foreign Wars.[12]

---

* The Americal Division was activated by General MacArthur in May 1942. It consisted of American troops who were already in New Calidonia.

FIDELE JOSEPH BASTARACHE
Theatre: Vietnam   Service: Army

I only have little more than 30 days left, Dad, and when I get out I am coming home and will go up to Canada and do some hunting. I am anxious to come home ... It has been one month since I have slept in a bed ... From one day to another we never know what is going to happen ... We stay awake at night and many times have to fight for our lives.

I saw one of our small jeeps run over a land mine. The explosion threw the jeep almost 20 feet in the air and killed the three soldiers riding in it. We had to pick them up in plastic bags.

That letter was written from Vietnam in May 1968. Later that month Fidele's army platoon was ambushed. He was severely wounded by shrapnel in a firefight and taken to a military hospital, where he died four days later at age twenty-two.

The Bastarache family, consisting of seven children, had moved from Saint-Antoine, New Brunswick, to Gardner, Massachusetts, on 6 July 1962 when Fidele was sixteen. The father, Ambrose, had been unable to find steady work until being hired by a furniture factory there.

Fidele's youngest sister, Dorilla, was fourteen when the family received word her brother was killed. It was her father's birthday. "My father was just leaving for work. I was in bed and I heard his screams. I thought I was dreaming. I wondered if I went back to sleep I'd find it was a nightmare, and when I woke up he'd be coming home. He was almost done. That's the worst part. He only had a month left ... "

Although drafted, Fidele could have avoided going to Vietnam. Since he was a Canadian citizen, his mother suggested he move back to Canada. He refused because he felt it his duty to serve.

Fidele took basic training at Fort Dix, New Jersey, in July 1966 and additional training at Fort Hood, Texas, beginning on 15 March 1967. He began his tour in October. A mortarman, he was assigned to Company B of the 1st Battalion, 6th Infantry Regiment, 189th Infantry Brigade. The Brigade had joined the 23rd Infantry Division (American) operating in the northern part of South Vietnam. Fidele survived until less than a month remained of his tour. He is buried in Gardner.[13]

SP-4 Fidele Bastarache, Vietnam, May 1968.
D. Bastarache

MICHAEL J. MASTERSON
Theatre: Southeast Asia   Service: Air Force

Lieutenant-Colonel Michael J. Masterson was born in The Pas, Manitoba, on 16 May 1937. His family moved to Ephrata, Washington. As a member of 602 Special Operations Squadron, Nakhon Phanom Airfield, Thailand, he was flying a Douglas A-IG Skyraider aircraft over Laos on 13 October 1968. While flying in loose formation with another A-IG, he radioed that he was getting out. No parachute descent was observed. Masterson was listed as missing until 20 November 1978, when his status was changed by the Department of the Air Force to killed in action.

His wife is following his directive: "If I become a POW I'll just wait for my government to come and get me. But if I become an MIA, I want you to find out what happened to me." Her search has led her to Laos and many times to Washington, D.C. After over twenty-five years the search continues. She writes: "I have had a live sighting report even last year when Michael Masterson and 41 other names came out."[14]

FREEDOM CHECK

PLEASE SIGN THIS CHECK
SEND IT TO YOUR CONGRESSMAN
OR SENATOR, ASK "WHERE IS HE?"

DO IT TODAY   19____

PAY
TO THE
ORDER OF   Lt. Col. Michael J. "Bat" Masterson   8 | 2,400 POW/MIA MEN & WOMEN |

ABANDONED IN SOUTHEAST ASIA   Oct. 13, 1968   Laos   DOLLARS

YOU CAN HELP TO SET THEM FREE

FOR   THE FUTURE GENERATION   NON-NEGOTIABLE   SIGNATURE

PAUL STUART LAVEROCK

Theatre: Vietnam   Service: Marines

Paul Stewart Laverock was born in Toronto on 27 October 1948. He grew up in Calgary. He enlisted in the U.S. Marines on 13 August 1968 in Perrysburg, Ohio. Paul had moved to Perrysburg in August 1966 to live with his aunt and uncle and attend school there. Private, First Class, Laverock was a member of the 1st Battalion, 3rd Regiment, 3rd Marine Division.

The following are some letters he wrote to his mother, aunt, uncle and sister.

Dear Mother,

As you already know I've joined the marines. I feel they will help me find something out for myself or in myself which I haven't been able to find. I will be stationed in San Diego for eight weeks and then I will have four weeks of jungle warfare training at Camp Pendleton in California. After that, I will be stationed wherever I am required.

Love,
Paul

Private Paul Laverock, 1968.
M. Laverock

Dear Sue,

If you didn't already know, I think you have gathered that I'm a private in the marine corps. Right now through boot camp all our time is on drill instruction. We generally get up at 10 minutes to 5 the morning and go to bed at 9 at night. We get an average time of 10 minutes per meal. As soon as we get up, we run a mile and then do exercises. We then clean up the area and after that have breakfast. We drill for half the day and do P.T. [physical training] for another one-third of the day. The rest of the time is spent in classes such as rifle and small arms, first aid, history and sentry duty. All this keeps us pretty busy. After supper we run another mile, take a shower and go to bed.

They have an L.D.S. Church (Church of Jesus Christ of Latter Day Saints) service here on base. The first service here they gave *The Book of Mormon* and *Principles of the Gospel.* We also got *The Improvement Era* and *The Church News.*

The marines are thinking of sending me to school to train me in the radio field or to be a war correspondent. October 17 is graduation day for us. We also have to go for 2 to 4 more weeks of advanced jungle warfare depending on where we are ordered to go. So I probably won't get my first leave till the first or middle of November.

Well, I must go now. Please write. Letters are sure good to get here. If you see any of my old friends, could you ask them to write and I'll answer them when I can?

Little bro,
Paul

Dear Sue,

Sorry I haven't written for a while but we were having tests, final drill inspection, etc. for graduation. We finally graduated Thursday. The first thing I want to tell you is that I won't be in Vancouver on the 1st of November. We are through with boot camp, but I'm now undergoing advanced infantry training.

What I'm slowly leading up to is that I'm going to Vietnam in December or January. Like I said it's not what I was counting on. Getting to the present, this advanced training is really rough. We are at Camp Pendleton which is the centre of the foothills. We walk at least 8 miles per day up these hills. A little later we will be camping out and going on night patrols simulating combat-zone conditions. Here at the base we fire weapons from the smallest pistol to flame throwers. We also experience firing artillery. We fire grenade launchers, machine guns, bazookas, etc.

Here at Camp Pendleton we are sleeping in tents. If you know anything about California weather, you know it's freezing at night and hot in the day time. Needless to say, I have a dilly of a cold.

Love,
Little brother,
Paul

Dear Mom,

Well, I managed to graduate Thursday. We are now at Camp Pendleton taking advanced infantry training. We have to take this training before leaving. It will last about four weeks. I told you I was hoping to get to go to school. Well, I'm afraid they are boosting the manpower in Vietnam, so all 2, 3 and some who enlisted for 4 years are going. This, of course, includes little old me. After my leave we will be heading out right away and stopping in Okinawa. By January 12 I will be in Vietnam. I don't really like the idea but I'm going to ride with the tide and be ready for just about anything. This place is starting to get me down, but after a couple of days I'll probably be enjoying it.

Well, I'm afraid I have about drained my supply of news. Please write soon.

Your son,
Paul

Dear Mom,

I am in Vietnam. We are about one mile south of the Demilitarized Zone [DMZ] which separates North Vietnam from the south. What we are doing is just basically camping out. We go on patrols every day or night sometimes for weeks looking for the "Luke the gook." I have only been here for a week so I haven't been on any extended patrols yet.

We are set up in lean-tos. There are four of us to a hole and one man on guard all the time. We are well fortified. We have an M-60 machine gun and five M-16 rifles all locked and loaded just outside the hole. Also, we have at least 50 grenades, an anti-tank weapon and in back about 25 metres are two tanks and an Ontos (lightly armoured tracked vehicle). This is just by our hole. However, this is not always the case. We are in a regrouping area and everything is available.

Mom, remember me in your prayers. I know that with that help from you and the church I will be back.

Well, there isn't too much I can tell you about except don't worry. This is really just like a boy scout camp only it's a little more organized.

Don't worry about sending anything if you can't afford it. I understand.

Your loving son,
Paul

Dear Sue,

I'm just writing you a quick note to tell you I'm OK. I haven't received any mail from anybody since January 28 probably because my address was always changing. I am in Vietnam. I was wondering if you could send me one or two packs of pre-sweetened Kool-Aid. The water we have to drink in the field is usually rice paddy water. The gooks use human waste to fertilize their fields. Thus, the water just isn't very good. Please write me soon. Although we are kept pretty busy, we can get pretty lonely.

> Your loving brother,
> Paul

Dear Mom,

I am in Quang Tri, Vietnam, which is just south of the Demilitarized Zone. Our company isn't seeing as much action as some, but it is getting its money's worth. It is very lonely here especially since I haven't received any mail since January 28, but my address has been changing. I will be back in the United States on February 22, 1970, and I will have only one address during that time.

> Love,
> Paul

Dear Aunty Joan, Uncle Mayo and Cousins:

We've been on this operation for about a month now and it will end tomorrow. All we've been doing is walking all over Vietnam hunting for those crazy, little slant-eyed people in black.

It is really hot today. Since we have been on this operation, we haven't washed or changed our clothes and have shaved infrequently. You can probably guess we are pretty grubby and I suppose smelly, but everybody stinks so you don't notice it. On our new operation we will be on a hill which is half in Laos and half in Vietnam. The hill is 948 metres high and is supposed to be very steep.

I'm sorry this letter is so sloppy but in this heat it's even hard to breathe. I have to sign off now as we have a patrol.

> Love,
> Paul

Dear Aunty Joan, Uncle Mayo and Cousins,

We are one mile south of the DMZ and have set up a perimeter. We will be waiting here for three days while we regroup and then go on to take a place called "Mother's Ridge," which is right on the DMZ.

On the way up, which is in a convoy, we stopped in one of the villes. The older people have black teeth not from rotting but from betel nut juice. They have no dentists so when they get a toothache they chew this betel nut which is a drug. It kills the nerves in their gums and the toothache goes away. They soon become addicted to it. We saw a real good looking babe in this ville and called her over. When she smiled, it was really sad because of this betel nut juice.

We had a tiger come into our lines last night which caused a lot of havoc. It gets so dark here you can't see ten feet in front of you. Last night or the night before we had our trip lines cut around the perimeter by the gooks. Other than that there hasn't been much excitement.

All we have to eat around here is C rations so I hope I can take you on your offer for baked goods. It sure would be appreciated.

Love,
Paul

Dear Aunty Joan, Uncle Mayo and Cousins,

I'm sorry I haven't written in a little while. I'll explain. We left LZ (landing zone) Vandigriff around the 15th by chopper. It took us to Saigon which is about 7 kilometres from the Laotian border near the DMZ. To help explain what happened I'll tell approximately what I was carrying. I had on jungle utilities and boots, of course, a cartridge belt with five canteens of water, 400 rounds of machine-gun ammo, 450 rounds of M-16 ammo, three frags (grenades), one illumination grenade, two pop-up flares, two sticks of C-4 (plastic explosive), my M-16 rifle, 11 magazines, a poncho and poncho liner, a pack with three C-ration meals and five long rations, letter-writing gear, my pictures and address book, rifle-cleaning gear, machete, bayonet, and last but not least, my helmet. Everybody was humping approximately the same amount.

We left LZ Saigon about two hours after we got there and started walking to LZ Paris, which is one half a kilometre from the Laotian border. The first day was uneventful except that it was about 110 Fahrenheit and we were running out of water. It is very dry here now and the terrain is hilly, or mountainous thick jungle, so it was slow moving. The next day we started out again about six in the morning while it was cool, hoping we would run into water. Well, I was completely out of water by eight and so was nearly everyone else. At about one that afternoon we started getting heat casualties. It was the same temperature as the day before but more humid and we were trying to move too fast, so we stopped and set up a defensive perimeter. I got heat cramps in my arms, face and feet so I took off my shirt and boots to get them a little cooler. Meanwhile, they had called in a medevac (medical evacuation) chopper for the more serious cases. The chopper had to lower a pulley because the jungle was too thick to land. It took quite a while to get four people on the chopper. The gooks had seen it come down. They started firing 82-mm shells on us. Everyone had taken off their gear to help these 20 casualties from the heat and had moved them to the best clearing we could find, so our gear was about 100 metres away from where the chopper had tried to come down. It was so dry there that the mortar rounds had started a big fire which completely engulfed our gear. We retreated and about 500 metres down the trail we ran into some muddy water which everybody went wild over. I never thought I'd end up drinking that crud, but I did. I was still in bare feet but a buddy of mine had some sandals he took off a dead gook and I used them for the rest of the hump. By this time the hill was two and a half kilometres away. We arrived there without incident. We stayed on LZ Paris for three days and it was still hotter than blazes, but we had choppers bring in water which was rationed out. From our foxhole on top of the hill we could see the great big river that divides Laos from Vietnam. It sure looked good, but it was crawling with gooks.

The day after we reached LZ Paris we had to go back and try and salvage gear, so I borrowed a pair of boots and a rifle from the company that was on the hill before us. When we got to our gear, there was very little left except ashes and a few odds and ends. I found my rifle in good shape. As for my boots, all that was left of them was a melted sole. We were resupplied back at LZ Paris and we set out for LZ Tiger, which was 2 1/2 kilometres away. We travelled at night so we were cool. We ran patrols and ambushes from LZ Tiger and then moved on to LZ Chaplain. There weren't any real incidents there. We were returned by chopper to LZ Saigon, where we are running patrols and waiting for our next orders.

It's a good idea to get in the army. The marines go to an area, clear it of gooks and secure it. Then the army brings in all their gear and takes over. All the LZs I mentioned are now occupied by the army. My gear was lost in the fire, including my address book. Yours is the only address I can remember.

I am doing fine here, but I'm a little dirty and downhearted at times. The mail doesn't get here too often. Please write.

Love,
Paul

Paul Stuart Laverock was killed on 1 May 1969, at Cam Lo in Quang Tri Province, by rifle fire while on patrol. He had been in Vietnam for about two months.[15]

GARY BUTT

Theatre: Vietnam   Service: Army

Gary Butt was born on 9 May 1951 in Chateauguay, near Montreal, Quebec. His father, Gordon, had served overseas with the 17th Hussars and met his wife, Elsie, while stationed in England.

Gary wanted to learn to repair helicopters and saw service in the U.S. Army as a way to achieve this ambition. He enlisted at Plattsburgh in 1968. Gary and his family surmised that the Vietnam War would soon be over.

The U.S. Army felt that Gary could best be used as a rifleman with the 173rd Airborne Brigade. Gary went to Vietnam because he felt he owed it to the U.S. government, which had invested considerable funds in his training. He served in Vietnam from July 1970 to April 1971. He was killed 3 April while a sergeant with the 4th

Sergeant Gary Butt feeding monkey, 1970–71. He was killed in action on 3 April 1971.
E. Butt

Battalion, 503rd Infantry, 173rd Airborne Brigade.
One of his friends explained the circumstances of his death in a letter.

11 May 1971

Dear Mr. and Mrs. Butt,

I don't know if Gary ever mentioned me to you or not, but I was one of his closest friends over there. Gary wished that if something happened to him that I would write you. If something had happened to me, he would have done the same.

It was on the morning of 3 April that we engaged the enemy of approximately regimental strength. We moved out that morning – 2nd Platoon, then 1st Platoon five minutes later; 3rd Platoon stayed on a ridge to give us cover. 2nd Platoon spotted three North Vietnamese Army troops and gave chase. They were led into an ambush. The NVA were in bunker complexes and when the first GIs appeared, they blew Claymore mines and opened up with automatic-weapons fire.

Our squad was on point for our platoon. We heard the fighting and took cover. The enemy began firing mortars and rockets at us, pinning us down. They had wounded several of our friends who had walked into the ambush.

The commanding officer then asked for a volunteer squad to go down and try to bring up the badly wounded. Our squad volunteered and Gary took off first. He was greatly upset because our buddies were lying down there screaming for help.

The NVA had cleared out an opening. We crossed that opening and one fired at us. We then found a wounded man and Gary and I put him on a poncho and began dragging him back. The enemy were waiting for us at the clearing and opened up with machine gun and automatic-weapons fire. It was there that Gary fell. He was shot through the heart and died instantly.

Your son was one of the bravest persons I've ever known. He did not hesitate to give his life to save his fellow man. I'll never forget Gary.

Yours truly,
Charles Tegarden[16]

THE GULF WAR

On 2 August 1990 Iraq invaded Kuwait. When President Saddam Hussein ignored the United Nations' 15 January 1991 deadline for an Iraqi pull-out, the UN coalition began an aerial bombing campaign lasting thirty-seven days. Continued refusal by Hussein to heed the deadline to get out of Kuwait brought on-the-ground war on 23 February. During the Persian Gulf crisis American recruiters faced a flood of inquiries from young Canadians anxious to serve in the U.S. forces and see action in the Gulf. Most of the Canadians who would serve in the American forces during the Gulf War were already members of those forces when war broke out. The rest were Canadian citizens who were on assignment from their own forces to the U.S. Air Force.

Some forty-two Canadian air force personnel normally assigned to 552 AWACS (Airborne Warning and Control System) Wing at Tinker Air Force Base, Oklahoma, were assigned to the Gulf with their American crewmates. They were air defence operators and pilots who now helped staff AWACS aircraft flying from bases in Saudi Arabia and monitored air activity throughout the area. In addition, Canadian air force personnel assigned to the NATO Airborne Early Warning Force at Geilenkirchen, Germany, were redeployed to Konya, Turkey. This force, also flying AWACS aircraft, monitored air traffic over northern Iraq.

On 24 February the land war began – "the mother of all battles." On 28 February the land war was over and had become "the mother of all defeats." After about 100 hours into the ground war, President George Bush declared the Iraqi army defeated. According to American accounts, the 675,000-strong coalition of air, land and naval forces had suffered only 148 dead in combat. In contrast, the Iraqi force of some 540,000 had lost over 100,000 killed and 175,000 captured. Although Hussein was driven out of Kuwait, he was left in power.

The burned-out hulks of vehicles used by Iraqis escaping on the highway from Kuwait City to Basra.
D. Potvin

GULF WAR EXPERIENCES

BRIAN BUCKNA
Theatre: Persian Gulf   Service: Navy

I was born in Trail, British Columbia, on 3 October 1960. My parents still reside there. My mother was a U.S. citizen born in Northport, Washington.

Layoffs and no jobs were the factors in my leaving Trail. I joined the U.S. Navy in June of 1984 after moving down to Richland, Washington. I chose the navy because of its better offer of schooling. I had always been interested in the medicine field and it offered the best training.

I enjoy being a hospital corpsman – never a dull moment, plenty of travel and, at times, real excitement. I am a combat navy corpsman trained for assignments with the Fleet Marine Force. Prior to the Gulf, I was assigned to the 1st Marine Expeditionary Brigade, Brigade Service Support Group-1, 3rd Alpha Medical Company.

During the Gulf War, I was assigned to the 1st FSSG, CSS D-91, which stands for the 1st Fleet Service Support Group, Combat Service Support Detachment-91. It was composed mainly of U.S. Marine Corps military police and a detachment of military police of the Puerto Rican National Guard and eighteen active duty navy medical staff. As a result of Iraq's invasion of Kuwait, all those in my category were rounded up and assigned to marine units (1st, 2nd and 3rd FSSG). During the Gulf War, I was a hospital corpsman, second class (E-5).

Let me relate to you our living conditions in the Gulf. We lived in a general-purpose tent buried in a ten-foot-deep trench with a bunker located out to the rear of the tent. Sand was everywhere and when a sandstorm blew up, which happened four times when I was there, you had to cover your mouth in order to sleep inside the tent. The sand is so fine it is like graphite dust and even now I still can pound some out of my sea-bag. Our showers were provided by the decontamination unit, once every two weeks and for four minutes – one minute to get wet and lather up, then three to rinse.

The supply system for desert uniforms was completely screwed up. We spent the entire war dressed in jungle camouflage. This was due to the fact that everyone in the rear had two to four sets of desert cammies while we at the front ended up sitting around like shrubbery.

Our camp was located forty-two kilometres west of Al-Rah-Mashab. During the Battle of Kafji (30 January), it was overrun twice by Iraqi tank columns trying to outflank the 1st Marine Division.

Food at the front was also a horror story. The prisoners were fed better than us. One memorable incident was when two large flat-bed trucks delivered pink salmon – for the prisoners. Can you believe it? Here we were eating monotonous rations and the prisoners were enjoying delicious salmon. Needless to say, some nocturnal scrounging forays provided some salmon for the medical staff.

As for the prisoners themselves, they could be classed in three

Hospital Corpsman, Second Class, Brian Buckna, forty-seven
kilometres west of Al-Rah-Mashab, near Kabrit, Saudi Arabia,
2 February 1991.
B. Buckna

categories. The first category were those who either were captured
prior to the ground offensive or gave up voluntarily. Many of these
prisoners hadn't eaten in several days. A lot were veterans of the
Iran-Iraq war. All bore scars from the previous fighting, and many
were crippled.

The second category of POW, taken after the start of the

ground war, was only slightly better off than the first POWs. They too suffered from general unhygienic conditions, lice infestations and exposure. A lot were also suffering from combat stress and related psychological problems. Many of these Iraqi prisoners arrived without gas masks and boots. The age of these POWs ranged from thirteen to sixty-five. Also included in this group were those with war-related wounds. We treated what wounds we could and those deemed to be severe were "medevacked" to a mobile surgical hospital at Kabrit for treatment.

Category three were POWs from Kuwait City. These were the death squads or Republican Guard units that had been captured in or around Kuwait City. Their overall physical condition was very good. All were fully equipped with complete uniforms. Many spoke English and seemed somewhat relieved at being captured.

I treated one Iraqi prisoner of the first category who had had part of his right arm shot and because of this was unable to straighten his arm. I doubt that this individual could have fired his AK-47 rifle, but Saddam Hussein used him nevertheless. Most of these POWs were glad that the war was over for them.

Another story that comes to mind from this group is of an Iraqi pay officer in the first category of POWs. After putting up with round-the-clock bombing and shelling, he decided one day to give up. This he accomplished after dodging mines and Republican Guard patrols. Upon arrival at our camp, he was still in possession of his personal effects. During the interrogation and medical screening, it was discovered that he had also brought his brigade's entire payroll with him. The amount was equivalent to $20,000 in American currency. As a POW he could only keep sixty dinars. Any additional funds and possessions were generally kept in a vault until the prisoner's liberation. The pay officer expected the payroll money back upon release. He didn't get it.

I recall one incident about this second category of POW. Our medical officer brought me an eighteen-year-old Iraqi supposedly suffering from dysentery. The prisoner was brought in on a stretcher with stomach cramps and unable to keep anything down. I was chosen to sit up and observe him overnight. The prisoner seemed to be improving until he reached into his dirty uniform and took a big bite of some Redman chewing tobacco. Apparently after capture, the Iraqi prisoner had watched the marines putting the stuff in their mouths and he thought it was food. He asked for and the marine guard had given him some.

I entered the war with the general attitude that I was going to do whatever it took to come back. I was going to kill the enemy with no remorse. This attitude soon dissipated as I witnessed in horror the conditions under which these people had been driven. I could not help but feel sorry for them. These were people like myself, only they were abandoned out in the desert with one purpose – to fight and die as they were ordered. Surrender meant food and life but in order to get it they had to cross their own defences and avoid Republican Guard patrols looking for deserters. These were people truly in the middle.

I was a Canadian citizen until 30 November 1988, when I became a naturalized U.S. citizen. I am now back at Beaufort, South Carolina.[17]

LORNE SAMAHA
Theatre: Persian Gulf   Service: Marines

I was born on 29 September 1970 in San Anselmo, California. My mother is a Canadian Indian and my father is Lebanese. I have dual citizenship. I consider myself Canadian because I grew up mainly near Kamloops, British Columbia, among an Indian band. I joined the U.S. Marines on 5 July 1989 because I wanted to be a part of the corps. I enlisted for eight years – four active, four inactive. My specialty is radio operator. I was a lance corporal in Saudi Arabia for seven months as part of "Task Force Ripper" – our purpose was to rip through Iraqi lines. The force included tanks, amphibious assault vehicles, helicopters, jets and infantry. My unit, Delta Company of the Amphibious Assault (Vehicle) battalion, was attached to the 1st Battalion, 7th Marine Regiment, 1st Marine Division. We were an average of ten to twenty miles from the Kuwaiti border and moved around the desert some forty times in seven months. Between moves we trained and trained some more.

Over the period in the Gulf a lot of interesting things happened. I can still recall two incidents very vividly.

It was Christmas morning. Three other marines and I set off in our reconnaissance vehicle (HMMWV). It was 0630 hours and our mission was to find the wife of one of the marines. She was also a marine, but with another unit somewhere in the desert. We knew the name of her unit but it's a big desert. After losing our tailpipe and almost running out of fuel we finally found her at 1930 hours that night. After the visit we had to return to our camp. I'm not going to say when we got back, only the guard knows. Put it this way – if there were such things as desert roosters, they would have been crowing!

On another occasion, around 1400–1430, we had to drive into the smoke from the burning oil fields. It got darker and darker as we drove. Soon we could see nothing. Even night-vision goggles didn't work. We called it going into the "Twilight Zone" after the television program – only here there were no stars or whistling.[18]

Lance Corporal Lorne Samaha, a member of Delta Company, 3rd Amphibious Assault Vehicle Battalion, 1st Marine Division, at the port Al Jubail, 5 March 1991. He is waiting to be flown to the United States.
L.G. Samaha

CONCLUSION

TIES THAT BIND

The 10,000 or so Americans who served in the Canadian Expeditionary Force in the First World War and the some 30,000 Americans who joined one or other of the three Canadian services in the Second serve as an important link between both countries. Such links continued after the Second World War. At reunions, anniversaries and meetings of veterans' associations, bonds forged in wartime are still apparent. Ties created by common service proved the forerunner of closer political cooperation and economic association.

Since 1860 at least 60,000 Canadians and Americans have served in one another's military forces. That figure is an important reminder of our mutual support in time of war as we mark the fiftieth anniversary of the end of the Second World War. This book is a monument to their sacrifice and achievements.

The service of Canadians and Americans in one another's armed forces is but one facet of the military connections between the two countries. Relations on the personal level among citizens of both nations have proven more enduring over the long term than political differences.

War brings out the best and the worst in people. In times of crisis, to have neighbours at the individual as well as national level come forward to help is important morally and psychologically. In 1939–40 Great Britain and the Commonwealth stood alone against Nazi Germany. For Americans to have volunteered in significant numbers was a great morale booster. This country remains indebted to those who stepped forward to serve. We are the richer for having had them in this country's military forces.

APPENDIX A

CANADIAN MEDAL OF HONOR RECIPIENTS

CIVIL WAR

Name	Rank	Unit	Birth	Date of Action
Asten, Charles	Quarter Gunner	USS *Signal*	Halifax, 1834	5 May 1864
Bois, Frank	Quartermaster	USS *Cincinnati*	1841	27 May 1863
Brown, John H.	Capt	12th Kentucky Infantry	New Brunswick	30 Nov. 1864
Buckley, Denis	Pvt	136th New York Infantry		20 July 1864
Cayer, Ovila	Sgt	14th Volunteers	St. Remi, Canada East	19 Aug. 1864
Chapman, John	Pvt	1st Maine Heavy Artillery	Saint John, N.B.	10 May 1865
Chaput, Louis G.	Landsman	USS *Lackawanna*	Nova Scotia	5 Aug. 1864
Coffey, Robert J.	Sgt	4th Vermont Infantry		4 May 1863
Dodd, Robert F.	Pvt	27th Michigan Infantry		30 July 1864
Dodds, Edward E.	Sgt	21st New York Calvary	Hope Township, Canada West	19 July1864
Fitzpatrick, Thomas	Coxswain	USS *Hartford*	1837	5 Aug. 1864
Flannigan, James	Pvt	2nd Minnesota Infantry		15 Feb. 1863
Gilmore, John C.	Maj	16th New York Infantry		3 May 1863
Hagerty, Asel	Pvt	61st New York Infantry		6 April 1865
Higgins, Thomas J.	Sgt	99th Illinois Infantry		22 May 1863
Houghton, George L.	Pvt	104th Illinois Infantry		2 July 1863
McIntosh, James	Capt	USS *Richmond*		5 Aug. 1864
McMahon, Martin T.	Capt	U.S. Volunteers	La Prairie, Canada East 21 March 1838	30 June 1862
McVeane, John P.	Cpl	49th New York Infantry		4 May 1863
Murphy, James T.	Pvt	1st Connecticut Artillery		25 Mar. 1865
Neil, John	Quarter Gunner	USS *Agawam*	Newfoundland, 1837	23 Dec. 1864
O'Connor, Albert	Sgt	7th Wisconsin Infantry		31 March–1 April 1865
O'Neill, Stephen	Cpl	7th Infantry	Saint John, N.B.	1 May 1863

Name	Rank	Unit	Birth	Date of Action
Pelham, William	Landsman	USS *Hartford*	Halifax, N.S.	5 Aug. 1864
Pickle, Alonzo H.	Sgt	1st Minnesota Infantry	Dunham, Canada East	14 Aug. 1864
Powers, Wesley J.	Cpl	147th Illinois Infantry		3 April 1865
Rich, Carlos H.	1st Sgt	4th Vermont Infantry		5 May 1864
Scott, Alexander	Sgt	10th Vermont Infantry		9 July 1864
Shivers, John	Pvt	Marine Corps		15 Jan. 1866
Young, Benjamin	Cpl	1st Michigan Sharpshooters		17 June 1864

INDIAN CAMPAIGNS

Name	Rank	Unit	Birth	Date of Action
Anderson, James	Pvt	6th Cavalry	Canada East	5 Oct. 1870
Gay, Thomas H.	Pvt	8th Cavalry	P.E.I.	Aug. to Oct. 1868
Harding, Mosher A.	Blacksmith	8th Cavalry	Canada West	20 Oct. 1869
Kilmartin, John	Pvt	3rd Cavalry		5 May 1871
Mahers, Herbert	Pvt	8th Cavalry		25 Aug. 1869
McCarthy, Michael	1st Sgt	1st Cavalry	St. John's, Nfld.	June 1876 to Jan. 1877
Morgan, George H.	2nd Lt	3rd Cavalry		17 July 1882
Robinson, Joseph	Pvt	6th Cavalry		17 June 1876
Wortman, George G.	Sgt	8th Cavalry	Moncton, N.B.	Aug. to Oct. 1868

INTERIM 1871–1898

Name	Rank	Unit	Birth	Date of Action
Denham, Austin	Seaman	USS *Kansas*	England, but lived in Woodstock, Ont.	12 April 1872
Everetts, John	Gunner's Mate	USS *Cushing*	Thorold, Ont. 25 Aug. 1873	11 Feb. 1898
Kersey, Thomas	Ordinary Seaman	USS *Plymouth*	St. John's, Nfld.	26 July 1876
Low, George	Seaman	USS *Tennessee*	1847	15 Feb. 1881
Maddin, Edward	Ordinary Seaman	USS *Franklin*	Newfoundland 1852	9 Jan. 1876
Moore, Philip	Seaman	USS *Trenton*	Newfoundland 1853	21 Sept. 1880
Noil, Joseph B.	Seaman	USS *Powhatan*	Nova Scotia 1841	26 Dec. 1872

Name	Rank	Unit	Birth	Date of Action
Sweeney, Robert	Ordinary Seaman	USS *Kearsage*	Montreal 1853	26 Oct. 1881
Williams, Henry	Carpenter's Mate	USS *Constitution*	1833	18 Oct. 1884

SPANISH-AMERICAN WAR

Name	Rank	Unit	Birth	Date of Action
Campbell, Daniel	Pvt	Marine Corps	P.E.I.	11 May 1898
Cooney, Thomas C.	Chief Machinist	USS *Winslow*	Westport, N.S. 18 July 1853	11 May 1898
Miller, Harry Herbert	Seaman	USS *Nashville*	Noel Shore, N.S. 4 May 1879	11 May 1898
Miller, Willard	Seaman	USS *Nashville*	Maitland, N.S.	7 July 1899
Phillips, G.F.	Machinist 1st Class	USS *Merrimac*	St. John, N.B.	4 June 1904
Russell, Henry P.	Landsman	USS *Marblehead*	Quebec 10 June 1878	11 May 1898

MEXICAN CAMPAIGN (Vera Cruz)

Name	Rank	Unit	Birth	Date of Action
Grady, John	Lt	Navy	25 Dec 1872	22 April 1914

SECOND WORLD WAR

Name	Rank	Unit	Birth	Date of Action
Munro, Douglas Albert	Signalman, 1st Class	Coast Guard	Vancouver, B.C. Oct. 1919	27 Sept. 1942
MacGillivary, Charles A.	Sgt	44th Infantry Division	Charlottetown, P.E.I. Jan. 1917	1 Jan. 1945

KOREA

Name	Rank	Unit	Birth	Date of Action
Millett, Lewis L.	Capt	Army	Mechanic Falls, Maine Dec. 1920	7 Feb. 1951

VIETNAM

Name	Rank	Unit	Birth	Date of Action
Lemon, Peter C.	Sgt	8th Cavalry, 1st Division	Norwich, Ontario June 1950	1 April 1970

APPENDIX B

CANADIAN CASUALTIES OF THE VIETNAM WAR*

VIETNAM VETERANS MEMORIAL

Name	Rank	Service	Panel	Line	Date of Birth	Date of Death
ANDERSON, John Austin	SP-4	Army	59E	16	10 Feb 47	13 May 68
BARTALOTTI, Alfonso Paul	PFC	Army	30E	95	02 Apr 43	27 Nov 67
BASTARACHE, Fidele Joseph	Cpl.	Army	65W	5	11 Feb 46	27 May 68
BEAUDOIN, Gaetan	Sgt.	Army	19W	16	05 Sep 48	26 Aug 69
BENCHER, Alvin Kenneth	Sgt.	Army	54W	36	03 Apr 40	02 Jul 68
BERNARD, Vincent	L. Cpl.	USMC	43W	51	07 Sep 45	21 Sep 68
BLANCHETTE, Guy André	Sgt.	Army	19W	17	30 Nov 46	26 Aug 69
BOLDUC, Daniel Alphonse	Cpl.	Army	20W	13	03 Feb 46	29 Jul 69
BOMBERRY, Gregory Lee	Sgt.	Army	45W	48	04 Apr 47	06 Sep 68
BROEFFLE, Ivan Clifford	Cpl.	Army	57E	15	20 Mar 46	09 May 68
BROWN, Thomas Edward	S. Sgt.	Army	15W	13	21 Mar 46	02 Dec 69
BRUYERE, Peter Norbert	SP-4	Army	10W	94	15 May 51	25 May 70
BUTT, Gary	S. Sgt.	Army	4W	103	09 May 51	03 Apr 71
CAMPBELL, Michael Frances	PFC	Army	52E	15	08 Apr 42	26 Apr 68

* The list originally appeared as an appendix to my *Unknown Warriors* (1990). Some readers have sent in additional names. Should anyone know of others, please contact the author.

Name	Rank	Service	Panel	Line	Date of Birth	Date of Death
CAMPBELL, Randall Kenneth	L. Cpl.	USMC	1E	109	18 Sep 44	25 Apr 65
CARON, Bernard John	S. Sgt.	Army	38E	48	10 Oct 36	09 Feb 68
CHAMBERLAIN, Dale Stewart	SP-4	Army	7W	91	08 Jul 49	25 Sep 70
COLLINS, Larry Richard	SP-4	Army	26W	90	15 Jul 46	01 May 69
COLLINS, Mark Paine	SP-4	Army	64E	12	01 Oct 46	21 May 68
CONRAD, Andrew Charles, Jr	SP-5	Army	24E	94	07 Nov 31	09 Aug 67
CORBIERE, Austin Morris	L. Cpl.	USMC	7E	42	19 Feb 43	09 May 66
CORBIN, Normand Alfred	L. Cpl.	USMC	20W	00	16 Jun 48	06 Aug 69
CRABBE, Frank Edward	PFC	USMC	5E	40	20 Jun 46	16 Feb 66
DAVIES, Donald Paul	SP-5	Army	21W	32	05 Oct 48	29 Jun 69
DEARBORN, Patrick John	L. Cpl.	USMC	29E	9	17 Nov 48	02 Nov 67
DELMARK, Francis John	L. Cpl.	USMC	2E	5	05 Nov 42	18 Aug 65
DEVANEY, Brian John	CWO	Army	10W	120	14 Jun 46	30 May 70
DEVOE, Douglas Wayne	PFC	USMC	41W	15	02 Nov 48	05 Oct 68
DEXTRAZE, Richard Paul	L. Cpl.	USMC	26W	31	09 May 47	23 Apr 69
DICKIE, Guy Douglas	Pvt.	USMC	38E	25	04 Mar 48	08 Feb 68
DUNN, Michael John	SP-4	Army	34E	76	20 Sep 46	19 Jan 68
EADIE, Gordon Patterson	L. Cpl.	USMC	24E	113	11 Apr 47	15 Aug 67

Name	Rank	Service	Panel	Line	Date of Birth	Date of Death
FRANCIS, John Fredric	Lt.	Navy	11E	109	12 Apr 33	26 Oct 66
FRASER, Thomas Edwin	Pvt.	USMC	12W	92	16 Jun 51	04 Apr 70
FRIGAULT., Joseph O.	S. Sgt.	Army	20E	15	12 Oct 26	17 May 67
GAUTHIER, Gérard Louis	AlC	USAF	25E	99	24 Mar 46	04 Sep 67
GENERAL, Leslie Neil	Cpl.	USMC	53E	31	26 Jun 46	01 May 68
GOODWIN, Danny Eric	L. Cpl.	USMC	25E	38	28 Apr 47	24 Aug 67
GRAHAM, Gilbert James	SN	Navy	27E	24	24 Feb 46	28 Sep 67
GREEN, Larry	PFC	USMC	35W	60	15 Jun 45	09 Jan 69
HATTON, Randolph Edward	PFC	Army	39W	16	15 Dec 39	14 Nov 68
HAWES, Wayne Lindsay	SP-4	Army	35W	16	03 Sep 34	01 Jan 69
HOLDITCH, Robert Wilson	CWO	Army	21W	45	04 Feb 33	02 Jul 69
HOUSE, Willis Francis	M. Sgt.	Army	29W	30	30 May 24	13 Mar 69
JMAEFF, George Victor	Cpl.	USMC	30W	4	14 Aug 45	01 Mar 69
JOBEY, Andrew John	PFC	Army	52E	2	15 May 49	29 Apr 68
KELLAR, Harry David	PFC	USMC	31W	51	05 May 49	25 Feb 69
KELLY, John William	Cpl.	Army	13W	15	19 May 45	15 Feb 70
KENNEDY, Bruce Thomas	PFC	USMC	46W	31	08 Jan 49	26 Aug 68
KENNY, Robert W.	Sgt.	Army	14E	74	19 Mar 42	24 Jan 67
KMETYK, Jonathan Peter	L. Cpl.	USMC	29E	96	17 Aug 47	14 Nov 67

Name	Rank	Service	Panel	Line	Date of Birth	Date of Death
KROISENBACHER, Adolf J.	L. Cpl.	USMC	30W	66	26 Nov 38	07 Mar 69
LAVEROCK, Paul Stuart	PFC	USMC	26W	91	27 Oct 48	01 May 69
LAWSON, Darryl Dean	Cpl.	USMC	26E	79	26 Dec 42	16 Sep 67
LOW, Kevin Douglas	Sgt.	Army	21W	29	24 Apr 49	28 Jun 69
LUKEY, Geoffrey John	L. Cpl.	USMC	17W	46	6 Aug 49	06 Oct 69
MacGLASHAN, John Williams	T. Sgt.	USAF	74E	73	27 Jun 29	03 Aug 67
McINTOSH, Ian	WO	Army	6W	9	21 Sep 45	24 Nov 70
MANNING, David Karl	L. Cpl.	USMC	35W	6	17 Jun 48	10 Jan 69
MARIER, Maurice John	SP-4	Army	15W	48	09 May 48	16 Feb 67
MARSHALL, Joseph Kenny, III	1 Lt.	Army	5W	118	30 Dec 48	18 Feb 71
MASTERSON, Michael John	LTC	USAF	41W	61	16 May 37	13 Oct 68
McSORLEY, Rob George	SP-4	Army	12W	107	26 Mar 51	08 Apr 70
MARTIN, Alan, Jr.	Sgt.	USAF	29W	15	21 Jul 46	08 Mar 69
MITCHELL, Cyril, Jr.	SP-4	Army	44W	27	16 Aug 47	11 Sep 68
MONETTE, R. Albert	SP-4	Army	28W	113	28 Feb 50	06 Mar 72
MORIN, Donald William	L. Cpl.	USMC	13W	20	26 Feb 49	16 Feb 70
NESBITT, Calvin Ian	PFC	USMC	52E	22	07 Jan 49	26 Apr 68
NICHOLSON, James Paton	PFC	USMC	54E	14	29 Jan 48	02 May 68
PERSICKE, Allan Wayne	SP-4	Army	18W	55	25 Jan 49	07 Sep 69

Name	Rank	Service	Panel	Line	Date of Birth	Date of Death
PISACRETA, Roger Melvin	CWO	Army	4W	45	06 Jun 40	10 Mar 71
PRICE, William Marshall	1 Lt.	USMC	1W	82	24 Aug 45	12 Oct 72
REEVES, John Howard	L. Cpl.	USMC	37E	76	28 Oct 43	23 Dec 66
ROBSON, William Reid	Lt.	Navy	37E	67	22 Nov 28	06 Feb 68
RODEN, John Joseph	Sgt.	Army	17W	69	02 Mar 43	11 Oct 69
SANTORO, Robert John	SP-4	Army	48W	15	19 May 46	14 Aug 68
SAULER, Charlie F.	SP-4	Army	27E	50	22 Sep 39	04 Oct 67
SAUVE, Daniel Louis	PFC	USMC	6E	127	15 Oct 47	21 Apr 66
SCOTT, Steven Joseph	L. Cpl.	USMC	52W	32	30 Jan 50	14 Jul 68
SEMENIUK, Larry Stephen	Cpl.	Army	34E	64	14 May 49	17 Jan 68
SCHMIDT, Dennis Richard	Cpl.	USMC	9E	117	06 Jan 45	08 Aug 66
SHARPE, Edward Gerald	PFC	USMC	18E	88	30 Apr 48	25 Apr 67
SHAW, Gary Francis	PFC	Army	29E	76	13 Mar 48	11 Nov 67
SHERIN, John C., III	WO	Army	42W	64	09 Jun 41	02 Oct 68
SMITH, Eldon Wayne	Sgt.	USMC	41W	20	13 Jul 47	06 Oct 68
SOMERS, Frank J.	S. Sgt.	Army	14E	77	24 Jun 36	25 Jan 67
SOSNIAK, Tadeusz	M. Sgt.	Army	45W	10	09 Jan 41	30 Aug 68
STALINSKI, Stefan Z.	PFC	USMC	2E	32	29 May 45	08 Jul 65
STEEL, Robert James	PFC	Army	11E	47	28 Mar 47	04 Oct 68

Name	Rank	Service	Panel	Line	Date of Birth	Date of Death
STURDY, Alan MacDonald	Sgt.	Army	22E	116	21 Jan 45	02 Jul 67
SUTHONS, Melvin Harold	PFC	USMC	2E	13	03 Feb 44	18 Jun 65
THORSTEINSON, Vernon J.	Cpl.	USMC	24E	104	07 Feb 45	12 Aug 67
VIDLER, Murray D.	PFC	USMC	32E	28	06 May 46	14 Dec 67
WARREN, Baxter	Sgt.	Army	12W	50	02 Apr 48	27 Mar 70
WELSH, Rutherford J.	WO	Army	4E	82	09 Jun 42	27 Jul 66
WHITE, Gordon Glenn	L. Cpl.	USMC	29W	26	25 Sep 45	12 Mar 69
WILLIAMS, Richard C.	PFC	Army	15W	127	18 Jun 45	04 Jan 70
WILLIAMS, Thomas Murray	Sgt.	Army	9E	35	27 Apr 28	18 Jul 66
YOUNG, Gerald Francis	L. Cpl.	USMC	48E	37	10 May 47	06 Apr 68

APPENDIX C

MEDAL OF HONOR RECIPIENTS INTERRED IN CANADA

Name	Edward E. Dodds
Place and Date of Birth	Hope Township, Canada West, 1845
Unit	21st New York Cavalry
Place and Date of Action	Ashby's Gap, Virginia, 19 July 1864
Date of Death	12 January 1901
Place of Burial	Canton Cemetery, near Port Hope, Ontario

Name	George F. Phillips
Place and Date of Birth	Saint John, 19 March 1864
Unit	USS *Merrimac*
Place and Date of Action	Santiago de Cuba, 2 June 1898
Date of Death	5 June 1904
Place of Burial	Fern Hill Cemetery, Saint John, New Brunswick

Name	Charles Robinson
Place and Date of Birth	Scotland, 1832
Unit	USS *Baron de Kalb*
Place and Date of Action	Yazoo River, Mississippi, 23-27 December 1862
Date of Death	21 April 1896
Place of Burial	Holy Cross Cemetery, Halifax

Name	Horatio N. Young
Place and Date of Birth	Calais, Maine, 19 July 1845
Unit	USS *Lehigh*
Place and Date of Action	Charleston, South Carolina, 16 November 1863
Date of Death	3 July 1913
Place of Burial	Rural Cemetery, St. Stephen, New Brunswick

APPENDIX D

AMERICAN VICTORIA CROSS RECIPIENTS

Name	Frederick George Coppins
Place and Date of Birth	San Francisco, 25 October 1889
Unit	8th Battalion
Place and Date of Action	East of Amiens, 9 August 1918
Date of Death	30 March 1963
Place of Burial	Greenlawn Cemetery, Livermore, California

Name	Bellenden Seymour Hutchison
Place and Date of Birth	Mount Carmel, Illinois, 16 December 1883
Unit	Canadian Army Medical Corps (attached to 75th Battalion)
Place and Date of Action	D-Q Line, France, 2 September 1918
Date of Death	9 April 1954
Place of Burial	Mount Carmel Cemetery, Mount Carmel, Illinois

Name	William H. Metcalf
Place and Date of Birth	Lewiston, Maine, 29 January c. 1897–98
Unit	16th Battalion
Place and Date of Action	D-Q Line, France, 2 September 1918
Date of Death	8 August 1968
Place of Burial	Bayside Cemetery, Eastport, Maine

Name	George H. Mullin
Place and Date of Birth	Portland, Oregon, 15 August 1892
Unit	Princess Patricia's Canadian Light Infantry
Place and Date of Action	Passchendaele, 30 October 1917
Date of Death	5 April 1963
Place of Burial	South Cemetery, Moosmin, Saskatchewan

Name	Raphael Louis Zengel
Place and Date of Birth	Fairbault, Minnesota, 11 November 1894
Unit	5th Battalion
Place and Date of Action	Warvillers, 9 August 1918
Date of Death	22 February 1977
Place of Burial	Errington, B.C.

NOTES

Abbreviations

AO   Archives of Ontario
CHR   *Canadian Historical Review*
NA   National Archives of Canada

Part One: From the American Civil War until the Second World War

1. *Encyclopedia Americana*, 1962, see "Civil War in America," 7.
2. See Robin Winks, "The Creation of Myth: Canadian Enlistments in the Northern Armies during the American Civil War," *CHR* 39 (March 1958): 24–40; Robin Winks, *Canada and the United States* (Baltimore, 1960), chap. 10; Ella Lonn, *Foreigners in the Union Army and Navy* (Baton Rouge, 1951), 2 and Appendix A.
3. See Betty Fladeland, "Alias Franklin Thompson," *Michigan History* 42, no. 4 (December 1958): 435–62; G.L. Sylvia Dannett, *She Rode with the Generals* (New York, 1960); and S.E. Edmonds, *Nurse and Spy* (Hartford, 1865).
4. Robin Winks, *The Blacks in Canada: A History* (Montreal, 1971).
5. Alfred F. Armstrong Diaries, AO, MU-838.
6. Mary L. Mark, *Dr. Newton Wolverton* (Woodstock, 1985); F.B. Heitman, *Historical Register and Dictionary of the United States Army* (Washington, 1903), 324.
7. G.L. Trigg, *Huff Genealogy: Descendants of Engelbert Huff of Dutchess County, New York* (Bowie, Md., 1992).
8. NA, Carman Miller's Guide and RG 38, Attestation Papers for South African War; see also C. Miller, *Painting the Map Red* (Montreal, 1993), 446.
9. S.F. Wise, *Canadian Airmen and the First World War* (Toronto, 1980), 88–89.
10. R.G. Haycock, *Sam Hughes*, Canadian War Museum Historical Publication No. 21 (Waterloo, 1986), 220–21.
11. NA, RG 24, vol. 6561, Colonel H.C. Osborne, secretary, Imperial War Graves Commission, report for the minister (Americans in Canadian forces), 14 October 1927.
12. G.W.L. Nicholson, *Canadian Expeditionary Force* (Ottawa, 1962), 347.
13. *Selective Service Regulations*, 2d ed. (Washington, D.C.: U.S. Government Printing Office, 1918), 122–23.

14. James Farrell, "Oliver C. 'Boots' LeBoutillier," *Cross and Cockade Journal* 24, no. 3 (Autumn 1983). See also D. Hist., Biog. File, Leboutillier, Oliver; Curtis Kinney, "I Fought the Red Baron," *The American Legion Magazine*, December 1968, 30–45.

15. See R.T. Chandler's record of military service, National Personnel Records Centre (Ottawa) and "R.T. Chandler," *Encyclopaedia Britannica*, vol. 2, 15th ed., 1979.

16. NA, George V. Bell fonds (MG 30, E 113), excerpts from the unpublished manuscript, "Back to Blighty."

17. Letter from Claire Leblanc, senior research clerk, National Personnel Records Centre, 24 July 1991.

18. John Swettenham, ed., *Valiant Men: Canada's Victoria Cross and George Cross Winners* (Toronto, 1973), 83, 115, 135, 139; George Machum, *Canada's V.C.'s* (Toronto, 1956), 86, 118, 132, 142. See also VC files, Canadian War Museum Archives.

19. NA, RG 24, vol. 6561, file HQ 899–90, vol. 2, H.C. Osborne, secretary, Imperial War Graves Commission (Canada), to J.L. Ralston, minister of national defence, 14 October 1927; see also RG 24, vol. 1753, DHS 27-25, Colonel A. Fortescue Duguid, director historical section, to Dr. A.G. Doughty, Dept. of Public Archives, 7 June 1933; see RG 24, vol. 6561, file HQ 899–80, vol. 2. Notes compiled by Historical Section (General Staff), Department of National Defence, 17 October 1927.

20. *Gazette* (Montreal), 15 November 1927.

21. NA, RG 24, vol. 6530, HQ 512-27-1, D.F. Davis, 11 November 1927; Vincent Massey, *What's Past Is Prologue* (Toronto: Macmillan, 1963), 141–43; see file, Canadian Cross of Sacrifice, Center of Military History, Dept. of the Army, Washington, D.C.

Part Two: The Second World War, 1939–1945

1. Originally, the U.S. military aviation division was part of the signals branch of the army. In the light of American experience in the First World War, the United States Army Air Service came into existence as a separate arm of the U.S. Army. On 2 July 1926 it became the U.S. Army Air Corps, and on 9 March 1942 the U.S. Army Air Forces (USAAF). The United States Air Force came into being on 18 September 1947.

2. NA, RG 24, vol. 18,826 (formerly D. Hist. file 133.065, D667); Recruiting in the United States of America, unpublished narrative (1945), D. Hist. 74/7, vol. 3, 542, 605–12.

3. W.A.B. Douglas. *The Creation of a National Air Force* (Toronto, 1986), Appendix C.

4. Letter from Claire Leblanc, senior research clerk, National Personnel Records Centre, 12 October 1993.

5. U.S. Selective Service System, *Problems of Selective Service,* vol. 1 (Washington, 1952), 123–24.

6. Letter from Richard Dunham, 18 June 1991.

7. Letter from Ben Brinkworth, 13 March 1991.

8. Letter from Terry Goodwin, 4 June 1991.

9. Letter from John Dacy, 5 April 1991.

10. Interview with James Hunter, 14 May 1992.

11. Letter from Hollis Hills, 15 June 1994.

12. Letters from Robert Gladnick, 13 March and 15 April 1992.

13. Excerpts from Gwilym Jones, *To the Green Fields and Beyond: A Soldier's Story* (Burnstown, Ont.: General Store Publishing Co., 1993).

14. Letter from Lionel Proulx, 13 July 1992.

15. Letter from Malcolm Hormats, 25 October 1993.

16. Letter from Betty Compton, 15 October 1991.

17. Letter from Clyde East, 21 April 1994.

18. D.A. Munro file, U.S. Coast Guard, Washington, D.C.

19. Letters from John Reynolds, 20 April and 7 May 1991.

20. Letters from Hubert Lewis, 17 and 19 March 1991.

21. Letter from Don Vogel, 26 June 1992.

22. Letter from Bruce Betcher, 16 May 1994.

23. Letter from Harold Makinson, 11 July 1991.

24. Letter from Bud Milligan, 4 February 1992.

25. Letter from Billy Hopkins, 8 July 1991.

26. Letter from John Wright, 28 December 1992.

27. Letter from Gerald Clough, 10 October 1991.

28. Letter from Craig Smith, 17 March 1992.

29. Letter from David Lewis, 29 July 1991.

30. Letter from John Tate, 6 October 1993.

31. Letter from William Fossey, 13 April 1991.

32. Letter from Harold Wilson, 22 February 1994.

33. Letter from Beryl Diamond, 19 April 1991.

34. Letter from Malcus Horton, 11 November 1993.

35. Letter from Charles A. MacGillivary, 16 January 1991.

36. Letter from Lucien Thomas, 11 August 1992.

Part Three: From Korea and Vietnam to the Persian Gulf

1. Letter from Frank Cassidy, 16 June 1994.

2. Letter from Peter G. Chance, 18 January 1993.

3. *Ottawa Citizen,* 8 April 1978.

4. D. Hist., Biog. File, Commander Peter G. Chance of Sidney, B.C.

5. Letter from Lewis Millett, 15 February 1991.

6. Letter from George Odom, 8 January 1991.

7. Letter from Keith Daniels, 4 July 1994.

8.   Letter from Bernard Schmidt, 18 March 1993.
9.   Letter from James MacKay, 10 February 1994.
10. Letter from David Ford, 6 June 1994.
11. Letter from Alex Kandic, 7 March 1994.
12. Letter from Kenneth Lewis, 7 October 1992.
13. Letter from Dorilla Bastarache, 19 July 1993; James Dempsey, "Veterans Without a Country," *Worcester Telegram and Gazette*, 30 June 1993.
14. Letter from Mrs. Fran Masterson, 12 August 1993.
15. Letter from Margaret Laverock, 12 March 1993.
16. Enclosed in a letter from Mrs. Gordon Butt, 10 October 1990.
17. Letter from Brian Buckna, 18 June 1991.
18. Letter from Lorne Samaha, 10 July 1991.

BIBLIOGRAPHY

PRIMARY SOURCES

National Archives of Canada (NA)

MG 40 DI, vol. 15, contains photocopies of correspondence between British and American officials relating to training facilities in Texas. The originals of the copies are held by the Public Record Office.

RG 24, Department of National Defence – Army Series.

Contingents – 213th Battalion CEF (American) – General /1916/ RG 24, vol. 4435, file MD3 26-6-75, pt. 1.

Disposition of American Officers who have resigned or who have been struck off strength of the CEF /1916/ RG 24, vol. 1127, file HQ 54 21-50-14, pt. 1.

97th, 211th, 212th, 213th and 237th Battalions (American Legion) / RG 24, vol. 1827, file GAQ 71, pt. 1.

Americans in Canadian Army to be released to serve with United States / 1916–17/ RG 24, vol. 1127, file HQ54 21-50-10, pt. 1.

Proposed acceptance of Americans, Russian, Serbian and Poles from United States for Overseas Services /1914–1920/ RG 24, vol. 2543, file HQS 1562.

Number of Americans enlisted in the CEF and list of casualties of those enlisted /1917–1921/ RG 24, vol. 288, file HQ13, 145, pt. 1.

Army – Misleading inducements to American Recruits /1916–1917/ RG 24, vol. 182, file HQ 19-82-156, pt. 1.

American flags not to be used by American Battalions, CEF vols. 2–5 /1916/ RG 24, vol. 5912, file HQ 501 23, pt. 2.

Discharge of Americans in CEF /1917–1919/ RG 24, vol. 4364, file MD2 34-7-14-2, pt. 1.

Return of Recruits enlisted in the U.S., boxes 4312–13 /1917–1918/ RG 24, vol. 4312, file MD2 34-1-59 R1.

Recruiting U.S. recruits /1917–1918/ RG 24, vol. 4585, file MD102R7, pt. 1.

Recruiting in the United States /1916-1917/ RG 24, vol. 4552, file MD6 12-51-66, pt. 1.

Cross of Sacrifice, Arlington Cemetery, Persons born in U.S. enlisted in CEF /1927–1933/ RG 24, vol. 1753, file DHS 7-25, pt. 1.

Citizens of U.S. serving with Canadian contingent WW I /1914/ RG 24, vol. 1241, file HQ 593-1-43, pt. 1.

Offer of Canadians in St. Louis, Missouri, United States to purchase and equip an Armoured Motor Car and men to operate same for WWI /1914–1915/ RG 24, vol. 1037, file HQ 54-21-33-18, pt. 1.

Diaries

Alfred F. Armstrong Diaries, 5 vols., Archives of Ontario (MU 838).

George V. Bell. "Back to Blighty," NA, MG 30 E 113.

Clayton Knight Papers. U.S.A.F. Historical Research Center, Maxwell Air Force Base, Alabama.

SECONDARY SOURCES

Articles

Armstrong, Kenneth. "Canada and the Civil War." *Jackdaw*, no. C17, Clarke, Irwin, 1969.

Boebert, Earl. "The Eagle Squadrons." *American Aviation Historical Society* 9, no. 2 (1st quarter, 1964): 3-20.

Bovey, W. "Confederate Agents in Canada during the American Civil War." *Canadian Historical Review* 2, no. 1 (March 1921): 46–57.

Brooks, Tom. "British North Americans (Canadians) in the American Civil War." *Camp Chase Gazette*, June 1991.

Browning, R.M. "Semper Paratus: Douglas Munro." *Naval History*, Winter 1992, 73–74.

Christie, Carl. "Ferry Command." In *The Canadian Encyclopedia*, 2d ed., vol. 2 (Edmonton, 1988), 760.

Farrell, James. "Oliver C. 'Boots' LeBoutillier." *Cross and Cockade Journal* 24, no. 3 (Autumn 1983): 285.

Fladeland, Betty. "Alias Franklin Thompson." *Michigan History* 42, no. 4 (December 1958): 435–62.

Fleming Doris, ed. "Letters from a Canadian Recruit in the Union Army." *Tennessee Historical Quarterly* 16 (June 1957): 159–66.

Gaffen, Fred. "Yanks in Canada's Fighting Forces." *VFW Magazine* 79, no. 3 (November 1991): 22–41.

Garnett, Stephen. "John Magee – The Pilot Poet." *This England Magazine*, Spring 1989.

Granatstein, J.L. "The American Influence on the Canadian Military, 1939–1963." *Canadian Military History* 2, no. 1 (Spring 1993): 63–73.

Gundy, H. Pearson. "A Queen's Medical Student in the Army of the Potomac, 1863–64." *Douglas Library Notes* 6 (December 1957): 3–8.

————. "A Kingston Surgeon in the American Civil War." *Historic Kingston* 7 (1958): 43–52.

Halliday, Hugh A. "Canada's Yank: Lieutenant A.A. Harrington." *Aerospace Historian* 18, no. 2 (June 1971): 75–80.

Hamer, M.B. "Luring Canadian Soldiers into Union Lines during the War between the States." *Canadian Historical Review* 27, no. 2 (June 1946): 150–62.

Hatch, F.J. "Recruiting Americans for the Royal Canadian Air Force, 1939–42." *Aerospace Historian* 17 (March 1971): 12.

Haycock, Ronald G. "The American Legion in the Canadian Expeditionary Force 1914–1917: A Study in Failure." *Military Affairs* 43, no. 3 (October 1979): 115–19.

Katz, M. "The Mysterious Prisoner: Assassination Suspect J.G. Ryan." *Civil War Times Illustrated* 21, no. 7 (November 1982): 40–43.

Kinney, Curtis. "I Fought the Red Baron." *American Legion Magazine*, December 1968, 30–45.

Lammers, P. "Alias Franklin Thompson: A Female in the Ranks." *Civil War Times Illustrated* 22 (1984): 24–31.

Levin, A.L. "The Canada Contact: Edwin Gray Lee." *Civil War Times Illustrated* 18, no. 3 (1979): 5–8, 42–47.

McCulloch, Ian. "Canadians in Blue and Grey." *Civil War* 11, no. 5, issue 43 (September-October 1993): 18–22, 52–53.

Milani, Lois Darroch. "Four Who Went to the Civil War." *Ontario History* 51 (Autumn 1959): 259–72.

Morgan, Len. "Harvard Graduate." *Flying* 116, no. 2: 82–83.

Moxley, Andrew, and Tom Brooks. "Drums Across the Border: Canadians in the Civil War." *Canadian Military Then and Now* 1, no. 6 (November 1991): 59–60.

Raney, W.F. "Recruiting and Crimping in Canada from the Northern Forces, 1861–1865." *Mississippi Valley Historical Review* 10, no. 1 (June 1923): 21–33.

Saunders, Andy. "John Gillespie Magee." *After the Battle*, vol. 16 (1989), pt. 63, 43–54.

Shannon, Norman. "Strong Deliverers." *Esprit de Corps* 2, no. 10 (March 1993): 22–24.

Sweetman, John. "Canadian Target: RCAF Attacks on the Sorpe Dam, 17 May 1943." *Canadian Defence Quarterly* 22, no. 6 (July 1993): 31–36.

Taylor, Stewart K. "Filley: America's First RFC Warbird." *Over the Front*, Winter 1992, 328–37.

Books

Alexander, R.L. *They Called Me Dixie*. Hemet, Calif.: Robinson Typographics, 1988.

Axelrod, Alan. *The War between the Spies: A History of Espionage during the American Civil War*. New York: Atlantic Monthly Press, 1992.

Berman, Susan. *Easy Street: The True Story of a Mob Family*. New York: Dial Press, 1981.

Blais, Pierre. *Loup solitaire. Un mercenaire québécoise pleure le Viêt-Nam*. Montréal: VLB éditeur, 1991.

Bothwell, Robert. *Canada and the United States: The Politics of Partnership*. Toronto: University of Toronto Press, 1992.

Burke, L.G., and R.C. Curtis eds. *The American Beagle Squadron*. Lexington, MA: The American Beagle Squadron Association, 1987.

Caine, Philip D. *Eagles of the RAF: The World War II Eagle Squadrons*. Washington D.C.: National Defense University Press, 1991.

Callender, Gordon W., Jr., and Gordon W. Callender, Sr., eds. *War in an Open Cockpit*. West Roxbury, Mass.: World War I Aero Publishers, 1979.

Cardoulis, John N. *A Friendly Invasion: The American Military in Newfoundland, 1940–1990*. St. John's: Breakwater Books, 1990.

Childers, J.S. *War Eagles*. New York: D. Appleton-Century, 1943.

Cleveland, Bill. *Mosquitos in Korea*. Farmington, Conn.: The Mosquito Association, 1994.

Crichton, Robert. *The Great Impostor*. New York: Random House, 1959.

Cuff, R.D., and J.L. Granatstein. *Ties That Bind: Canadian-American Relations in Wartime from the Great War to the Cold War*. 2d ed. Toronto: Samuel, Stevens, Hakkert and Company, 1977.

Curtis, Lettice. *The Forgotten Pilots*. Henley-on-Thames, England: G.T. Foulis, 1971.

Dannett, G.L. Sylvia. *Noble Women of the North*. New York: Thomas Yoseloff, 1959.

———. *She Rode with the Generals*. New York: Thomas Nelson and Sons, 1960.

Darroch, Lois. *Four Went to the Civil War*. Kitchener, Ont.: McBain, 1985.

Douglas, W.A.B. *The Creation of a National Air Force: The Official History of the Royal Canadian Air Force*. Vol. 2. Toronto: University of Toronto Press, 1986.

Dziuban, S.W. *Military Relations between the United States and Canada, 1939–1945.* Washington, D.C.: Department of the Army, 1959.

Edmonds, S. Emma E. *Nurse and Spy in the Union Army: Comprising the Adventures and Experiences of a Woman in Hospitals, Camps and Battlefields.* Hartford, Conn.: W.S. Williams and Co., 1865.

Empey, A.G. *From the Fire Step: The Experiences of an American Soldier in the British Army.* New York: G.P. Putnam's Sons, 1917.

————. *Over the Top by an American Soldier Who Went.* New York: G.P. Putnam's Sons, 1917.

Franklin, H. Bruce. *MIA or Mythmaking in America.* New York: Lawrence Hill Books, 1992.

Gaffen, Fred. *Forgotten Soldiers.* Penticton, B.C.: Theytus Books, 1985.

————. *Unknown Warriors: Canadians in the Vietnam War.* Toronto: Dundurn Press, 1990.

Granatstein, J.L., and Norman Hillmer. *For Better or for Worse: Canada and the United States to the 1990s.* Toronto: Copp Clark Pitman, 1991.

Hartney, Harold E. *Up and At 'Em.* Harrisburg, Pa.: Stackpole Sons, 1940.

Haughland, Vern. *The Eagle Squadrons: Yanks in the RAF, 1940–1942.* New York: Zift-Davis Flying Books, 1979.

Hillmer, Norman, ed. *Partner Nevertheless: Canadian-American Relations in the Twentieth Century.* Toronto: Copp Clark Pitman, 1989.

Hoehling, Mary. *Girl Soldier and Spy: Sarah Emma Edmundson.* New York: Julian Messner, 1959.

Hudson, James J. *In Clouds of Glory: American Airmen Who Flew with the British during the Great War.* Fayetteville: University of Arkansas Press, 1990.

Johnson, Charles Monroe. *Action with the Seaforths.* New York: Vantage Press, 1954.

Kennerly, Byron. *The Eagles Roar!* Washington D.C.: Zenger Publishing, 1941.

Lambert, W.C. *Combat Report.* London: William Kimber, 1973.

Lynch, John William. *Princess Patricia's Canadian Light Infantry, 1917–19: The Exciting Story of an American Volunteer in the Canadian Army during World War I.* Hicksville, N.Y.: Exposition Press, 1976.

MacShane, Frank. *The Life of Raymond Chandler.* New York: E.P. Dutton, 1976.

Mark, Mary L. *Dr. Newton Wolverton: A Life of Service.* Woodstock, Ont.: Nethercott Press, 1985.

Milberry, Larry, and Hugh Halliday. *The Royal Canadian Air Force at War, 1939–1945.* Toronto: CANAV Books, 1990.

Murphy, Edward F. *Korean War Heroes*. Novato, Calif.: Presidio, 1992.

Preston, R.A. *The Defence of the Undefended Border: Planning for War in North America, 1867–1939*. Montreal: McGill-Queen's University Press, 1977.

Roberts, E.M. *A Flying Fighter: An American above the Lines in France*. New York: Harper and Brothers, 1918.

Shores, Christopher, and Clive Williams. *Aces High: The Fighter Aces of the British and Commonwealth Air Forces in World War II*. London: Neville Spearman, 1966.

Smith, Donald B. *Long Lance: The True Story of an Imposter*. Toronto: Macmillan, 1982.

Smith, Joseph S. *Over There and Back in Three Uniforms: Being the Experiences of an American Boy in the Canadian, British and American Armies at the Front and Through No Man's Land*. New York: E.P. Dutton, 1918.

United States Selective Service System. *Problems of Selective Service*, 3 vols. Washington: United States Government Printing Office, 1952.

Valencia, Gene. *Fred Libby: The Flying Buckaroo*. Chula Vista, Calif.: Valor Productions, 1970.

Wheelwright, Julie. *Amazons and Military Maids: Women Who Dressed as Men in the Pursuit of Life, Liberty and Happiness*. London: Pandora, 1989.

Winks, Robin W. *Canada and the United States, the Civil War Years*. Baltimore: John Hopkins Press, 1960.

———. *The Blacks in Canada: A History*. Montreal: McGill-Queen's University Press, 1971.

Wise, S.F. *Canadian Airmen and the First World War: The Official History of the Royal Canadian Air Force*. Vol. 1. Toronto: University of Toronto Press, 1980.

Wolverton, A.N. *Dr. Newton Wolverton*. Vancouver: privately published, 1933.

CONTRIBUTORS

Fidele Bastarache

Bruce Betcher

Ben Brinkworth

Brian Buckna

Gary Butt

Frank Cassidy

Gerald Clough

Archie Melville Compton

John Dacy

Keith Daniels

Beryl Diamond

Guy Dickie

Richard Dunham

Clyde East

William Fossey

Robert Gladnick

Terry Goodwin

Hollis Hills

Billy Hopkins

Malcolm Hormats

Malcus Horton

James Hunter

Gwilym Jones

Alexander Kandic

Paul Stewart Laverock

David Lewis

Hubert Lewis

Kenneth Lewis

Charles A. MacGillivary

James M. MacKay

Harold Makinson

Michael J. Masterson

Lewis Millett

Bud Milligan

George Odom

Lionel Proulx

John Reynolds

Lorne Samaha

Denis Richard Schmidt

Craig Smith

John Tate

Lucien Thomas

Don Vogel

Harold Wilson

John Wright

INDEX